THE RULE OF THE MANY

Fundamental Issues in Democratic Theory

Thomas Christiano
UNIVERSITY OF ARIZONA

WestviewPress
A Division of HarperCollinsPublishers

To Dorothea van den Oever Christiano
and to the memory of
Joseph Francis Christiano

Focus Series

Copyright © 1996 by Westview Press, A Division of HarperCollins Publishers, Inc.

Published in 1996 in the United States of America by Westview Press, 5500 Central Avenue, Boulder, Colorado 80301-2877, and in the United Kingdom by Westview Press, 12 Hid's Copse Road, Cumnor Hill, Oxford OX2 9JJ

Library of Congress Cataloging-in-Publication Data
Christiano, Thomas.
  The rule of the many : fundamental issues in democratic theory /
Thomas Christiano
    p. cm. — (Focus series)
  Includes bibliographical references and index.
  ISBN 0-8133-1454-2. — ISBN 0-8133-1455-0 (pbk.)
  1. Democracy. I. Title. II. Series: Focus series (Westview
Press)
JC423.C567 1996
321.8—dc20   96-8404
                                                            CIP

The paper used in this publication meets the requirements of the American National Standard for Permanence of Paper for Printed Library Materials Z39.48-1984.

10   9   8   7   6   5   4   3   2   1

CONTENTS

PART THREE
PRINCIPLES AND PROBLEMS OF
DEMOCRATIC INSTITUTIONS

ACKNOWLEDGMENTS

Research for the book was supported by a summer stipend from the National Endowment for the Humanities in 1992, the Philosophy Department of the University of Arizona, a fellowship from The Udall Center for Studies in Public Policy at the University of Arizona, and a junior sabbatical from the School of Social and Behavioral Sciences of the University of Arizona.

I would like to express my appreciation for the help and encouragement I received from friends and colleagues. My intellectual debts to Russell Hardin should be evident in every chapter of this book. Russell's ideas have provided simultaneously the basis of many of my views and many of the challenges to which I have attempted to respond, and despite many lasting disagreements on fundamental issues he has been an unfailing source of encouragement. He also gave me valuable comments on the whole of the penultimate draft. John Christman's friendship and philosophical acumen have been indispensable sources of inspiration and intellectual stimulation for me over the years. I had many provocative conversations with Allen Buchanan on the ideas of the book. David Estlund read the whole manuscript and provided an insightful and challenging set of comments. Three anonymous reviewers at Westview Press gave me thorough and very helpful comments on drafts of the manuscript. John Armstrong, Harry Brighouse, Chris Griffin, Jean Hampton, Thom Hudson, and John Schwarz generously provided me with helpful comments on individual chapters of the book. I also benefited immensely from discussions on individual chapters with Patrick Croskery, Helen Ingram, Michael Hechter, Arthur Kuflik, Julian Lamont, Deborah Mathieu, Ken O'Day, David Snow, and Robert Varady. My thanks also go to Spencer Carr at Westview Press for his generous and patient editorial supervision during the writing of this book. Mark Patterson and Dale Cooke assisted with the proofreading and indexing of the book. I also want to express my gratitude to Aline Stevens for her love and support through the many ups and downs involved in my intellectual endeavors.

Thomas Christiano

Introduction

The Justification and Elaboration
of the Democratic Ideals

Any society is organized in many ways by rules that constrain the lives of its citizens and by which each expects others to abide. We are constrained by traffic rules, tax laws, regulations on our economic activities, laws protecting property and punishing offenders as well as laws regulating education and health care. Our society is constituted and regulated by a constitution, laws, and government. Every citizen is obligated to comply with these laws and expects others to do the same. The laws that bind us are not, however, inevitable. We live under one set of laws now, but in the past we lived under different laws, and in the future we may be bound by others. In addition, other societies have different laws. For example, in the United States the laws permit advertisers to promote their clients' products on television with certain important restrictions, but those laws could be changed to forbid advertising on television as some countries have legislated, or they could be altered to allow people to advertise without any restrictions.

Since a society can be organized in different ways, we can ask two distinct questions about its organization. First, How well is it organized? To answer this question we will evaluate the quality of the laws and policies a society has and their impact on the well-being of the population, and we will compare them to possible alternatives. We may say that a society fares best when it permits private property and free trade, or we may disagree with this assessment. We can debate the relative merits of different sets of laws. Second, we can

1

ask, Who chooses these terms of association? The organization of society is artificial; it comes about by choices people make. Who makes laws and policies? Since the laws and policies made by one group of persons will often be different from those made by another group, it is essential to ask, Who rules?

The people is one answer to this second question. It contrasts with a monarch and an oligarchy. In a monarchy, a single individual or family makes the laws under which all are to live. In an oligarchy, a group of individuals is charged with the task of legislation. A democracy is a society in which the people rule. The people are charged with choosing between different terms of association in a democracy as a king is charged with such choices in a monarchy. The issue I will explore in this book is not who in fact rules but who has the *right* to rule? This question is about how the decisionmaking in a society *ought* to be made. Who has the right to define the terms of association for a society? Ought the rules be made by a royal family? Should they be made by a body of experts? Or should the rules that we live by be made by the most wealthy members of the society? Or does the whole of the people have the right to choose?

Most believe in the democratic idea that the people have a right to rule, that decisions about what laws and government a people live under ought to be made ultimately by it or at least by individuals the people have chosen. We are deeply opposed to the thought that some person or group of persons has a right to tell us what to do without our having any say. This latter form of rule is known as despotism, dictatorship, or tyranny.

By what method can a people make decisions? There is rarely universal agreement on what laws we ought to live under, so the people do not usually have a unified view of what to do and thus cannot make decisions the way individual persons do. We must be able to make decisions even when there is substantial disagreement over the best course of action. Those who disagree must comply with the decisions if we are to live in a society ruled by law. How ought we make these decisions? We think that these decisions ought to be made in general by majority rule among equal citizens. When there is disagreement, we think that the larger number ought to prevail and the smaller number ought to go along. Yet we do not think that this is dictatorship or tyranny of the majority over the minority. It is a legitimate way of making decisions. These kinds of beliefs come automatically to most citizens of Western states. My purpose in this book is to examine their basis and to discern some of their implications.

Let us focus more closely on the basic ideals of democracy. First, in a democracy, the people rule. *Popular sovereignty* implies that all minimally competent adults come together as one body to make decisions about the laws and policies that are to regulate their lives together. Each citizen has a vote in the processes by which the decisions are made and each has the opportunity to participate in the deliberations over what courses of action are to be followed. Second, each citizen has the right to participate as an equal. *Political equality* implies equality among citizens in the process of decision-making. Of course there are different kinds of equality here. Political equality assigns each citizen an equal vote and requires that decisions be made by a majority. In addition political equality includes the more robust requirement that citizens be equal in the control they exercise over the decision-making process. Third, each citizen has the right to an opportunity to express his or her opinions and supporting reasons to every other citizen as well as a right and duty to hear a wide spectrum of views on subjects of public concern. Each has a right, as well as a duty to participate in open and fair *discussion*. These are the ideals of democracy.

These ideals are partly realized in features of modern democratic societies. One-person one-vote is observed in the process of electing representatives to the legislative assembly; anyone may run for election to public office; in elections, a number of political parties compete for political power by advocating alternative visions of the society; the political campaigns of candidates and parties consist in large part in discussion and argument over the worth of these opposing views, and everyone is permitted to have a say in this process; and the society tolerates and often encourages vigorous debate on all issues of public interest. All these features provide concrete evidence of commitment to democratic ideals in contemporary political communities.

These aspects of modern democratic societies represent great accomplishments, but they are not the last word on democracy. They constitute a kind of minimal conception of democracy in modern societies. Democracy embodies moral ideals to which most people in modern society have a deep and abiding allegiance. These ideals go beyond the minimal conception of democracy. In particular the ideals of political equality and of rational social discussion among citizens seem to require a more substantive equality than the practice of one-person one-vote. A society may be minimally democratic while not fully living up to democratic ideals. Consider a citizen who has a vote and is not forbidden to say something in the process of deliberation. But suppose that because of poverty, lack of education, and lack of organization this citizen is unable to understand the issues involved in the decisionmaking or have a clear idea of what her interests are or how to articulate them to others. Such a citizen is not the political equal of the citizen who is wealthy, well educated, whose interests and points of view are supported by organization, and who is able to understand issues as well as clarify and articulate his interests. A society that permits this kind of inequality may well be democratic in the minimal sense described above, but most of us would believe that it does not live up to the democratic ideals of political equality and participation in rational social deliberation.

This is an intuitive judgment with which most will concur, and it will be defended at length in this book. This judgment uses ideals of democracy to scrutinize practices and institutions. Underlying this judgment is the conviction that the ideals of political equality and rational deliberation require that citizens have more equal resources for developing their understanding of their society and their interests. Equal citizens must also have the resources to make their points of view known to others as well as to listen to what others have to say in turn. And they require that citizens have a robust equality of control over the ultimate decision. A process of decisionmaking that satisfies these requirements is intrinsically just. The laws on which a democracy decides are legitimate to the extent that they are made through an egalitarian and rational process. Other values may compete with democratic ideals and sometimes override them, but they are themselves intrinsically valuable. In the first part of this book, I will examine the meaning and basis of democratic ideals. I will inquire into whether and how democracy is a just or fair way of making decisions about the laws and policies that bind us all. I will explore the arguments political thinkers have offered to justify and explain our allegiance to democratic ideals. And we will find that the principles that provide the rationale for the familiar aspects of democratic government adumbrated above point beyond them to robust ideals with which we can take a critical stance on our society.

Democratic Ideals and the Modern State

The ideals of democracy suggest that citizens ought to play a very substantial role in the governance of their society. The trouble is that the ideals appear quite unrealistic in a modern democratic state. Our society is extremely complex. The systems of taxation, education, and military defense as well as the regulation of the economy and the structure of the criminal law are vitally important to social and political life but are very sophisticated. Exercising control over any of these complex institutions requires a great deal of knowledge. In our own society individuals devote their careers to developing expertise in these and other areas. Some specialize in developing policy in education, others specialize in economic policy, and others in foreign policy. Each person can specialize only in a few areas if he or she is to be able to do a thorough job. The complexity of modern society requires that tasks be divided up and that individuals specialize narrowly in them. Our society requires a division of labor wherein each must be assigned a narrowly defined role that is associated with a narrowly defined kind of expertise. Moreover, most ordinary citizens have tasks that they must perform in the society that have little to do with making law and policy. Businessmen, farmers, workers, and professionals all have important tasks to fulfill that demand a lot of time and energy. In general, they do not have the time to assess the intricacies of economic and foreign policy. Given these facts of the modern state it is hard to see how most ordinary citizens can play a large and important role in the formulation of the laws and policies that govern a large modern state.

In addition, it would appear that ordinary citizens do not have much reason to inform themselves about politics anyway. Each citizen in the United States has one vote out of over 100 million with which to influence the outcomes of elections. What benefit is the citizen likely to reap from casting such a vote? The outcomes of elections are usually determined by many thousands of votes, so it looks like each citizen has a minuscule say in what happens. So why should a citizen spend the precious little time he or she has away from work trying to understand the difficult issues of politics when his or her vote makes so little difference? It would appear that most citizens have reason to be ignorant about politics in a democracy.[1] Most seem to have reason to leave the difficult questions for experts and special interests to resolve.

These two factors suggest a picture of the ordinary citizen as almost entirely outside of the process of democratic decisionmaking. Yet decisions must be made. When citizens ignore the complex tasks of government and leave discussion and decisionmaking to experts and special interests, the result must be a society in which a few rule and the rest obey. The ideal of citizens participating in serious and rational discussions about the organization of society seems to be a pipe dream, and the ideal of political equality seems deeply unrealistic and perhaps even incoherent.[2]

These worries depend on assumptions that should be scrutinized. First, the assertion that citizens will not do much to inform themselves when they see that the benefit to themselves of voting is not very significant presupposes a conception of how citizens are motivated and what they see as good reasons for acting. Here we must ask whether these assumptions are correct and whether an alternative view of citizens is not a superior one. Second, if the division of labor is here to stay, we must inquire into the proper role of citizens in the decision-making processes in a modern democratic society. Is there a role ordinary citizens can play in the division of labor that is compatible with a robust conception of political equality? Is there a way to conceive of citizens so as to make sense of their participation as equals in a common process of rational discussion about their collective decisions? At first it might appear that these questions must be answered in the negative. But answers can be given to these questions that are plausible and that reconcile the conditions of the modern state with the ideals of democracy. The task of Part Two of this book will be to set up and answer this challenge of modern society to the democratic ideals.

The great diversity of peoples in modern societies creates another fundamental challenge to the ideal of political equality. Let us consider two examples of this kind of problem. First, consider the problem of representation. In modern democracies, citizens cannot make the laws themselves; they must have representatives who make laws for them in a legislative assembly. In this instance a division of labor is needed in society. But a familiar problem arises in the theory of representation. Consider the electoral system in the United States in which representatives are elected to the House of Representatives by majority rule from each district. Each district is of equal population size so each person's vote for a representative is roughly equally weighted. If there are a number of ethnic groups in the society and one is in the minority, legislative districts can be arranged so that there is only a small number of the minority members in each district. In some cases this minority group will not have any representatives in the House. If this minority has distinctive interests and concerns, this lack of representation will be a serious setback to their interests. We may think that these people are not being treated as political equals. In the United States judges have been assigned the task of making sure that districts are properly apportioned so that the legislative assembly properly reflects the distribution of groups in the society. The question that arises is, By what criterion do they decide that the districts are properly apportioned? They may simply try to make the proportion of minority representatives to the total number of representatives in the legislative assembly the same as the proportion of members of the minority to the population as a whole. The trouble with this as a general principle is that there are many minorities in our society and to some extent they overlap. To ensure that women, African Americans, Polish Americans, Italian Americans, as well as Jews, Catholics, Protestants, and other minorities are proportionally represented in the legislature is impossible. In response we might say that only some groups ought to receive special attention whereas others do not need it. But which ones do we choose? By what criteria are they chosen? Giving the power to decide these matters to judges involves a massive transfer of power from citizens. In effect, judges would be making decisions about whose interests matter and whose don't. We need an account of what political equality re-

quires in these contexts. The problem may appear insoluble, but in
fact I think we can answer these questions in a plausible way that is
guided by a robust conception of political equality as well as by a
conception of citizenship designed to answer the first set of problems I elaborated.

Finally, in a democratic society every individual or at least every
group with distinctive interests ought to have a hearing in the
process of discussion leading up to the choices that must be made.
Individuals or groups with important and distinctive points of view
who are not able to have their views heard are surely not being
treated as equal citizens in a democratic society. I will defend this
thesis in some detail in the book. Yet, obvious questions arise.
Which groups have the distinctive interests that ought to be taken
into account and which groups have something important to say?
We must answer these questions before we say that the process of
discussion has taken proper account of all the relevant points of
view. We need a principle that tells us what equality among individuals in a process of discussion requires, and we need to elaborate an
account of institutions that can satisfy this conception of equality.
These last two problems will be discussed in Part Three.

The Plan of the Book

In this book we will see how strong political equality among citizens can be reconciled with the conditions of the modern state and
can provide guidance in the design of just democratic institutions.
The project of reconciliation will be made in three parts. The first
part will defend a theory of democratic equality that supports the
ideals of popular sovereignty, political equality, and rational democratic discussion. In Chapter 2, the foundation of this defense will
be shown to be in the principle that each person's interests ought to
be given equal consideration in society. Such equal consideration is
essentially embodied in the ideals of democracy. The basic principles of democratic equality will then be laid out. We will come to
these arguments only after a review and assessment, in Chapters 1
and 2, of some main alternative efforts to provide foundations for
democracy. Those theories fall short of what is necessary for this
task primarily because they are unable to handle the immense plu-

rality of opinion and interest in any reasonably complex society.
Our review of them will allow us to take stock of the questions that
a theory of democracy must answer. In particular, the facts of disagreement and conflict that undermine the theories of Chapter 1 can
be fully accommodated in the theory proposed in Chapter 2. Other
basic defenses of democracy will be considered throughout the
book. In particular, I shall be discussing aspects of the contractarian,
or economic, defenses of democracy primarily in Chapter 4, where I
shall provide a critique of these views.

The second part begins with a chapter on the first challenge to the
democratic ideals that arises in the modern democratic state. We will
see how the principle of political equality defended and elaborated
in Chapter 2 appears to be undermined when we try to implement it
in contemporary political societies. And we will discuss how rational democratic discussion about matters of public concern seems to
be entirely inconsonant with the conditions of modern societies.
The basis of these two fundamental challenges resides in some important assumptions that are made about citizens and the society.
Citizens are assumed to be self-interested in the first problem, and
in the second the idea that society is a division of labor appears to be
incompatible with rational deliberation. These two problems will
compel us to discuss the nature of democratic citizenship and its
prerequisites.

Chapter 4 reviews economic conceptions of citizenship embodied
in theories that take the self-interest of citizens as the mainspring of
motivation in politics. We will see that theories of political ideals
that presuppose a conception of citizens as primarily self-interested
individuals are ultimately self-defeating. Finally, we will review evidence for and against the self-interest axiom and see that it ought to
be rejected on empirical and methodological grounds. Once we
have established the idea that citizens can be and are motivated by
moral principle, we have cleared the way for a precise and thorough
discussion of the appropriate role of ordinary citizens in the process
of collective decisionmaking in society. In Chapter 5 we will see that
the business of democratic citizenship in society is to choose the
basic aims of society. We will discuss in great detail the nature of this
contribution as well as what citizens are expected to do in order to
fulfill this role. We will conclude this discussion with a defense of

some basic standards that citizens ought to be able to live up to in carrying out their role. I shall argue that if citizens are the basic choosers of aims in the society and are able to live up to the standards outlined, then they are in a position to be sovereign over the society as well as to be political equals.

Part Three is concerned with the kinds of institutions that are necessary to enable citizens to carry out their role. Citizens can play their role in society only if others are playing complementary roles. Institutions of legislative representation, electoral systems as well as interest groups and political parties specify the complementary tasks of other actors in the political system. These institutions are all necessary to assure citizens of the opportunity to play the role of choosers of basic aims. They are also necessary to provide access for citizens to the cognitive conditions necessary for performing this role adequately.

Chapter 6 advances a conception of the functions of legislative representation and electoral systems. We will see that our ideals of democracy coupled with the conception of citizenship and the fact of pluralism of opinions and interests in society provide clear guidance as to how these democratic institutions ought to be designed. In this chapter I will characterize equality in a system of representation. I elaborate criteria for an egalitarian system of representation on the basis of the conception of political equality defended in Chapter 2 as well as the conception of citizenship in Chapter 5. I will show that these criteria provide definite guidance in justifying electoral and legislative institutions.

The last two chapters discuss the deliberative aspect of democratic equality. Deliberative institutions provide the conditions in which citizens become informed about their own interests as well as those of others and about the requirements of justice so that they can properly fulfill their role as choosers of the aims of society. The ideas outlined in Chapter 2 about the nature of equality in social discussion will help us see the kinds of principles necessary for evaluating such institutions as interest groups and political parties as well as such practices as electoral campaigning. We then explore the institutional conditions necessary to establish egalitarian institutions of discussion. The last chapter attempts to elaborate general criteria for egalitarian institutions of discussion and then explores alternative institutional arrangements that can satisfy these criteria.

Parts One, Two, and Three fit together as a unit. Part One supplies the fundamental principles of democracy but suggests that their coherence is challenged when they are to be applied to the conditions of modern society. Thus conceptions of citizenship and the companion democratic institutions outlined in Parts Two and Three are necessary to provide a defense for the principles outlined in Part One. At the same time the principles of democratic equality provide guidance and support for the ideas elaborated in the rest of the book. Furthermore, Parts Two and Three are inextricably linked insofar as the conception of citizenship can only be fully supported when the other parts of the political division of labor have been outlined. We will also see that the conception of citizenship provides support and guidance in the outline of the principles for evaluating institutions discussed in Part Three.

Notes

1. See Anthony Downs, *An Economic Theory of Democracy* (New York: Harper and Row, 1957), p. 244.

2. Downs, *An Economic Theory of Democracy.*

PART ONE

Foundations of Democracy

CHAPTER ONE

Self-Government

In the history of political thought, justifications of democracy begin with the defense and articulation of certain basic political values and argue that democratic decisionmaking embodies or promotes them. There are basically three kinds of arguments. The first is that democracy is based on self-government. Some thinkers claim that _liberty_ is the preeminent political value and argue that democratic society embodies the liberty of its citizens more than any other kind of society. They argue that democratic government is the only kind of government wherein individuals freely impose laws on themselves. Government and law are necessary to solve certain basic problems in social interaction. Without government and law, individuals find themselves in an unpredictable world of conflict and violence. Conversely, government and law impose constraints on individual action. Only when these constraints are self-imposed do individuals remain free when living under law. Inasmuch as liberty is intrinsically valuable, democracy is intrinsically valuable.

The second kind of argument is that democracy is founded on the _equality_ of citizens. These theorists argue that equality is the fundamental political value and that democratic decisionmaking embodies the equality of citizens. Decisions about the terms of association under which we must live affect the interests of all the citizens. When decisions must be made that affect the interests of all, then each has a right to an equal say in making these decisions. The only alternative is that some have more say than others, as in monarchy or aristocracy. These first two arguments suggest that democracy is intrinsically worthwhile because it embodies certain intrinsically worthwhile properties. They each argue that the citizens have a right to rule because the right embodies the liberty or the equality of citizens. Even if citizens make bad decisions on certain occasions, it remains that the mistakes are rightfully theirs to make.

A third kind of argument is *instrumentalist*; it states that democracy is good not because of any of its intrinsic properties but because democracies just tend to choose the best terms of association for a society. This kind of argument bases the right to rule on the assessment of the terms of association that are chosen by the rulers. Democracy is not a good in itself; it is the most reliable political method to produce good decisions. For instance, some argue that democratic institutions promote the greatest happiness of citizens either because the legislation is good or because of the effect the institutions have on the participants.[1] Others argue that democratic institutions tend to produce just legislation or protect civil and economic liberty.[2] A benevolent monarchy would be just as good as democracy if it could reliably make good legislation, instrumentalists argue, but it is highly unlikely that it could. So instrumentalists are not primarily concerned with who will rule; they are concerned exclusively with how well the ruler rules. They base assessments of methods of rule on the quality of the ruling itself and ultimately on the likely quality of the terms of association that are chosen.

In the next two chapters, I will examine varieties of the liberty-based argument and the egalitarian argument. My procedure will be a limited one. I will work from the assumption that democracy is an important political ideal, and I will explore the arguments mentioned above in terms of how well these different conceptions can make sense of democracy. My main purpose will be to determine whether either liberty or equality can be thought of as the basis of any recognizably democratic ideal. So I will not inquire into the ultimate values of liberty and equality except as is necessary to my main purpose. I will be asking whether the idea of a right to rule based on the ideal of either liberty or equality is a coherent one. Surprisingly, most of the arguments that are offered cannot provide a coherent basis for democratic rule. They fail to acknowledge one or another essential feature of democratic societies in a way that vitiates the basic argument. However, once we have put aside a number of inadequate egalitarian arguments, I conclude that equality is the fundamental value underlying democracy. Individuals in a society have equal rights to vote, to organize political parties and interest groups, and to contribute to discussions on how the society would best be organized.

Finally, in my view, the best argument against instrumentalism is the demonstration of the intrinsic value of the democratic process as well as the coherence of the ideals that regulate that process. Thus I shall not explicitly treat the arguments for instrumentalism in any specific section of this book. Instead, the arguments of the next two chapters and mainly of Chapter 2 will establish the intrinsic importance of democratic equality, and I will note along the way where I think that instrumentalists have gone wrong. The arguments of Chapters 4 through 9 will establish the coherence of these ideals in the face of the problems that instrumentalists have thought undermine the ideals of equality.

Self-Government and Democracy

Here is a schema of the basic arguments from libertty: One, a fundamental value in politics is that of freedom; two, freedom must ultimately be understood as self-development; three, each has an equal right to the conditions of self-development; four, participation in determining common activities is a necessary condition of self-development. Therefore, each person has an equal right to participate in determining the course of common activities in which he or she is involved. Political liberty is a necessary component of liberty overall.[3]

That freedom is a basic value in politics is taken as given for the purposes of our discussion. So the first premise of this argument will not be questioned. Only the implications of this premise for democratic theory will be addressed in this book.[4] The second premise gives us a conception of what freedom is. Very briefly, it involves four main conditions. It is perhaps uncontroversial that being free implies that one is capable of making choices. Someone who is comatose or deeply mentally disabled is not a free human being. In addition, being free requires that others do not interfere with the choices that I make. I am not free to travel to other countries if the laws prohibit my doing so. Some have argued that these two conditions alone are sufficient for being free, but a person cannot really be said to be free if that person lacks the means for acting as she would choose. If I lack the money to pay for travel, I am unfree to travel in a society where such payment is required for traveling. This condition is closely connected with the conditions stated previously, since if I lack the money to pay for a ticket to travel by plane to another country, someone will interfere with my attempt at air travel by stopping me from getting on an airplane without a ticket.[5] So if I am to be as free as you are, then I must have the same socially important means at my disposal as you to carry out my choices. The fourth condition of freedom is more difficult to explain and plays a role in only some of the arguments I will discuss. A free person is one who is, in a sense, the author of his or her own life. Such persons live in accordance with projects of their own invention as well as principles they adopt upon due reflection. They decide what kinds of persons they want to be and shape their personalities by their own action.[6] This is freedom as self-development.

In support of the third premise, since freedom has great value, each person has a right to freedom. Since all human beings have the same basic capacity for self-development and the possession of that capacity gives a person a right to the conditions of self-development, they each have a prima facie equal right to the conditions of self-development.[7] This is a principle of equal freedom for each person. Note that the liberty-based arguments for democracy require a principle of equality in order to ensure that each person has an equal right to participate. They are incomplete without a principle of equality. The fourth premise of the argument links the requirement of equal self-development with democracy. The self-government argument states that because the laws provide the framework within which citizens shape their lives, to be free they must be the authors of those laws. Democratic participation enables them to be authors of the laws. Each must have political liberty and personal liberty. I explore this premise most in what follows.

Combining this premise with the principle of equality in the conditions of self-development, each person has an equal right to participate in determining the course of common activities he or she engages in. In particular, each person has an equal right to participate in the making of the laws under which he or she lives. Thus concludes the general liberty argument for democracy.[8]

In the rest of this chapter, we will examine three different versions of the liberty, or self-government, argument: the direct, the epistemic, and the constructive conceptions of the self-government arguments. Telescoping a bit, we will see that such theories consistently face two serious problems of coherence. (1) They cannot explain why the liberty involved in participating in ruling the society is more important than the individual liberty involved in more nonpolitical pursuits. They must explain why political liberty is essential to liberty overall. Why, for example, is a person more free when she has the opportunity to participate in politics than when she has the choice between partners in marriage? Hence, even if democracy represents a kind of freedom, it is not clear why democracy is essential to being a free person. Why can't a person conceivably get a greater liberty overall by giving up political liberty altogether? This is the trade-off problem. (2) There is a deep tension between the idea that an individual should be free to govern the world he shares in common with others and the claim that every citizen should have this freedom. I cannot be free to have my way with regard to the common world when what occurs must be the result of the assent of many others. Yet democracy essentially involves sharing power with other citizens. Democracy seems to be incompatible with liberty.

These difficulties are addressed by those who assert an epistemic relation between participation and self-government as well as those who assert the constructive view. But these views rely too heavily on the possibility of an underlying consensus for them to give us even an ideal account of democracy. Also they do not escape the problem of trade-offs. Furthermore, the very ideal of an association of individuals devoted primarily to public discussion and deliberation as the bases for deciding how they will live together proves to be untenable once we appreciate the impossibility of consensus.[9]

Participation and Self-Government

Historically, the most important argument for democracy is based on a principle of self-government.[10] The self-government argument begins with the premise that human beings are social beings in three main ways. First, their characters, goals, and knowledge are socially conditioned; what I know and what I value as well as what kind of person I am depends in numerous ways on the social environment in which I live as well as my particular place in that environment. Second, the wealth, institutions, education, and other means by which individuals advance their goals are based on the activities of many people working in concert. Third, the careers, plans, and projects people have are to a great extent defined in terms of a set of social relations; for example, one cannot be a father or a mother in a society where there is no institution of the family, and one cannot be a teacher or a lawyer in a society that has no educational institutions or law courts.[11] These phenomena are shaped and constituted by our social world; they are dependent on the actions of many individuals.

These actions of many people, which play such a large role in shaping our lives, are coordinated and regulated by a system of law. Without such coordination each person would suffer from uncertainty in his or her expectations and would be unable to give shape to his or her life. Individuals' lives would be subject to the vagaries of chance. When citizens live under the rule of law, by contrast, they gain security and the ability to control their lives within the system of laws. They can form long-term projects on the assumption that other people will act within the framework established by law. But, although laws make a robust freedom possible, they structure the three forms of social conditioning described above. They play profoundly formative and constraining roles in each person's life by shaping, creating, or destroying the opportunities available.

From these observations self-government theorists argue that only when citizens have control over the laws and policies of their society are they truly masters of their own lives and free. Citizens who do not participate in making the laws that have such a powerful influence on the shape and direction of their lives have little control over their lives and are mostly the passive subjects of those who do make the laws. Joshua Cohen gives a compelling description of this view:

> A [self-consciously free] person wants more than the availability of alternatives within a system of laws and institutions that they view as a set of constraints imposed by others on their action. Rather, they

want to be able to regard those institutional constraints as themselves conforming to their own judgments of what is right. . . . The free person wants to affirm the framework of rules itself; they want to "have their own will as a rule."[12]

Let us explore these ideas a bit more closely. What does it mean to have one's own will as a rule? I have a will when I choose an action or set of actions in accordance with a *plan* that I wish to carry out. The plan conforms to *rational principles* of which I approve and implements those principles. When I act in accordance with my will, I act in accordance with my best judgment about what to do. This is in contrast to mere desire. I may plan to pursue a course of action and while I am pursuing it experience desires that pull me away from my plan. Desires are often mere momentary impulses that are not connected with any plan or conception of what is best for me to do. For example, I may pursue a course of studies at the university. This requires a plan of action and is in accordance with my sense that an education is for my own good. The night before a final exam, some friends of mine may come to me and attempt to persuade me to come out drinking with them. I may be sorely tempted to join them, but I believe that it is not what is best for me. Here my will to successfully complete my course of studies conflicts with the momentary desire to join my friends in an evening of revelry. Another example is the case of a person who tries to stop smoking. He sets out a plan for himself that is justified by his sense that smoking is bad for him. At the same time he is tempted by his mild addiction to cigarettes to smoke another cigarette. Here again, will and desire conflict. Sometimes we do what we will, and at other times we succumb to our opposing desires. What we will is somehow closer to what we are whereas our desires seem opposed to us when they oppose our will. In the case of addiction to smoking we feel somehow assailed by an alien force; we feel a threat to our ability to control our lives. But since we feel impelled in part to act in accordance with our desires, our will constrains us. We feel constrained by a rule that we impose on ourselves. Therefore, to do what we will is to have our own will as a rule, to be master of ourselves and to be free. To follow the desires we are tempted by but recognize as opposing our good is to be a mere "slave to appetite."[13] The conflict between will and desire is not always present (we often will that our desires be satisfied), but it is with our will that we identify.

Almost all of us agree that it is best to live in a society governed by law; thus, it is in accordance with our will that we are constrained by law. And these legal constraints may conflict with what we desire in particular cases. Furthermore, we realize that laws make it possible for us to plan our lives and thus contribute to our freedom. So the rule of law is not incompatible with our freedom. The rule of law in a society is a constraint we impose on ourselves that is similar to the personal constraints we impose on ourselves. The issue for self-government theorists is, How can we make sure that the laws we live under are in accord with our own will? But first, let us look at one nondemocratic attempt at ensuring self-government.

A Nondemocratic Method of Ensuring Self-Government

Social organization could accord with our own will if society were like a club that we could join or leave at will. If we could enter societies that have laws of which we approve and leave societies that have laws of which we do not approve, then we would be self-governing on this view. This conception of self-government does not require democratic participation; it merely requires that we be able to leave one society to join another. We do not need the right to a vote to satisfy this liberty but merely rights to enter and exit. Even a world of small dictatorships is compatible with this liberty as long as each person can leave one for another.[14]

There are three basic difficulties with this attempt to reconcile liberty and government. One is that it is quite costly for most persons to move from one state to another since each person must pay for the movement and frequently must learn a new language and cultural traditions, as well as leave family, friends, and even a familiar beloved environment behind. These costs are very difficult to measure, but they seem high enough on many occasions to undermine the idea that persons are freely endorsing the laws of a state merely by their continued residence.[15]

A second related difficulty is that some individuals will experience much higher costs of exit than others. Those who are poorer will experience much higher exit costs than those who are wealthy. Those who are attached to the land will lose much more in moving than those who are not. The consequence of these differences in the costs of exit may in many cases be that those who experience the lower costs will be able to exact concessions from those who would experience high costs. For example, consider a large corporation with ample ability to move from one region to another but on which the local population depends for jobs; the corporation may say, "If you do not comply with our wishes, we will move elsewhere." In these cases, the poorer members of the society may be constrained to accept unfavorable terms of agreement. In general, if we think of societies as voluntary clubs, we are in danger of turning many members of these societies into second-class citizens who are constrained to accommodate the wishes of more powerful citizens. Making the right of exit the chief instrument of each person's liberty, therefore, threatens equality of liberty for citizens and ultimately equality of citizenship itself.

We might attempt to accommodate at least the financial aspect of the problem of cost by making the states much smaller than they currently are and more accessible to everyone. Thus the world would be made up of political units the size of counties in the United States. However, having small political units leads to the third difficulty. Very small states would be highly interdependent in such a way that they would have little control over what happens within their territory. Only if the relationships between states were regulated by laws would citizens have the security and control over their lives that we expect from the rule of law. We would then want to know how these interstate laws would be made. The argument from self-government would require that these relations between states be regulated by laws in accordance with the wills of the citizens. The smaller entities would have to be supplemented and superseded by a more powerful overarching political entity, which in turn would have to be ruled by citizens if they were to be self-governing. Thus the model of the state as voluntary club will not be sufficient to ensure the self-government of citizens.

In contrast to the preceding position, those who would defend democracy on the basis of self-government argue that only if citizens participate in making the laws under which they live can they

be said to have imposed the laws on themselves and be self-governing and subject to their wills alone. Having one's will as a rule implies both that one lives in accordance with plans one can justify on
the basis of one's own rational principles, and that the laws of the
society that shape and constrain one's plans by making certain alternatives available and others unavailable are also justified on the basis
of rational principles to which one adheres. Each citizen can affirm
the laws because each has participated in making those laws.

There are, however, three different conceptions of the relation between the democratic participation of citizens and their wills: the direct, the epistemic, and the constructive conceptions. The *direct*
conception is that one's participation in making laws is a direct expression of one's will. The *epistemic* conception is that one's participation is an attempt to discover what one wills with regard to political society. The *constructive* conception is that one's participation is
an attempt to define what one wills. Each of these conceptions defines a distinctive version of the self-government argument, and I
will discuss each in turn.

The Direct View of Democratic Participation and Self-Government

The direct self-government argument states that when I participate
in making the laws I directly express my will concerning the laws I
will live under. Thus when I vote for a law, I express my will in
favor of that law. When I live under laws for which I have voted,
then I have my own will as a rule inasmuch as my participation contributes to the making of the law.

There is an obvious difficulty here. I cannot be free to determine
the course of an activity I choose in common with others in a
democracy. For whatever I want done must acquire the assent of
some proportion of the other participants. This seems like a para-
digmatic case of unfreedom. With regard to the common activity C
(such as the legal organization of society), which is democratically
controlled by all the participants, I may be free to participate or not
and to participate in whatever way I wish, but I am not free to dispose of C as I wish. If I share roughly equal control over the common activities, then I am not free with respect to C since I must se-

cure other people's agreement if I wish to pass a law. I will often be unable to find enough people to support my position, and I will be in the minority. But if I am free with respect to C, which implies that I can choose it myself, then I have more than equal control. This situation, the incompatibility problem, asserts an incompatibility between democracy and self-government.

There are two ways in which one might try to bolster the direct conception of the relation between participation and self-government. The first account of the direct relation between self-government and participation is that participation *maximizes* self-government. Keith Graham argues that in choosing common activities, individuals' desires and goals are likely to conflict, and insofar as their desires conflict, their autonomous activities conflict.[16] As we have seen, there is no way to make good on the idea that each person freely chooses each law. Since conflict among wills is inevitable and must be resolved somehow, we must opt for the principle that each ought to have his or her own will as a rule as much as possible. This resolves conflicts of will. The best way to maximize self-government is to introduce majority rule. In each case, conflicts of will among different individuals are resolved in favor of the greater number of individuals so that a greater amount of self-government is achieved.

The argument assumes that even though you would not have gotten what you want if others did not vote with you, getting what you want is a case of freedom if you participate in the action that satisfies your desire. Contrary to this assumption, if I must depend on others' agreement to get the outcome I want and those others are independent of me, then I am not free to have that outcome. For example, I am not free to take your shirt from you if you have not already chosen to give it to me. Democracy is a system of decisionmaking where each is dependent on the assent or actions of many others to secure what they want. This is really only a repetition of the incompatibility problem.

Perhaps we could say that once I have the assent of others to my choosing between *a* and *b*, then I am free to choose between *a* and *b*. Hence, once a seller has agreed to sell me an object at a price, then I am free to buy the object at that price, even though I was not free to do so before. In the democratic case I am free to choose between

two outcomes when my vote is the deciding one. The trouble with
this argument is that this condition is virtually never satisfied. In
large democratic societies, the winning option almost never wins by
less than a thousand votes or so. In those cases, my vote does not
decide the issue. Since I rarely, if ever, cast the deciding vote I will
virtually never be free to choose the outcome. Moreover that freedom, if it arises, will be extremely limited since it will only exist
after the agenda has been formulated and the alternatives are supported evenly by all the other members. On this account, democracy grants little or no liberty over the common activity.[17]

These points are compatible with people having a lot of personal
freedom. My choice of scientific, religious, political, or moral beliefs
need not depend on anyone else's assent. My choices about what to
do with my life are free when I have received the assent or can count
on the assent of others. I am free to choose whether to marry a person when she agrees or asks me to marry her and not before.
Whether I marry depends on me once she desires it. I am free to buy
things because others are willing to sell them to me at a certain price.
Again, once the object is for sale, the decision is up to me. I am in
this position all the time in the case of personal liberty, but (virtually) never in the case of politics. In my personal life I am free to
make, to accept, and to reject proposals; in politics I am free only to
make proposals but never to accept or reject them. In my personal
life, I am free to speak and act; in politics I am free to speak but not
to act, unless I am a king.

Graham's argument also implies that a great deal of democracy
will always maximize freedom. But we can be free in ways that are
independent of political participation, and democratic decisionmaking may restrict that freedom. And even in a dictatorship, each person can pursue activities freely in the private sphere. I may not be
able to choose the laws, but I can choose my friends, my career, my
place of residence, and many other things as long as I mind my own
business. Indeed, some may care only about this private freedom
and not at all about political freedom. If we suppose that freedom
has both a private component as well as a political component, we
need an argument that shows why it isn't possible for a society to
have enough private freedom so that freedom is maximized without
political freedom. In other words, even if democratic participation

constitutes some kind of free activity, we need to know why political participation is a necessary condition of a society having as much freedom as possible. Only then will we know that democracy maximizes freedom overall, something the argument we have canvassed above cannot show. This is a version of the trade-off problem. The question is, Even if democratic participation contributes to freedom, why is it necessary to freedom? Why can't a little political freedom be traded off for a lot of private freedom?

The second account of the direct relation between participation and self-government is that my freely chosen participation constitutes a kind of free endorsement of the outcome of the joint decision-making process even when the decision is not the outcome I voted for. Individuals *indirectly consent* to the outcomes of decision procedures when they freely participate in the procedure. Hence, they freely impose the laws on themselves by voting even when they don't get what they want. The trouble with this view is that it is false to say that individuals necessarily consent to the outcome of a procedure through their participation. Someone can say, without incoherence, that he withholds his consent to the outcome until he sees it.

To remedy this defect in the argument Peter Singer advances the idea of *quasi-consent*. For example, suppose a number of friends have gone to a bar and they are taking turns paying for rounds of drinks. Suppose that each person is tacitly expected to pay for a round and that everyone relies on that fact in participating. But when it comes to Jill's turn to pay for a round, she protests by saying that she was never asked whether she would pay and she will not do it. One might say of Jill that though she was never asked, she still consented because of her knowing participation in the practice and everyone's reliance on her. She has done something very much like consent, and it is reasonable for everyone to expect her to follow through. If Jill had told everyone in advance that she could not pay and they nevertheless included her, then her nonpayment would be acceptable, but since she knowingly got others to rely on her, she would be remiss in backing out now. This practice, quasi-consent, generates a voluntarily assumed obligation.

Singer says there is a parallel in the case of voting: Participating in voting is like accepting drinks, and compliance with the outcome of the vote is like having to pay for a round at one's turn. A participant does something *like* freely consent to the outcomes when she participates and thereby voluntarily imposes an obligation on herself to comply with them. She voluntarily imposes the rules of the common activity on herself. Here is the argument: (1) If there is a continuing system of voting then that system must be such that individuals generally comply with the outcomes of the votes. Otherwise, the system would go out of existence. Therefore, (2) if X votes it is reasonable to expect that X will comply with the results and to rely on that compliance. Now, given the principle of quasi-consent defended in the previous paragraph, (3) if by X's conduct, one is reasonably led to rely on X's compliance with the results of the vote and X knows this, then X has an obligation to comply with the results of the vote. Therefore, X has voluntarily imposed an obligation on herself to comply.[18]

This argument rests on an equivocation. Premise 2 is not equivalent to the antecedent of premise 3. It may be true that we can expect participants in a voting system to comply with the outcome of the vote, but this does not imply that each of them puts me in the position of relying on him or her by participating in the voting procedure. Only the latter supports an obligation to comply with the outcome of the vote. The above argument may work for small groups where participation may be the best sign that each is willing to comply with whatever choice is made and where that sign is crucial for relying on the participant; however, the argument does not generalize to larger groups and in particular not to the state since citizens hardly can or do rely on each others' compliance with the law on the basis of their participation. Most citizens do not know about others' participation. Most citizens rely on each others' law-abidingness merely because the law coordinates their activity and because the law is enforced. Voting may generate voluntary obligations to comply with the outcome in cases where there are few participants but not in any democratic state that we know of.

Therefore, the direct conception of the relation between participation and self-government fails to found democracy on liberty. Either this approach is fundamentally unable to overcome the problem of incompatibility between liberty and democracy or it can overcome the difficulty only by making false assumptions about democracy.

The Epistemic View of Democratic Participation
and Self-Government

The epistemic conception of democratic participation attempts to overcome the problem of incompatibility of democracy with liberty by asserting that democratic participation is a process of discovery of one's own will. It is the most reliable process for discovering one's will, and it is a process that essentially transforms it. It requires a conception of the will that is quite different from that of the direct view. This conception goes beyond mere reflective choice and implies a substantive commitment to promoting the common good. Every rational person wills that the common good be promoted. And so, the freedom of each requires that the common good of all be promoted. That is the first stage of the argument. The second stage of the argument shows that the participation of each citizen in social deliberation and collective decisionmaking is essential to the discovery and promotion of the common good.[19] Democratic participation is a necessary component of what a rational person wills. Therefore, democratic participation is an essential part of self-government.

The argument for the first stage relies on four premises: (1) It is a condition of one's own full, secure self-possession of one's personhood that one acknowledge and meet others as free and equal persons. The argument for this is that one's recognition of oneself as a person with aims worth pursuing depends on one's having some significance for others. We depend crucially on the esteem and respect of others to have a conception of ourselves as worthy persons. If nothing one does commands respect from others or moves others to action on a voluntary basis, one's conception of oneself will be incapacitating. One will lack the self-confidence and the sense of the worth of one's projects necessary for full personhood. The respect and esteem one needs from others can only be provided if they share an equal status with oneself. The approbation of children or insane persons is not sufficient for one's self-respect. One needs the respect of equals in moral and intellectual capacity. And one is not moved by the apparent esteem of those who are forced to say good things. Others must have the liberty to express their approval and disapproval in actions or words. One cannot treat the interests, needs, and understanding of others as completely insignificant, for then one stands alone without the respect one needs. The freedom and equality of others is a necessary part of our own secure sense of self.[20]

(2) If one can reasonably act only by reference to the being and needs of others, then one must act in accordance with those rules that are for the common good and not merely one's own isolated good. It is important for the sense of self-respect of each person that he or she lives in a society that is regulated by equitable laws that promote the common good. A further premise (3) states that a free person must have full and secure possession of personhood, and so the conditions of such a full and secure possession of one's person must be conditions of one's freedom. If a sense of one's self-worth is necessary for one's self-development, the conditions that are necessary for a sense of self-worth must be necessary to self-development as well. Therefore: (4) Being required to follow a rule that is for the common good is a necessary component of one's freedom.

There are some difficulties that should be noted with the first stage of the argument. First, it is not clear that the equality among persons that is required for a sense of self-worth is strong enough to motivate a concern for the common good in the rational person. It might still be rational to will that one be preeminent among persons who have the minimal capacities to appreciate one's projects. Secondly, it does not appear necessary to one's self-worth that all persons or even all members of one's society be free and equal. Perhaps it is sufficient that one have some companions who are free and equal. The universal equality that seems to underlie a concern for the common good does not seem to be necessary for one's self-esteem. An aristocratic society founded on inequality among classes of persons does not seem inconsistent with the need of its members to be associated with equals. Thus, it is not clear that the premises of the first argument are strong enough to support the conclusion. Let us leave them for now and discuss the second stage.

The second stage of the argument is as follows: (5) Deciding and acting in accordance with the common good not only involves obedience to rules that are for the common good but also consists in trying to discover these. The common good is not immediately evident to individuals. If they do not attempt to discern what it is, they will not be able to make laws that promote the common good. So citizens must participate in a process of discussion and decision-making to discover the rules that promote the common good.

Democracy is the only reliable method for discovering the common good. So: (6) Participation in the democratic process will realize each person's interest in promoting the common good. To illustrate this epistemic conception of democracy, it is useful to compare democracy to a criminal trial process. Just as a criminal trial process is designed to discover who in fact commits crimes and who does not, so democracy is designed to discover what the common good is. Just as the guilt or innocence of the defendant is independent of the trial process but ideally is discovered by it, so whether a policy or law is for the common good is independent of the democratic process that attempts to ascertain this fact. And finally, just as the trial procedure that is most reliable in discovering guilt and innocence is imperfect, so democracy, though the most reliable method for understanding and implementing the common good, is an imperfect method and will produce mistakes sometimes.

The epistemic approach to democracy is defended in two ways. First, citizens participate in democratic processes ideally by advancing opposing conceptions of the common good and trying to secure reasoned agreement on these conceptions. Discussion and deliberation greatly improve each citizen's understanding of the common good particularly when all the citizens are involved. The reason is that each citizen alone tends to be biased in favor of his or her own interests and will conceive of the common good in ways that inordinately favor them. When all citizens participate in discussion, the effects of these biases are reduced or canceled out. Through discussion individuals give up or modify those aspects of their views of the common good that tend to disfavor the interests of others or that betray misunderstanding of the interests of others.[21] So when discussion on alternative policies includes all citizens, the results are likely to be better than if it merely includes some of the citizens. These theorists argue that a society ruled by experts will not be one that advances the common good but will more likely advance the good of those experts; a society with a ruling class will advance the interests of that class.

Second, when discussion and deliberation end, citizens vote on the basis of what they *judge* to be the correct conception of the common good. Drawing on the analogy between voters and jurors, jurors vote on the guilt or innocence of the defendant; they express their judgments on the matter, not their own interests or wills. Similarly, citizens do not merely express their will that a certain policy or law be chosen, they express their judgments that the policy or law is for the common good. And, most important, the position that garners the most support among voters is the one for which there is the most evidence that it is for the common good. It has the forces of the better arguments on its side. When the citizens are roughly equally competent in determining what the common good is and each has a more than fifty-fifty chance of being right about the common good in each case, the policy or law that receives the most support will be the most likely to be for the common good.[22]

These claims would solve the problem of incompatibility between liberty and democracy since they imply that each citizen can affirm the proposal that receives a majority because she has reason to believe that it is the most likely to be for the common good. Even those who voted against a proposal can say to themselves: "When the opinion that is contrary to my own prevails, this proves neither more nor less than that I was mistaken, and that what I thought to be the general will was not so. If my particular opinion had carried the day I should have achieved the opposite of what was my will; and it is in that case that I should not have been free."[23] This does not imply that groups never make mistakes; they do. But the majority and the minority have reason to think that the majority choice is the best judgment about the common good. The dissenting voters have good reason to think that they have made a mistake and that the majority is right. Therefore, both those who have voted for the proposal that has passed as well as those who voted against it can "affirm the framework of rules itself" and "have their own will as a rule." Hence, participation in democratic processes is compatible with freedom with regard to the common activities we engage in.

Difficulties with the Epistemic View

The first difficulty is that it is still the case that a person or group of persons might prefer to pursue more fervently their own personal good rather than deliberate over conceptions of the common good. As long as it is thought that there are two different contexts for self-development, as all these theorists think, it is possible for there to be a trade-off between the freedom that is had in participation and the freedom that can be experienced in the pursuit of one's own personal projects. If so, it will still not be true that participation is a necessary condition of freedom overall.

The first stage in the argument has two crucial weaknesses. On the one hand, we noted that the sense of self-respect so important to each person can be sustained in the context of smaller, private groups in the society. As long as one is free to pursue private association with others and thereby enjoy the esteem of one's colleagues, friends, and family, it is not clear that it is necessary to liberty that one live in a society where everyone is able to bolster one's self-respect. Hence, it is not clear why following a rule that is for the common good of everyone is a necessary component of one's freedom.

On the other hand, the social world one lives in is inevitably affected by many more things than the social and political institutions under democratic control, especially in a pluralistic society. A member of a pluralistic society will be a member of voluntary and involuntary groups, including universities, families, religious groups, and so on. Some aspects of these groups will be shaped by the basic social and political institutions, but many will not. These groups have a serious formative effect on their members. They also have a large effect on nonmembers. Furthermore, the impact that social and political institutions have on the characters of private associations as well as other social phenomena are frequently diffuse and unintended, whereas each person's contribution to political decisions is likely to be very small for any sufficiently large society. Hence, it is simply not clear that a person must participate in choosing those institutions in order to be free, given the ample opportunities for pursuing self-development in private associations.

Putting these two points together, a diversity of private associations in a society should be sufficient to provide each person with the social conditions of self-respect necessary to freedom, and such associations should provide each person with enough control over the social aspect of their lives to offset any lack of political liberty. Hence, it is not clear why political liberty is necessary to liberty overall on this account.

A second problem is with the role of the epistemic conception of democracy in the argument. The epistemic conception of voting is meant to provide a link between a dissenting person's judgment and that of the majority by means of the claim that the majority vote will provide the best evidence for judgments about the common good when there is disagreement. In this way the dissenter may justifiably adopt the majority judgment as his own insofar as he wishes to affirm the most reasonable judgment about the common good. But this argument requires two premises that may be false. The first is that individuals have roughly equal competence not only overall but on each issue, and the second is that they have a better than fifty-fifty chance of being right on the issues. The first is unlikely to be true. More often than not, some citizens have more competence on some issues and other citizens have more on others, even though overall they are equally competent. In such cases, dissenting individuals may be justified in thinking that the choice of the majority was wrong and hence be unable to affirm that choice as their own.

Even if there is equal judgmental competence, there is a difficulty with the second claim that everyone has a better than fifty-fifty chance of being right. This claim requires that the issue space be relatively simple. There cannot be a great number of proposed alternatives on each issue. The more alternatives, the smaller the chances that individuals will make the right choice, and hence the less reason there is for affirming the choice of the majority, if there is one. In politics issues do not come neatly packaged with two alternatives apiece; there are usually many alternatives among which to choose. Also, usually people disagree about what the real issues are, and the agenda for decisionmaking is itself controversial. Sometimes the issues are simplified by discussion, but in many instances discussion makes the issue space more complex. In any case, even when the issue space is simplified by discussion, it is virtually never reduced to neat two-alternative issues. In those cases, it is unlikely that individuals, on average, will be right more than 50 percent of the time. Therefore, it is not the case that each citizen has reason to believe that the majority is usually right in its choices about the common good. So dissenting citizens must view the decisions as constraints on their actions that they cannot affirm as their own. Of course, this problem is overcome when there is wide agreement on what the issues and relevant alternatives are. But in modern societies, we rarely see this kind of agreement. Clearly, then, this solution to the incompatibility problem depends too much on the possibility of consensus.

From this brief review, it is apparent that the proposed epistemic connection between each person's will and participation cannot hold. In addition, the argument fails to establish the claim that liberty requires that individuals participate in democratic politics. It also fails to overcome the incompatibility problem except under rare circumstances of considerable consensus.[24]

The Constructive View of Democratic Participation and Self-Government

One way to overcome the difficulties of the epistemic approach is to argue that democratic discussion, deliberation, and decisionmaking under certain conditions are what *make* the outcomes legitimate for each person. The epistemic account sees democratic participation by all as a method of discovering the common good. What is discovered by democratic participation is independent of that participation. The common good, in the epistemic account, is not merely whatever the people decide after discussion and voting; it is something independent that these processes attempt to uncover. In the epistemic account, democracy is, as we noted above, like a criminal trial procedure that is used to discover who is guilty and who is innocent. By contrast, the constructive view says that whatever the results of discussion, deliberation, and decisionmaking are, they are legitimate. The results are made legitimate by being the results of the procedure.[25] Such a view automatically ensures the importance of democracy and deliberation as necessary conditions of a legitimate political order. To participate in democratic discussion and decisionmaking under certain conditions is simply what it means to be self-governing. The issue is to define the conditions that confer legitimacy on the outcome.

The relation between democracy and the legitimate common good is not like that of a trial procedure to the guilt or innocence as in the epistemic view; it is more like the relation between the rules of a game and the winner of the game. The rules of the game do not help us discover the winner of the game as if that were an independent fact; the rules define who the winner is. The winner of the game logically cannot be determined by any other method. Similarly, the constructive view is that the democratic process makes the outcomes legitimate; they constitute what a legitimate outcome is. The legitimate outcome logically cannot be brought about by any other procedure.

Joshua Cohen states that: "Outcomes are democratically legitimate iff [if and only if] they could be the outcome of a free and reasoned agreement among equals."[26] This principle states the conditions under which democratic participation makes legitimate outcomes. The basic idea is that individuals are self-governing if they base their terms of association on consensus. If they agree to the terms of association, then the citizens are self-governing members of that association. In addition, of course, agreement must come about only in a certain way. It must be agreement among free persons. Individuals are *free* in the sense that they are bound only by the results and preconditions of their own discussion and decisionmaking, and the participants can take their deliberation as sufficient grounds for complying with the result of the deliberation. They are not required to accept any prior norms aside from those that are necessary to the process of discussion itself. The discussion is *reasoned* in the sense that only the force of the better argument is exercised and that the decisions are the outcome of actual deliberation among individuals who have different preferences and ideals but who want to reach agreement on principle and not merely arrive at a compromise. Citizens do not come to agreement by making deals with each other, and they do not get other citizens to agree to the terms of association by making threats. The only basis on which citizens agree to the terms is that they can now justify the terms to themselves from principles they believe. This suggests that every citizen has good reason for adhering to the consensus that is formed. Agreement among citizens is like agreement among scientists after a successful discussion; it is based on reasons, not on coercion or bribery. The discussion takes place among citizens who are *formally and substantively equal*. They have equal opportunities to contribute at all levels of discussion and decisionmaking so that differences of power and wealth as well as in ethnic or religious affiliation do not shape their chances to contribute to the discussion. Finally, free and reasoned *consensus* among equals is the fundamental aim of everyone's participation in the discussion. And when consensus cannot be had, the citizens have recourse to majoritarian procedures. What is envisioned here is that a group of citizens get together and discuss among themselves what terms they are to live under. After a certain period of free and open discussion of alternative views, reasoned agreement on terms arises and each citizen is satisfied that the terms are the right ones.

It is clear how this resolves the incompatibility between liberty and democracy. The fact of reasoned consensus ensures that each person adopts those terms in accordance with his or her own will. Each has his or her own will as a rule. It is also reasonably clear why participation in discussion is necessary for arriving at this consensus. Though discussion is not logically necessary for arriving at reasoned consensus, it would be absolutely extraordinary if reasoned agreement on terms of association were reached in any other way. And since there is no independent source of legitimacy aside from reasoned consensus, participation seems to be necessary to complete self-government and liberty.

Objections to the Constructive View

The chief difficulty with this view is its heavy reliance on the possibility of consensus. It appears to ignore the facts of the ubiquity and pervasiveness of disagreement that characterize every citizen's experience in a democracy. As noted above, discussion only rarely eliminates differences of opinion on matters of politics. When discussion does resolve differences, it rarely produces anything more than partial and temporary consensus. Often, discussion produces more disagreement and greater diversity of opinion.

If the possibility of consensus is rare, does the constructive view have anything to say about real democratic societies? One possible response is that when disagreement remains after discussion, decisions must be made by majority rule. But this is an entirely unexplained addition. It is a mere afterthought. One advantage of the epistemic view was that it attempted to explain how a member of the minority might be satisfied with the decisions of the majority. Under certain circumstances, the minority might reasonably think that the majority was right in its assessment of the common good and thus could affirm the decision of the majority. The constructivist has no such recourse. There is no independent truth about which to be right that confers legitimacy on the decision. Only actual agreement confers legitimacy.

The need for actual agreement is obscured by the use of the term *could* in the conception of legitimacy. The phrase "iff they could be the outcome of free and reasoned agreement" suggests that outcomes might be legitimate even if they are not in fact the outcomes of free and reasoned agreement. They simply could be. If this interpretation is correct then we might have a conflict between actual democracy and the demand to bring about laws and policies that "could" be the outcome of the ideal deliberative procedure. We might evaluate institutions in terms of whether they brought about decisions that could have been the outcome of the ideal deliberative procedure. Such institutions might not require that everyone actually participate or even that everyone have a right to participate. Such an interpretation would be fatal for the claim that the theory shows how democracy is compatible with self-government.

In the light of pervasive disagreement, the ideal deliberative procedure might be taken as a *model* for social institutions of collective decisionmaking. Actual democratic institutions are justified to the extent that they approximate the ideal deliberative procedure. But once we have abandoned reliance on consensus, the demanding ideal of active citizenship implied by the model becomes less appealing. There are two reasons for this. First, discussion and deliberation are important in this view inasmuch as they contribute to free and reasoned consensus. Consensus among citizens is the chief aim only when that consensus is reasoned. Reasoned consensus is what ensures that citizens are self-governing. When we abandon the idea that consensus is possible on the great majority of issues and we abandon the epistemic approach, then the rationale for extensive discussion and deliberation diminishes and the attractiveness of the constructivist ideal fades.

Second, once we abandon consensus, we notice that severe limits are imposed on the importance of participation in public discussion. Participation in discussion and deliberation are costly and time-consuming activities for individuals as well as groups. There are four important implications of this. (a) An individual citizen must forgo other opportunities when she participates in public discussion. Participation in public discussion could be the sole focus of a person's life in modern society. Such a person would have to forgo other possible careers and other pursuits. (b) The society suffers opportunity costs when individuals participate extensively in public discussion. When someone participates in public discussion extensively, he does not have the time to engage in economic production, artistic activity, or the like. When a person is particularly adept at political discussion and not other activities, these are costs the individual and society wisely accept. But in most cases, the opportunity costs to the citizen as well as to the society are too great. A society must have a division of labor and can ill afford the prospect of everyone constantly engaged in discussion about the common good and ignoring the tasks of production, defense, education, and the like. (c) When there are irresolvable differences of opinion we need a principle that will justify cutting off debate and leaving the decision to the force of the majority. Efficiency or some other measure of the quality of the decision might be the answer, as it is in ordinary individual and social deliberation. The value of deliberation must compete with the importance of other activities, including the implementation of policy and all the other activities that people must perform in the society at large. (d) The value of deliberation depends crucially on the value of the information and understanding to be acquired from the deliberation. A lot of deliberation for the sake of an increase of understanding about a small matter or extensive deliberation for the sake of a minor increase in understanding will be a waste of time.

These four observations suggest that the value of deliberation is limited by other values of individuals and society as well as the value of the information and understanding that comes from deliberation. The society and the citizen face trade-offs between the amount of time individuals are to participate in public discussion and in other matters. A democratic theory must address how these trade-offs ought to be made and according to what standard.

The constructivist's only view on these issues is that "members are bound only by the results of deliberation and by the preconditions for that deliberation." Participation in public discussion and deliberation is the overarching value. This view appears to be intolerably demanding when the other activities that must be taken care of are considered. Two replies are available to the constructivist. He can answer that all the limitations above can be justified on the grounds that they enhance the quality of public discussion and deliberation overall, much as rules of order enhance the quality of debate in a committee. A division of labor that assigns some a large role in deliberation while assigning others a small role may be justified by pointing to the advantages of discussion in smaller groups as well as of specialization. The truth of this claim, however, relies in part on the fact that we find it greatly desirable that most people spend their time doing other things. These other activities advance other values aside from deliberation that we take to be important. Our commitment to these limits shows that we do not see deliberation as the overarching value.

The second reply the constructivist might offer is that the very limits that are imposed on discussion and deliberation ought to be the result of prior reasoned discussion and deliberation. Thus, we limit public discussion by means of institutions that we have justified through prior public discussion. The division of labor is itself the result of deliberation; the limits on discussion on particular issues are themselves the results of deliberation. Constructivists might distinguish between *first order* discussion on particular issues and the *second order* discussion and deliberation concerned with deciding the proper trade-offs between the value of first order discussion and other values.

This reply must come in one of two forms. On the one hand, second order deliberation might take place locally, as it does when a group decides to stop discussing a particular issue and votes on it. Here the trade-offs between spending more time in discussion on a subject and discussing or doing something else would be made in each particular circumstance, and new decisions about trade-offs would have to be made in every new circumstance. This kind of second order deliberation, however, is deeply impracticable. It would itself consume too much of the citizens' time and often not leave enough time for other activities. In our own society some institutions are constructed precisely so as to limit even this kind of deliberation. We do not want individuals constantly reassessing their role in society or the rules of debate. These roles and rules would not have much force if that were how individuals related to them. These roles and rules serve to cut off first order and second order discussion. Conversely, members might deliberate about how the values of free and equal rational deliberation ought to be balanced with other values in all the institutions of society all at once. Here they would deliberate essentially about a constitution for the society. This role for deliberation is compatible, however, with the almost total suspension of first order discussion and deliberation since it states that if citizens decide that a deliberative constitution is not desirable then it should not be brought about. This view departs greatly from the ideal of democracy in all but the basic constitutional issues. Thus the second order deliberation reply cannot be used to save the idea that rational deliberation among free and equal persons is the preeminent ideal of a society.

In my view the preceding observations suggest that public discussion and deliberation are of primarily instrumental value in a democratic society. First, participation in deliberation is likely to figure in different ways in the different conceptions of the good that individuals have, and a principle of pluralism and toleration ought to respect that. Assigning a general intrinsic value to participation in public deliberation and active citizenship militates against this pluralism. Second, we noted earlier that the value of deliberation is essentially tied to the expected increase in our understanding, to the importance of the understanding, and to the trade-off between the value of the understanding gained and the opportunity costs of engaging in the discussion. This suggests that discussion and deliberation have little worth (except to those who particularly enjoy conversing) when no new important understanding is to be acquired. Thus the processes of discussion and deliberation ought to be thought of as instrumental in acquiring understanding about one's interests and one's society. They are not the principal values of a democracy but only helpful instruments for achieving understanding on matters of importance to the citizens.

One final question about the constructivist view under discussion is, Why majority rule? Given the high level of disagreement we see in societies, consensus will virtually never arise on issues. This is what makes democracy incompatible with the various ideals of self-government that I have discussed. A fair and reasonable process for making decisions in the absence of consensus (such as majority rule) plays a much more important role than constructivists allow. Such a process requires a principled elaboration and defense; it ought not be left as an afterthought. Indeed, the fact of conflict over the common life of citizens is so great that any ideal that does not take it into account cannot be thought of as a complete ideal for a democratic society.

What I wish to argue in the next chapter is that majority rule is a reasonably egalitarian method of resolving conflict in the midst of disagreements. In the face of deep disagreements, individuals can still be treated fairly if they are treated as equals. Though they cannot be self-governing, they can be treated fairly and this is what is essentially attractive about democracy. Public discussion and deliberation are essential tools in a democratic society. Majority rule is deeply unsatisfying when the participants to the procedure are uninformed about the issues they are deciding or when there are serious inequalities in their understanding or access to understanding. Thus it is important that individuals be informed about the policies they prefer and the significance of these policies for themselves and others as well as the justice of these policies. Deliberation can help individuals become informed about their interests, the interests they share in common with others, as well as the differences between their interests and others. Furthermore, deliberation forces individuals to think of reasonable accommodations of their interests to others. They must attempt to find fair resolutions to the conflicts between their interests and others. Hence, deliberation plays a part in a learning process and a process of moral accommodation to others that is vital to a democratic society. Also, since participation in public deliberation enhances a person's ability to have a beneficial effect on the outcome of collective decisionmaking, and the ideal of political equality recommends that individuals have equal resources for determining the outcomes of collective decisionmaking, political equality will require that the resources for participating in social deliberation be equally distributed. These are the main functions of deliberation in a complex democratic society.

Conclusion

Liberty-based arguments found democracy on the basis of the claim that democratic participation is a necessary component of liberty or self-government. All of these fail to establish that democratic participation is a case of self-government. They cannot establish this for two main reasons. First, they fail to explain why democratic participation is necessary to freedom since it is clear that one can be free in many ways, including by just minding one's own business. This is the trade-off problem. Second, they fail to show how democracy is not simply incompatible with self-government. This is the incompatibility problem. These two problems undermine the cogency of all the arguments we have discussed despite the efforts theorists have made to overcome them. The main reason why the incompatibility problem resists solution for the self-government theorist is that such views ultimately must rely on the possibility of consensus in our very complex societies to solve it, and that consensus does not and cannot exist in them. In the next chapter we will explore a more compelling account of the nature and value of democracy.

Notes

1. See John Stuart Mill, *Considerations on Representative Government* (Buffalo, N.Y.: Prometheus Books, 1991), for both these considerations.

2. See Richard Arneson, "Democratic Rights at National and Workplace Levels," in *The Idea of Democracy,* ed. David Copp, Jean Hampton, and John Roemer (Cambridge: Cambridge University Press, 1993); Brian Barry, "Is Democracy Special?" in *Democracy and Power: Essays in Political Theory I* (Oxford: Oxford University Press, 1991); William Nelson, *On Justifying Democracy* (London: Routledge and Kegan Paul, 1980); William Riker, *Liberalism Against Populism* (San Francisco: W. H. Freeman, 1982); Ronald Dworkin, "What Is Equality? Part IV: Political Equality," *San Francisco Law Review* 22 (1987): pp. 1–30, for examples of these arguments.

3. See Carol Gould, *Rethinking Democracy: Freedom and Social Cooperation in Politics, Economy, and Society* (New York: Cambridge University Press, 1988), chap. 1, for this argument.

4. See Gould, *Rethinking Democracy*, p. 63, for arguments in favor of this claim.

5. See G. A. Cohen, "Capitalism, Freedom, and the Proletariat," in *The Idea of Freedom*, ed. Alan Ryan (Oxford: Oxford University Press, 1969), for arguments to this conclusion.

6. This is what distinguishes Gould's view from that of MacPherson, who in *Democratic Theory: Essays in Retrieval* (Oxford: Oxford University Press, 1973) spells out a theory of essential human capacities that are exercised in the process of self-development. Gould seems to avoid this kind of theory out of a concern to avoid the objections of Isaiah Berlin in *Four Essays on Liberty* (Oxford: Oxford University Press, 1969).

7. Gould introduces some other potentially conflicting principles in chapter 7; hence the qualification "prima facie."

8. See Gould, *Rethinking Democracy*, p. 84.

9. I discuss another kind of liberty-based argument, which is tangential to our concerns here, in "Freedom, Consensus, and Equality in Collective Decision Making," *Ethics* October (1990): pp. 151–181, especially pp. 154–157, as well as in "Is the Participation Argument Incoherent?" in *Philosophical Studies* April (1996).

10. Jean-Jacques Rousseau, *The Social Contract and Discourses*, trans. G.H.D. Cole (London: J. M. Dent, 1967).

11. See George Sher, "Three Grades of Social Involvement," *Philosophy and Public Affairs* 18 (1989): pp. 133–157, for a good discussion of various forms of social involvement.

12. Joshua Cohen, "Autonomy and Democracy: Reflections on Rousseau," *Philosophy and Public Affairs* 15 (1986): pp. 275–297, especially p. 286.

13. Rousseau, *The Social Contract and Discourses*, p. 196.

14. For an extensive defense of this position, see Thomas Hudson, "Self-Determination, Decentralization, and Political Diversity" (Ph.D. thesis, Department of Philosophy, University of Arizona, 1994). See also David Osterfeld, "Radical Federalism: Responsiveness, Conflict, and Efficiency," in *Politics and Process: New Essays in Democratic Thought*, ed. Geoffrey Brennan and Loren Lomasky (Cambridge: Cambridge University Press, 1989), pp. 149–173.

15. As David Hume says: "Can we seriously say, that a poor peasant or partizan has a free choice to leave his country, when he knows no foreign language or manners, and lives from day to day, by the small wages he acquires? We may as well assert, that a man, by remaining in a vessel, freely

consents to the dominion of the master; though he was carried on board while asleep, and must leap into the ocean, and perish, the moment he leaves her," in "Of the Original Contract," in *Hume's Ethical Writings,* ed. Alasdair MacIntyre (South Bend, Ind.: University of Notre Dame Press, 1965), pp. 255–274, especially p. 263.

16. Keith Graham, *The Battle of Democracy* (London: St. Martin's Press, 1986).

17. It might be objected that my criticism relies on an identification of democratic participation with voting. And this is certainly not all that is involved in democracy. My response is that voting is an important part of democratic decisionmaking, especially in cases of conflict, and that any theory of democracy must give a reasonable account of its role.

18. Peter Singer, *Democracy and Disobedience* (Oxford: Oxford University Press, 1974), p. 50. See also J. Jenkins, "Political Consent," *Philosophical Quarterly* 1 (1970): pp. 60–66.

19. See N.J.H. Dent, *Rousseau: Psychological, Social, and Political Theory* (New York: Basil Blackwell, 1989), particularly chapters 4 and 5, for this account. See also Joshua Cohen, "Autonomy and Democracy."

20. Versions of this premise are also provided by John Rawls, *A Theory of Justice* (Cambridge, Mass.: Harvard University Press, 1971), pp. 178–179; Jon Elster, "Self-Realization in Work and Politics: The Marxist Conception of the Good Life," in *Marxism and Liberalism,* ed. John Arens, Fred Miller Jr., Ellen Frankel Paul, and Jeffrey Paul (New York: Basil Blackwell, 1986), pp. 97–126; as well as G.W.F. Hegel, *The Phenomenology of Spirit,* ed. A. V. Miller (Oxford: Oxford University Press, 1977), pp. 111–118.

21. See Rousseau, *The Social Contract and Discourses,* pp. 200–204, for this argument.

22. See Scott Feld and Bernard Grofman, "Rousseau's General Will: A Condorcetian Perspective," *American Political Science Review* 82 (1988): pp. 567–576; Joshua Cohen, "An Epistemic Conception of Democracy," *Ethics* 97 (1986): pp. 26–38. Such arguments were originally expressed by Aristotle in the *Politics,* Book III.

23. Rousseau, *The Social Contract and Discourses,* p. 278.

24. This argument does not imply that democracy is not epistemically superior to other forms of collective decisionmaking. I think that in the long run, democratic societies do tend to come to a better understanding of the common good. But the fact that the society I live in now is likely to come to a better understanding of the common good in the long run does not give me reason to affirm its current decisions when they seem wrong by my lights. The epistemic view is not in itself wrong, but it cannot solve the incompatibility problem.

25. See John Rawls, *Political Liberalism*, (New York: Columbia University Press, 1993), chapter 3, for an account of constructivism.

26. Joshua Cohen, "Deliberation and Democratic Legitimacy," in *The Good Polity*, ed. Alan Hamlin and Philip Pettit, pp. 18-27, especially p. 22. See also Iris Marion Young, *Justice and the Politics of Difference* (Princeton: Princeton University Press, 1991), p. 34, for a similar kind of principle for defining the nature of social justice. Actually, Young at one point advocates the more epistemic view in her "Polity and Group Difference: A Critique of the Ideal of Universal Citizenship," *Ethics* January (1989): p. 259, and at other points advocates the constructive view.

CHAPTER TWO

Equality

Society is organized by terms of association by which all are bound. The problem is to determine who has the right to define these terms of association. Democrats state that only the people have a right to rule over the society. And they argue that citizens ought to be equals in important respects in making these decisions. What is the basis of these views? We have seen that liberty accounts of democracy fail to provide a thorough understanding of the foundations of democratic decisionmaking. In large part this failure is due to the dependence of these conceptions on consensus within the society. They are unable to account for the basic democratic principle that when there are disagreements over what the terms of association are to be, that view that secures support from a majority of the citizens ought to be chosen. This is the problem of incompatibility. These theories also fail to account for the interests persons have in democratic decisionmaking that explain why a person ought to be allotted equal shares in political rule. This is the problem of trade-offs.

Although liberty over the common social world is incompatible with democracy, equality on its own may provide the basis. After all, democracy implies commitments to equality, such as equality in voting power as well as equality of opportunity to participate in discussion. Egalitarian theories attempt to derive a conception of democracy from a principle of equality among persons. They acknowledge fundamental conflicts of interests and convictions in society and assert that because of this lack of consensus, each person may demand an equal share in political rule.

At the same time an egalitarian conception of the foundations of democracy must include an important component of liberty views that is often left out by egalitarians. It ought to accommodate and explain the importance of the convictions citizens hold and the role of public discussion in democracy. Democratic decisionmaking is not merely a matter of each person voting his or her preference. Individual citizens' preferences are formed in society as a result of social interaction they have with others and the institutions that structure social interaction. It is important for them to reflect critically on and improve their preferences so as to have a sophisticated appreciation of their interests and ideals. A democratic theory ought to have something to say about what constitutes a reasonable and just context for the formation of these preferences.

In what follows, we will discuss three egalitarian views of the foundations of democracy. The procedure followed is dialectical. We will start with an examination of the idea of democracy as a kind of fair compromise among persons who have irresolvable disagreements about how to organize their common world. Problems with this idea will lead us to explore a view that democracy can be understood as a direct implementation of the principle of equal consideration of the interests of citizens. This view suffers from difficulties that do not beset the fair compromise view. After taking stock of these difficulties we will develop a view that accommodates the insights and overcomes the difficulties that are associated with the views of these two chapters in one systematic account. The defense and elaboration of the ideal of political equality will set the stage for discussion of the problems of citizenship and pluralism and the principles of institutional design that are the focus of Parts Two and Three of this book.

Democratic Equality as a Fair Compromise

One approach to democracy that attempts to deal with the problem of irresolvable disagreement head-on is the view of democracy as a fair compromise.[1] Recall the observation that among individuals there are often ineliminable differences of opinion concerning how society as a whole ought to be organized. Individuals are often unable, by rational persuasion, to get others to agree on the right way to organize society. The question is, When individuals differ concerning how to arrange things and some decision binding on all of them must be made, how are they to decide?

The natural response here is to recommend *compromise* among the differing parties. If two people irresolvably disagree about what common course of action to follow and they wish to act in concert, they ought to compromise. For example if you and I are friends and wish to spend our vacation together but want to do incompatible things during the vacation, such as swimming and mountain climbing, we should compromise by finding some way to do both. In addition, we ought to pursue some kind of *fair* compromise. It is unfair if I manage to get you to agree to virtually everything I want merely because I threaten to put up a big fuss if I do not have my way. This kind of hard bargaining will often fail to produce a just compromise. Intuitively, a reasonable compromise is to spend equal time together on the activities. This example also suggests the importance of equality in fair compromises. Equal division seems like a naturally fair solution to many problems of compromise. This instance of compromise doesn't tell us how to resolve disagreement because it does not involve disagreement at all; it is a case of *conflict of interests.*

The conflict presented above is over how to satisfy our various desires when they are in conflict. You desire to go to the beach and I desire to go the mountains, so we have to compromise. Now suppose that two people have a difference of opinion on what the right or fair course of action is and cannot persuade each other. For example, two people make an important contribution to science but they cannot agree on the amount of credit each deserves. They agree that each deserves credit in proportion to their contribution, but they disagree as to how much each has contributed. They have a *factual disagreement* about what's fair in this case. They discuss the point and remain in sincere disagreement. A third person acting as arbitrator might divide the credit equally as a kind of fair compromise if he too cannot determine who is right. Notice that one of the two persons may be right about what each deserves, but neither can persuade the other or the arbitrator. Most would agree that it is fair to divide the credit equally even though it may not be the absolutely fair division of credit since someone may in fact have made a larger contribution. We have a standard of fair compromise when there is disagreement on "absolute fairness."[2]

Peter Singer thinks that the idea of fair compromise applies when there is disagreement on the principles of fairness, or justice, as well as when there is factual disagreement. In the example above both agree to the principle that each should receive goods in proportion to their relative contributions; they merely disagree about who has contributed most. Regarding *principled disagreement*, if individuals disagree on the moral principles that ought to govern their relations and the disagreement cannot be resolved through rational persuasion, it makes sense to call for a fair compromise. Each must concede part of what he or she wants and be prepared to live under a compromise arrangement that is not fully satisfactory to him or her.

What kind of compromise is called for? Singer thinks that if we resolve the disagreement in favor of one of the principles, the individual who holds it gets his or her way on the matter. Getting one's way despite disagreement and regardless of the concerns of others is a kind of dictatorship over others. Since each party to the disagreement aims to have his or her principle implemented, each person in effect desires to be a dictator over the others. Obviously disagreement arises here because each thinks that he or she ought to rule and that the others' claims to authority are wrong. Notice that there are two sorts of disagreement in these cases. One concerns *what* decisions to make, or *substantive disagreement*; the other concerns *who* is to make decisions, or *procedural disagreement*. Singer thinks that the disagreement about how best to organize society implies a disagreement about who ought to decide: Each thinks he or she ought to rule. His proposal is to resolve the substantive disagreement with a fair compromise on the procedural disagreement.

The procedural interpretation of the dispute implies a kind of symmetry among the claims since each makes a claim to be dictator. Since each claims the same right to rule and there is no agreed upon way of determining whose claim is best, a fair compromise divides authority to make decisions into equal shares. Each must give up the same amount of his or her claim to rule in a way that can produce a workable decision procedure; so each receives an equal voice in the making of collective decisions, and the rule for deciding is majority rule. Hence the fair procedural compromise among persons who disagree fundamentally about the principles that are to regulate their society is democracy.

Problems with Democracy as a Compromise

This argument for democracy attempts to accommodate the problem of persistent disagreement that undermines the liberty arguments. It is founded on the inevitability of such disagreement. But there are a number of difficulties with this approach. First, there is no defense of the move from substantive to procedural compromise. Why interpret principled disagreement as an instance of who ought to rule rather than what ought to be done? Why not resolve principled disagreement by setting up a compromise on the issues? Such a compromise might be established by an outside arbitrator who could give each person's preference equal weight in deciding the arrangements. A substantive compromise would have the virtue of including everyone's preferences in the result, whereas the procedural compromise entails some winners and some losers on the substantive issues. For example, two groups disagree on principles of economic organization; one advocates a principle of minimal restriction on private property, and the other advocates state control over all economic decisions. A substantive compromise might be some kind of interventionist welfare state. A procedural compromise, conversely, would imply a kind of majority rule, so that the larger group would determine the economic arrangements. Moreover, the substantive compromise need not be chosen democratically. It does not require any particular distribution of authority; it could be selected by an arbitrator. Democracy may be a more reliable way of finding the best substantive compromise, but it is not thereby intrinsically fair. So, there is a serious gap in the argument for democracy. We must know why a procedural solution is necessary and should have priority.

Another problem with the idea of democracy as a fair compromise is that giving everyone an equal say in matters is not always a fair compromise. Singer defines a compromise as an arrangement in which each person concedes part of his or her claim. In a fair compromise the parties make equal concessions. Whether an arrangement is a fair compromise depends on the initial points of disagreement as well as the compromise procedure. The outcome of the procedural disagreement is egalitarian only because Singer assumes that the parties' claims must be symmetrical. But if we suppose that the parties to the dispute are not all equally megalomaniacal and that some wish to institute democracy whereas others have more oligarchical aspirations, then giving each an equal say will not constitute a compromise at all, let alone a fair compromise; the democrats will have their way, whereas the aspiring oligarchs will get nothing. The fair compromise on the procedural matter in this instance would be some mix of democracy and oligarchy.[3] Alternatively, if the members of the group mostly agree that one of the persons ought to rule, then the fair compromise principle will provide no basis for democratic rule. This is an unfortunate consequence for a theory that attempts an intrinsic defense of democracy. Thus Singer's argument cannot justify democracy except under special and unlikely circumstances.

A third difficulty is that Singer's account is marred by a kind of self-defeatingness. He argues that fair compromise is appropriate for resolving principled disagreement. However, since the principle of fair compromise is itself a moral principle, whatever problems attend the holding of moral principles in general should also attend the principle of fair compromise. If mere disagreement on moral principles suffices to call for fair compromise among the parties, what do we do when there is disagreement on the principle of fair compromise? Surely disagreement is likely to arise here as well. If there is something wrong about trying to implement one's preferred conception of justice when there is substantial disagreement on conceptions of justice, then it would seem to be wrong to try to implement a conception of fair compromise when there is serious disagreement on it. Whatever makes us hesitate about applying principles of justice ought to make us think twice about applying any controversial notion of fairness as a compromise. But given the ubiquity of disagreement, it appears that virtually any notion of fair compromise will be controversial. Hence, the idea that one can and ought to finally and fairly resolve political disagreements by means of a notion of a fair compromise seems to be self-defeating.

Moreover, if everyone does agree on a principle of fair compromise, they will probably disagree on some aspect of its application.

How can we be sure that everyone will agree that an equal say is a fair compromise? Such agreement is especially unlikely in view of some of the complexities we have noted concerning the notion of fair compromise. For example, why suppose people will favor procedural over substantive compromise? And since some will advocate democracy and others oligarchy, there is no reason to expect everyone to want to be dictator. Disagreement on these matters is as likely to arise as on the original principles of justice. The logic of Singer's argument compels us to seek a fair compromise for resolving these procedural questions as well. This process could easily go on ad infinitum. So we have a kind of regress problem from which the idea of fair compromise provides no relief.

In sum, the principle of fair compromise cannot provide a rationale for democracy since it cannot explain why disagreement must be handled by procedural compromise. And even if procedural compromise is called for, the principle of fair compromise cannot explain why it ought to be democratic. Finally, the principle of fair compromise either defeats itself in cases where people disagree with it, or it leads to a regress in those cases where individuals cannot agree on its application.

Equal Consideration of Interests

The view of democracy as a fair compromise, which I explored in the previous two sections, founds democracy on the idea that each person's *judgment* about what is right and wrong ought to be considered equally in a fair compromise when there is disagreement among the parties. We found the approach to be deeply flawed. In this section we will look at an egalitarian approach to democracy that requires that each person's *interests* ought to be given equal consideration in choosing the laws and policies of a society.[4] This approach begins with Thomas Rainsborough's observation that "the poorest he that is in England has a life to live as the greatest he."[5] It goes on to claim that democracy is founded on this principle of equal consideration of interests.

Let us explore the distinction between judgments and interests and show how it is related to the principle of equality as well as sketch the relation of judgments and interests to democracy. First, an *interest* is something that is a component of a person's overall well-being. I have interests in pleasure, friendship, knowledge, health, and so on. I am better off when my interests are satisfied and worse off when they are not. An interest is not the same as the satisfaction of desire. I may desire many things that do not contribute to my own good. I may desire that peace and justice reign forever over the world, but I am not better off if ten thousand years from now there is peace and justice, though this does satisfy my desire. I may knowingly desire things that harm me because I am addicted to them or simply because I have been raised in a way that encourages masochism. Interests also differ from judgments. An interest is something that can be attributed to me whether I believe it or not. Someone can coherently say of me that it would be better for me if I had more pleasure in my life even if I, because of certain religious convictions, abhor pleasure and believe it to be bad. In this case, I may judge falsely what is in my interest. A judgment is a belief about a fact of the matter or a principle of justice or one's interests. Interests are one kind of fact about which we make judgments. Judgments can be correct or incorrect, whereas interests are not correct or incorrect; they are simply attributes of a person.

Equal consideration of interests means that advancing the interests of one person is as important as advancing the interests of any other person. There is no reason why one person should have a fundamentally better life than others, because "each has a life to live." To the extent that social institutions have a great influence on how people's lives go, they are unjust when they unnecessarily make some people's lives go worse than others.

It is an elementary requirement of justice that individuals ought to be treated equally if they are equal in the relevant ways and may be treated unequally if they are unequal in a relevant way. Each person has an equally important life to live, so there is a strong presumption in favor of his or her interests being given equal consideration. Furthermore, there is no good reason at the outset for arranging things so that some persons' lives will go better than others. Let us consider why some have thought that the lives of some individuals ought to go better than the lives of others. Some have maintained that race or sex ought to determine how a person's life can go. They have thought that women's or blacks' interests are less important than those of men or whites because of the natural differences between them and that the lives of these could be worse without injustice. But this is false; the fact that someone is a woman or black is of no relevance to issues of justice. They each have a life to live and interests to satisfy, and it would be unjust to treat their interests as less important. Social institutions that systematically make it harder for women or blacks to live flourishing lives than for others to are unjust. Others have thought that there is no injustice in the fact that the children of poor parents are not likely to do nearly as well as the children of the wealthy. That growing up in poverty and without the benefits of education makes it much harder and much less likely for a child to live a satisfying life implies that the institutions that permit these great disparities are unjust. The wealth or poverty of the family into which one is born hardly seem relevant to whether one's life ought to go well or not. This kind of argument can be generalized. We find injustice in any society that systematically ensures that some persons' lives go worse than others'. Thus, if we take the standpoint of considering each person's life as a whole, we see no relevant reason for treating anyone's interests unequally.

How does all of this apply to democracy? Democracy gives individuals equal abilities to advance their concerns when decisions concerning the terms of association are made. For instance, each person is provided with an equally weighted vote in deciding the outcome of an election. We cry "foul play" when some are prohibited from voting or when the votes of some are not counted. Also, the democratic method is usually to decide by majority rule. Whichever alternative gets the most votes is implemented. Majority rule is a genuinely egalitarian rule because it gives each person the same chance as every other to affect the outcome. Thus each person's concerns are treated equally by this method. In addition, each person is thought to have an equal opportunity to run for office and to have a say in public debate. Those who are systematically unable to make themselves heard because of poverty or race or sex are treated unjustly. If nothing else, democracy is a deeply egalitarian method of organizing social decisionmaking.

It is important, however, to get clear on the relation between democracy and the principle of equal consideration of interests; a

large part of this chapter will pursue this issue. We might understand the principle to imply that everyone's interests are to be
equally advanced or that everyone is to be made equally well-off by
decisions. This is the *equal well-being* interpretation. On this account, justice demands that each person lives a life of the same total
level of well-being as everyone else. But if we interpret the principle
of equal consideration of interests as recommending that everyone
be equally well-off, then the relation between it and democracy is
rather unclear. Democracy is a method for making collective decisions in which everyone has an equal right to play a role. Democracy is an arrangement in which individuals have some equality in
political power. But the principle of equal well-being is not concerned with the *method* by which decisions are made. It does not
say anything about who has a right to rule. And it does not say anything about the distribution of power. Policies can be designed with
an eye to making everyone equally well-off without their being
democratically chosen. Such equality of well-being may be a good
thing, but it is not the same as democracy. Democratic processes
may be good methods to ensure that everyone's interests are equally
satisfied, but such an argument for democracy would be instrumentalist and not an intrinsic argument of the sort we are pursuing.
Again, to use a worn illustration, equal well-being is compatible
with the institution of benevolent dictatorship.

So if we are to understand democracy as based on a principle of
equal consideration of interests, we must have a different interpretation of that principle to work with. After the next section, I will lay
out a different interpretation of equal consideration that provides a
more defensible version of equality as well as a proper basis for
democracy.

Taking Stock

Let us take stock of the problems we have found in efforts to offer
philosophical foundations for democracy. This will provide us with
a list of issues to be resolved in the rest of this chapter. In the theories of democracy founded on liberty we found three difficulties.
The trade-off problem suggested that liberty accounts cannot de-
liver a rationale for political liberty in addition to personal liberty. A

general concern for liberty does not explain why it is important that there be equality in political liberty as well as personal liberty. Why couldn't trade-offs between these two kinds of liberty be possible? If a defense of democracy is to be successful, this problem suggests, we need a theory of the specific interests persons have in political life aside from their private lives. Such an account cannot be given in the liberty theories that eschew talk of conceptions of the good life. Furthermore, it should be clear that once we have a sufficiently specified conception of interests to explain the interest in democratic participation, the invocation of liberty as a founding principle will be otiose.

Second, liberty accounts fail to deal with the fact that equal political participation in collective decisionmaking is incompatible with liberty in the collective decisionmaking. When I participate in democratic politics, I depend on the actions of many others, over whom I have no control, in order to achieve desirable outcomes. I am not free to do what I believe is best, and I do not have leave to bring about what I prefer. I am bound by the actions of many people.

Some have supposed that democratic participation is really a matter of formulating judgments about the best way to organize society. They argue that a democratic society is one in which I live under institutions that correspond to my judgment of what is best. I am free on this account when the institutions that constrain my life accord with my freely arrived at judgments about what is best. But in order for this approach to be relevant, there must be substantial consensus of judgment on the proper terms of association we live under. This condition, however, flies in the face of the common and pervasive experience we have of disagreement and conflict in society and thus, must fail as a strategy for defending democracy.

From the failure of the last view, we know that our conception of democracy must not ignore the facts of deep disagreement on matters of principle in modern society. We have seen that some egalitarian theorists of democracy have tried to accommodate the idea that participation is based on judgment with the fact of disagreement. Disagreement on matters of principle, they argue, must be resolved by fair compromise. Such a fair compromise is that each has a say in making decisions. A number of difficulties afflict this view, but the most serious is that it is self-defeating. If all disagreements on matters of principle are to be met with fair compromise, what are we to do if there is disagreement on what the fair compromise ought to be?

From these failures we have learned that there is a basic problem with thinking of politics as a matter of judgment alone. Such an approach either presupposes consensus or it leads to a kind of self-defeating quest for compromise when there is disagreement. Thus, we must found a normative, intrinsic defense of democracy and politics in general on another principle altogether. We explored the possibility of equal consideration of interests as our basic principle. We observed, however, that a first interpretation of this ideal, that is, equal well-being, is an unsuitable basis for an intrinsic defense of democracy since it makes no provision for the kind of equal sharing in authority implied by democracy. Equal well-being can only be a general principle for evaluating the outcomes of political processes.

In what follows we shall see that these problems can be solved. First, we shall start with the basic argument for democracy. Democratic decisionmaking can be founded on a principle of equal consideration of interests. For this we need two things. First, we need a conception of the interests individuals have that are specifically related to their common lives together. Second, we must show that the best interpretation of equal consideration of interests requires that each has an equal share in authority over that common life. Such a conception of equality requires not that everyone be equally well-off but that citizens have equal resources for advancing their interests. Once we show that this is the best understanding of equal consideration of interests we can explain why it is so important that citizens have equal voting power as well as equal access to institutions of power and the processes of social discussion. Then, we shall see how this view of democracy can overcome the problems that beset the liberty-based views as well as the idea of democracy as a fair compromise. I will show how the view can accommodate the pervasive facts of moral disagreement while avoiding the problem of self-defeat. Then we shall see how the view avoids the trade-off problem. We will then see how the position I have sketched can account for the importance of democratic deliberation in democratic politics.

An Egalitarian Defense of Democracy

There are four steps in the basic argument that democracy is defensible in terms of a principle of egalitarian justice. First, justice requires that individuals be treated equally with regard to their interests. Second, there is a special category of interests that are deeply interdependent, so that what affects one, affects all; these are interests in the collective properties or features of society. Third, these interests can generally only be served through a collectively binding procedure. Fourth, the principle of equal consideration of interests requires equality of means for participating in deciding on the collective properties of society. Democratic decisionmaking is the embodiment of this equality of resources. Votes, campaign finances, and access to sources of information are all the kinds of resources that must be equalized in the process. Therefore, the principle of equal consideration of interests requires democratic decisionmaking on the collective attributes of society.

Collective Properties

Let us start with an explanation of the interest in collective features of society. Examples of collective properties are the arrangement of public symbols and spaces, the level of environmental protection, the geographical disposition of various elements of the community by means of zoning laws, the system of defense, the system of education, the laws regulating property and exchange as well as the enforcement of these institutions, and finally the method by which all the above activities are financed. We also have to include the distribution of wealth in society and the basic structure of civil rights of citizens. A society can have any one of a variety of collective features. With regard to property, one collective feature is a highly regulated system of private property, an alternative feature would be an unregulated system, and another yet would be a system of collectivized property. With regard to environmental protection, a society can have regulations that limit the amount of pollution or it might choose to permit a considerable amount of pollution. A society must make choices among the above institutions. And the set of collective features is what defines the common world that people share in a society.

I define "collective property of the society" in the following way: A property of individuals' lives in a society is a collective property or feature if and only if in order to change one person's welfare with regard to this property one must change all or almost all of the other members' welfare with regard to it. This definition implies that collective properties have the following four characteristics. First, they satisfy a condition of *nonexclusivity*. It is not possible to affect one person's life without affecting the lives of the others. Pollution control is the most obvious example of this. One cannot generally limit pollution in a society for the benefit of some but not for others. Everyone benefits from pollution control or no one does. Of course, not all collective properties affect citizens in the same way; some collective properties may benefit some citizens and harm others. What is important is that everyone be affected by the change in a collective property. Zoning, or the lack thereof, is a property of the whole community in which it is done. When one zones a community, one arranges the various parts in a certain way. A change in a zoning law is a change of collective property for the community being zoned; in principle, everyone is affected by the change. The same is true for public monuments and institutions as well as limitations on publicly displayed behavior. These sorts of concerns are cultural in nature. They are collective properties, but there is conflict over the goods themselves.

The second condition is *publicity*. The point of saying that everyone's well-being is affected rather than that their preferences are satisfied is that it rules out the possibility that the property satisfies purely nosy preferences. For example, it might be thought that homosexuality is a collective property when some members of the society desire that others participate in or abstain from this activity. But insofar as I can participate in, or abstain from, homosexual activities without affecting other people's interests, I do not affect others' welfare with regard to this property even if those others have preferences about what I do. Hence, collective properties must be public objects.[6]

Third, the fact that individuals share such a common world is *inevitable*. For example, every society has a public environment; we have no choice about whether our community will have air and water of some quality or another. That environment is characterized by its collective properties. It can have different properties, just as a surface can be different colors. It will have some such properties necessarily.

Finally, the properties of this common world are *alterable*. The issue for us is which among the alternative possible properties society will have. We have no choice about whether the community is arranged geographically in a particular way, but we can choose which among the many possible ways it is arranged. Thus, we cannot avoid the existence of a common world in which each person shares, but we may be able to decide what that common world is like.

These four conditions describe a high level of interdependence of interests. To affect one person's interests is to affect everyone's interests. Individuals have interests in these properties of society because they play such an important role in defining the basic environment in which individuals live. The common world frames each's relations with others and structures the possible courses of life each can lead. These features are also a source of a sense of belonging inasmuch as citizens understand, recognize, and adhere to the cultural and moral norms of the social arrangements that frame their lives. They can also be a source of alienation to those for whom these conditions do not hold. For each person, there is a lot at stake in how the common world is arranged.

However, in modern society there is substantial conflict over what collective properties to bring about. There are disagreements about the norms of justice, there are different cultural traditions that citizens identify with, and there are disagreements about the appropriate level of provision of public goods. Finally, there is substantial disagreement as well as conflict of interest over the total packages of collective properties. Some may think that certain issues are more important than others. Thus there is no consensus on these goods.[7] I will not go into what is the basis of this diversity in society except to observe that modern societies are the products of large movements of diverse peoples, they include highly differentiated divisions of labor, and they tend to be very large geographically. More generally, people are different from each other inasmuch as they flourish in different kinds of environments. To some degree these different needs can be handled in more private circumstances and voluntary associations without affecting the interests of others, so I do not wish to deny the private-public distinction or the importance of individual liberty. However, the whole environment of the society is at stake in many conflicts of interests in collective properties. So collective features are defined in terms of a deep interdependence of interests in certain features of society, though there is no consensus on which properties to choose for organizing the society.

One choice a community must make is whether to decide these issues in a centrally coordinated way or to leave the determination of these properties up to the free play of social forces. In the case of collective properties, the latter method will often lead to unpalatable results for all. To allow these to develop in an uncoordinated fashion will often lead to results of which no one will approve. For example, it is better to have some legal system of property than none at all. The absence of such a system would lead to confusion and uncertainty for everyone. The likely result will be worse for everyone than almost all the alternatives. In order to have a legal system, however, a society must have an authoritative process by which to decide on what the laws are as well as how to enforce them and judge when individuals have violated them. If a society is to advance the interests of all its citizens, it must have a collective decision-making procedure that binds citizens to its decisions.

So far, this collective decision-making procedure need not be democratic in order to play the role of choosing collective properties. Kings can choose collective properties; aristocracies can also do this. The question for us is, Is there anything special about democratic methods of making decisions on these matters? As we noted earlier, equality requires that citizens' interests be given equal consideration, but we have not shown yet why democracy is a unique embodiment of this equal consideration.

A Defense of Equal Distribution of Political Resources

The problem we need to address is, Why does equal consideration of the interests citizens have in collective properties imply that they ought to have equal votes in the collective decision-making process that chooses those properties? How can citizens complain of injustice if they are not given the means with which to influence the process of decisionmaking? A crucial step in the argument for democratic decisionmaking is to move beyond mere equal consideration of interests to equality in the process of decisionmaking. The reason for this is that democracy involves not just any equality, it requires equality in certain kinds of instruments or resources for achieving one's ends. For example, democracy is commonly thought to require that each person have one vote. A vote is a kind of instrument or resource for achieving one's aims. A vote is not by itself intrinsically desirable; it is not a piece of happiness or well-being itself. But it might help us achieve what is intrinsically worthwhile to us. If we have a vote in a decision, this vote will help us get the decision that we think best. Having equality in votes does not imply that there is equality in well-being; and having equality in well-being does not entail that there is equality in the vote. Our previous two conceptions of equality have failed to make the necessary move from equality to equality in the instruments for achieving one's aims that is required for a defense of democracy. Can this move be made? I believe it can.

What is the difference between equality in well-being and equality in resources? Here are some examples of this distinction. Well-being is usually thought to involve happiness, health, knowledge, friendship, pleasure, self-respect, and the respect of others, as well as a sense of belonging and community with others and a variety of other things that people desire for their own sakes. These are what make up a good life. They are the most basic interests that people have. On the other hand, resources are money, power, liberty, and opportunity, as well as votes and information that people usually desire for the sake of achieving greater well-being. They may be described as tools, instruments, or means for pursuing our aims. They do not by themselves make for a good life, but they are useful in helping us satisfy our interests.

Equality of well-being is equality in those things that make for a good life. Each person, in such a view, would have equal totals of pleasure, happiness, self-respect, and so on. Clearly the idea of equal consideration of interests is closely related to equality of well-being. However, equality of resources involves the equal distribution of money, power, opportunities, and so on. The relation between equal consideration of interests and equality of resources is more obscure. At the same time it is clear why democracy might constitute at least a partial realization of equality of resources since democracy involves the equal distribution of those means (e.g., votes) for influencing the collective decision-making procedure. We should note here that though resources themselves are not intrinsically desirable, equality in the distribution of resources may well be intrinsically just and valuable. If we start with a principle of equal consideration of interests, it is essential that we show that equality of resources is really the most plausible interpretation of this ideal.

Not only does equality of well-being not provide an account of democracy, I argue that egalitarian justice under circumstances of substantial disagreement and pluralism about well-being is best understood as equality of resources.[8] The problem with equality of well-being is that it runs afoul of a basic constraint in political theory. It appears to be a reasonable interpretation of the principle of equal consideration of interests, but upon closer inspection it is not. In political philosophy we cannot assume an equal well-being approach because we cannot make clear sense of the comparisons of well-being that must be made in order to sustain it. There is too little information about the alternatives and their comparisons, and there is a great deal of disagreement as to how they should be compared. First I will show how these claims are true, and then I will demonstrate their importance.

Three considerations motivate the rejection of equal well-being as a political principle with which to evaluate social and political institutions. The incompleteness of knowledge, the changeability of preference, and the contestability of comparisons of well-being all show that the distribution of well-being is not a reasonable standard for assessing social institutions. The main point is that equality of well-being and indeed any notion of equality in the satisfaction of interests is unintelligible as a political ideal. Thus it cannot provide an interpretation of equal consideration of interests for a political society.

The *incompleteness of knowledge* is that individuals do not have clear or fully worked out ideas of what their overall interests are. And no one else can have such an understanding about what individuals' overall interests are. But only if we do have such an understanding can we make sense of equality of well-being among citizens. There are two basic reasons for the incompleteness. The first reason is that human cognitive capacities are simply too weak to formulate such complex conceptions about all the possible interests persons have in all the relevant circumstances. The alternatives are themselves quite complex, and the number of possible different alternatives is very great, too great for a single mind to grasp. Let each person attempt to rank the goods I adumbrated above in all the different combinations in which they might arise. Each will find that they only have extremely crude ways of comparing the goods of love and self-respect as well as knowledge and pleasure. These ways are completely inadequate for attempting to evaluate many of the circumstances in which we find ourselves. This is so even when limited to the sphere of interests over collective properties of society.[9] It is not that we haven't tried to do this, it is simply that it is beyond our capacity to conceive of such a complicated ranking of all the different combinations of the things we think are important.

The second reason why knowledge of interests is incomplete is that individuals do not have complete understandings of most of their particular interests. Individuals are constantly in a process of improving and completing their judgments about what is good and just, and they do not come to an end in this process. It is ongoing and incomplete because of the cognitive limitations on persons. Much of our lives consists of learning new things about our good. None of us would claim that we have a full understanding of even the elements of our good. And if this is true of our knowledge of ourselves, it is even more true of our understanding of other people's interests. But if our knowledge of our own interests is so incomplete, then even if we have a metric for comparing interests, we do not have even the beginnings of a clear idea of what we are comparing. And if we do not know what we are comparing, then we certainly cannot say when we have equal amounts of those things.

To be sure, if we think of equal well-being as equal satisfaction of preferences, at least the second part of the above argument can be answered. It simply says that we ought to advance each person's preferences equally. But the *changeability* of preferences undermines this possible response. The problem is that persons base their preferences on their understanding of their interests and they are constantly changing their conceptions of their interests. Their understandings change as a consequence of the process of learning from experience and discussion with others, as well as from other causes. Their lives cannot be evaluated in terms of how well they live up to a preference ordering over a whole life because they cannot be identified with any single set of preferences since they change over time. Thus, even if we were to have a metric for measuring relative levels of preference satisfaction, we would not be able to figure out what equality of preference satisfaction for lives amounts to, given the mutability of these preferences.

The *contestability of comparisons argument* proceeds from the claim that there is considerable disagreement in any democratic society about what interests are most important as well as how to compare the relative worth of satisfying those interests. What constitutes an equal distribution for one person may not be equal in another's eyes. How to compare interests among individuals will be a deeply contested subject. The ideal of equality of well-being must be essentially ambiguous in a complex society. The same is true for any conception of welfare. What constitutes welfare is a matter on which persons will have serious disputes, and the metric for determining when people's interests are met is itself a matter of deep contestation.[10]

Hence, egalitarian institutions cannot depend on the notion of equal well-being to serve as a principle for solving political disputes. The metric for defining how much a person has gotten out of the democratic process must be essentially undefined since individuals cannot have fully articulated or constant preferences over results in general. There also cannot be uncontestable accounts of the bases of comparison on which any notion of equality of results must depend.

These difficulties may be thought to show that an outcome view like equality of welfare is a first-best solution, which, though unattainable, must be approximated by some second-best solution. On such an account equal well-being would be an unattainable but desirable political ideal and democratic equality would be merely a necessarily imperfect means to such an outcome. This would be much like a trial procedure which is thought to be an imperfect means to discovering the guilt or innocence of a person. Or some may think that economic markets are means for achieving efficient allocations of resources as well as technological progress. The market arrangement is not in itself just, these proponents would say, it is merely a good way to achieve good outcomes, given the ignorance of persons in figuring out how to do it in some other way. Similarly, these thinkers would argue that democratic institutions are not intrinsically fair or just, they merely are the best way to ensure a fair distribution of well-being. The fact that we do not know what such a fair distribution looks like in advance does not imply that it cannot produce it. Our ignorance is merely a contingent obstacle that ought not to come in at the level of defining the political ideal.

But in my view the rejection of equal well-being as a political ideal is not merely a matter of contingent fact. We are not merely ignorant of what the ideal would look like; we are ignorant of what increasing approximations to the ideal look like except in fairly crude cases. It is certainly as fundamental a fact as any that human beings are not able to come up with clear conceptions of their own interests and that they cannot compare those interests in any precise way amongst themselves. It would be absurd to evaluate political institutions on the basis of so unfathomable a standard.

One reason why this is absurd is that just institutions must not only be just by some standard, they must be capable of being manifestly just to each of the members. Partly this is because the justice of a social order ought not to be a complete mystery to the citizens of the society. No standard of justice can be in principle beyond the capacity of citizens to ascertain. It must be something they have a chance of knowing and celebrating; the justice of a society is a feature of that society that individuals can recognize and by which they can acknowledge each other as equals. Furthermore, each member of an egalitarian society has an interest in their equal public status being manifest to themselves and to everyone. Such *manifestness*[11] in equal status does not arise with the use of the inscrutable standard of equality in well-being or preference satisfaction for the various reasons identified above. But there is some reasonable chance that the manifestness of equality can arise as a consequence of the implementation of equality of resources. I can see if I have an equal vote with others. I can know if I am being discriminated against in an electoral scheme. I can have a sense of when the promotion of my interests and point of view have far less financial backing than those of others. Indeed, these are the stuff of the standard complaints of politics in a democratic society. These publicly observable inequalities are often raised against political systems as affronts to the principle that each person is to be treated and acknowledged as an equal citizen. But these complaints are related not to the distribution of well-being in the society but rather to the distribution of resources in the society. Hence, an egalitarian will be concerned to determine collective properties in accordance with an equality of resources scheme. That each person has a vote, has adequate means to acquire understanding of their interests, and has the means for making coalitions with others as well as getting equal representation in a legislature is a publicly manifest phenomenon. Without such manifest equality citizens cannot be assured of their membership in an egalitarian society.

Moreover, observe how we actually do evaluate institutions. Part of the function of political institutions is to distribute resources for collecting and processing information about interests. Ignorance is one of the reasons why human beings need political institutions. They serve as contexts in which individuals may learn about their interests. Institutions of education, deliberation, and communication are designed in part to help individuals determine where their interests and values lie. Because institutions are to provide the basis for discovering one's interests, and those institutions must treat individuals as equals, the idea of equality for such institutions must be defined in some other way than directly in terms of equality in interests. Indeed, the ideal of equality must be defined partly in terms of the resources that are necessary to undertake these learning tasks. Consider primary education. We do not evaluate it on the grounds of its ability to ensure that each has equal well-being in the end; that would be simply impossible. We judge the justice of primary educational institutions on whether they give each child an equal chance to learn. Generally we judge these institutions on whether they have devoted equal resources to each and every pupil. Sometimes we think more resources ought to go to the students who need more help as a result of previous deprivation in their backgrounds, but this involves compensating the students for the lack of resources in the past. Beyond that already difficult task we cannot go.

Furthermore, democratic institutions provide the means for fairly deciding on the relative importance of various interests once discussion and deliberation have failed to produce consensus. The question must be, when we must make a collective decision, How do we decide in the light of the fact that we disagree about considerations of justice as well as about the relative importance of various kinds of interests? If fairness in the method by which we decide these issues is important, it must be that the fairness is to be implemented by means of a distribution of resources and not on the grounds that one method is more likely to achieve the equal well-being outcome. The latter is something deeply contested, and the contest is part of the reason why we must make a decision.

We have shown the impossibility of establishing what people's interests are and the contestability of our ways of comparing people's interests, as well as the function of justice as publicly establishing the equal worth of the interests of each citizen in the society. The only publicly accessible way to implement equal consideration of interests is to give each citizen the means for discovering and pursuing his or her own interests. The only reasonable implementation of such a principle must be in the equal distribution of resources for making collective decisions. Such a distribution permits each of its members the chance to enhance their understanding of their interests as well as justice on a publicly available equal basis.

Justice, Collective Properties, and Political Equality

Now we are in a position to bring the strands of our argument together. A society must make certain collectively binding decisions about its collective properties in which each citizen has distinct and substantial interests. But consensus is not possible in a society; disagreement is inevitable. So how should that authority be shared among the citizens? Equal consideration of interests is a solution to the problem of the just division of benefits and burdens when there is a scarcity of goods. There is scarcity when the interests of individuals conflict and they cannot all be satisfied. For collective properties there is a serious problem of scarcity. For example, there is conflict over the level of provision of pollution control insofar as different levels of provision have different costs. In the case of the cultural goods, there is conflict over the very goods to be provided as well as the level of provision. And in the case of the laws of property and exchange, there is considerable disagreement as to what ought to be chosen. These concerns determine the whole nature of the community. Insofar as there is a diversity of opinion among the citizens on the issues of which collective properties to implement, few will get their way on any particular issue. Hence, there is a high demand (relative to what can be supplied) for having one's preferred possible collective property implemented.

These last claims provide reasons for thinking that collective properties ought to be subject to principles of just distribution. What does justice require in these circumstances, and why are properties that are not collective to be treated differently? Justice, we have seen, requires that each person's interests be given equal consideration. This equal consideration of interests implies that individuals be given equal resources with which to understand, elaborate, and pursue their interests. Insofar as individuals' interests are deeply interdependent concerning certain features of society and individuals cannot avoid conflicts of interests over those features, there ought to be collective decisionmaking about those features. Inasmuch as everyone has interests in making these decisions, the ideal of equality of resources ought to be applied to the collective decision-making procedure. Thus, each citizen ought to have equal resources to affect the outcomes of the collective decision-making procedure. This implies roughly that each ought to have an equal vote and other resources for participating in the collective decision-making procedure. This is the principle of *political equality*. Political equality implies that each and every citizen ought to have a say in the choice of collective features of society in a common decision procedure. Thus the principle implies a version of the idea of popular sovereignty. Who ought to make the decisions? The answer is, the people. How should they make these decisions? They ought to make the decisions in accordance with a principle of political equality so that each citizen has an equal say. To say that the people are sovereign is not to say that they all agree or that they all have a common will. It merely implies that all the citizens ought to come together in one group to make decisions together as a group.

Inevitably, many readers will have complaints with the argument that I have given. In what follows, I will show how my view avoids difficulties, such as the problem of regress and the trade-off problem, that I have observed in the other theories. I will show how justice in the distribution of resources for collective decisionmaking relates to issues of justice in the distribution of economic resources as well as civil justice. And I will show how my conception of democracy implies the best view of the function of social deliberation in democracy. After addressing these potential sources of difficulties, I will give a fuller elaboration of the nature of political equality, and, finally, I will show how my view avoids one of the main recent criticisms of democracy, the impossibility theorem of social choice theory.

Interests, Judgments, and Conflicting Conceptions of Justice

Democracy is a just way of making laws in the case of collective properties because citizens' interests are opposed on them. But here a difficulty arises. Society must make decisions on matters of civil and economic justice too. Citizens disagree on the justice of the laws of property, exchange, taxation, and the rights of citizens as well, and, clearly, these laws are about collective properties. But conceptions of civil and economic justice are not opposed in the same way that interests are. On the one hand, when there is a controversy on civil and economic justice, individuals try to get others to give up their conceptions by means of rational persuasion. Their first concern is to arrive at the right conception. So when two people disagree they are not primarily concerned that their own conception be advanced but that the right conception be advanced. Conceptions of justice are a matter of judgment. They can be correct or incorrect. The first interest of each person is to have the correct judgment. By analogy, if you and I disagree on the solution to a mathematical problem, we advance opposed conceptions of the solution. What we try to do is figure out who is right, if either of us is right. Our first interest in discussion and debate is not to advance our own view but to discover what is right. Each is willing to give up his or her view if he or she can be shown to be wrong. So it appears that there is no ultimate conflict of interest involved in controversies on civil and economic justice.

On the other hand, when our interests are genuinely opposed, there is no further possibility of rationally persuading one person to give up his or her interests as there is in the case of judgments. My interests are not correct or incorrect as judgments are. And it is precisely this irresolvability that leads to attempts to resolve the conflict by fair means of accommodation. For example, if two people go out while it is raining and they have only one umbrella, they have a conflict of interest in not getting wet. It would not make sense for one person to attempt to resolve the matter by persuading the other that her interest is incorrect or that she should give up her interest. What the two must do here is accommodate the opposing interests in some way.

So although the principle of equality applies to conflicts of interest and democratic decisionmaking is appropriate in these contexts, it is unclear how the principle applies to controversies over civil and economic justice. Since everyone has the same interest—to find the right conception of justice—there is apparently no conflict. If this is right, then the scope of democratic decisionmaking is severely limited since the issues of property, exchange, and taxation play a role in virtually every decision and these issues are almost always connected with matters of justice. If democracy is intrinsically just only in matters unrelated to civil and economic justice, then the thesis of the intrinsic justice of democracy is not a very important one. The effort to improve on Singer's idea of democracy as a fair compromise has eviscerated the view.

The way to show that the principle of equal consideration of interests does apply to such conflicts is to show that important interests do conflict when citizens advance opposed conceptions of justice. There are really four such interests. First, there is the interest in recognition. Each person has an interest in being taken seriously by others. When an individual's views are ignored or not given any weight, this undermines his or her sense of self-respect, in which each has a deep interest. Each has an interest in having his or her conception of justice heard and taken into account when there is irresolvable disagreement. These interests in recognition obviously conflict to the extent that individuals advance opposing conceptions of justice. Second, conceptions of justice often reflect disproportionately the interests of those who hold them. There is a tendency to cognitive bias in articulating and elaborating conceptions of justice, particularly in contexts of actual political conflicts. Cynicism is not necessary to observe this. Cognitive bias is natural given that individuals are likely to be more sensitive and understanding towards their own interests than those of others. And in a complex society

-where individuals' positions in society are quite different, this tendency to bias is increased. If many advance conceptions of justice that reflect their interests, those who lack opportunities to advance their own will lose out. To be sure, the process of rational persuasion should eliminate some of this cognitive bias, but it is unlikely to eliminate it all. Thus, serious conflict of interest is likely to accompany controversies on justice. A third interest associated with advancing a conception of justice is that a person will most likely experience a sense of alienation and distance from a social world that does not accord with any of her sense of justice. She will have a sense of nonmembership. That individuals have these kinds of difficulties can be seen from the experience of indigenous peoples in societies that are radically different from theirs. But this sense of alienation can be experienced to lesser degrees when there are lesser disagreements. The interest in a sense of membership is a source of conflict as well. A fourth interest is related to the interest in coming to have the right conception of justice. If persons are to be rationally persuaded, the arguments that lead them to the new belief must start by appealing to their initial beliefs. Persons are not persuaded by arguments based on premises they do not believe. As a consequence, the views of each person in a process of social discussion must be taken seriously if each is to have the opportunity to learn from that discussion. But a person's views will not be taken seriously in such a process if that person does not possess the power to affect political decisionmaking. Why should others try to convince someone who has no impact on the decision when there is so little time to persuade those who do have power? So each person has an interest in having his or her own view taken into account in discussion, and citizens' interests conflict to the extent that there is a limited space in which to discuss all views. The only way to treat these interests equally is to give them equal shares in political authority. I explore equality in discussion in more detail later in this chapter and in Chapter 8.

These four interests suggest that there is some similarity between advancing conceptions of justice and advancing one's interests. They suggest that there is some basis for applying a principle of equal consideration of interests when there is substantial disagreement over conceptions of justice. So democratic decisionmaking is the proper way of resolving conflicts over conceptions of justice.

To avoid misunderstanding here, when I say that individuals have interests in advancing their own conceptions of justice, I do not mean to say that their conceptions of justice are mere masks for their own interests. I also do not mean to say that individuals' conceptions of justice are mere tools for pursuing their own interests. I take it as a fundamental fact that human beings are deeply concerned with matters of civil and economic justice and are concerned with having the most accurate understandings of these matters. I defend this claim in detail in Chapter 4. Conflict in political society is often generated by pervasive but sincerely based disagreement on these matters. The four kinds of interests that I described above are interests that individuals pursue when advancing conceptions of justice; they are interests that are assured by giving each an opportunity to advance his or her own conception of justice in a world where there is uncertainty about the truth of any particular conception.

The contrast between interests and principles of justice drawn above was too great in another way. Citizens do not advance their interests directly; they advance what they believe to be their interests. So when there are conflicts of interests, they are conflicts between what citizens judge to be their interests. Of course, unlike issues of justice, they are not in conflict primarily because of disagreement as to how best to understand their interests; they are in conflict on the assumption that their conceptions of their interests are right. But the question still arises as to why it follows from a principle of equal consideration of interests that citizens ought to be given the right to advance what they *understand* to be their interests. Versions of the four reasons provided above give answers to this question. To treat a person as incompetent in discerning her interests is to undermine a fundamental support for her self-respect. It amounts to treating her as an inferior. Her interest in recognition gives us a reason to treat her as competent in judging her interests. Furthermore, individuals are more likely than others to understand their own interests. Obviously, each has a greater incentive to understand his or her own interests than those of anyone else. And each is better acquainted with the needs and vicissitudes of his or her life than anyone else. This is particularly true in a complex and highly diversified society wherein the contexts of people's lives are quite diverse.[12] Furthermore, analogs of the feelings of belonging and alienation accompany the lives of those who live in contexts that respond to their conceptions of their interests and those who live in circumstances that do not. Finally, people can learn best about their interests in discussions with others where their ideas are taken seriously.

We might ask what a person is more likely to understand about his interests than others. Some have a lot more technical and scientific knowledge than others. Many doctors probably understand many aspects of my health better than I do. But there are aspects even of my health that I understand best, such as how much time I wish to contribute to my health compared to other goods of mine or how well I feel. As Aristotle says: "There are some arts whose products are not judged of solely, or best, by the artists themselves, namely those arts whose products are recognized even by those who do not possess the art; for example, the knowledge of the house is not limited to the builder only; ... the master of the house will even be a better judge than the builder ... and the guest will judge better of a feast than the cook."[13] Thus, though citizens may not be the best judges of their interests in an unqualified way because they have little knowledge of how to satisfy them or the conditions under which they can best be preserved, they are the best judges with regard to certain essential features of their interests. Not all the aspects of my interests are a matter of technical knowledge that can be had by anyone. Some knowledge of a person's interests is essentially more available to him or her than to anyone else. Though each can improve on his or her knowledge of interests by reflection and even discussion with others, others are not likely to be better informed in general. An important task of democratic theory is to separate out those aspects of a person's interests that a person is likely to be most knowledgeable about and those that he or she is not. This subject will be pursued in greater detail in Chapter 5, where the problem of how to deal with expertise in a democracy will be explicitly treated.

Democratic Equality and the Problem of Regress

We have seen how disagreement on matters of justice call for a democratic solution, but the problems of infinite regress and self-defeatingness that undermined fairness as a compromise may appear to afflict our theory as well. Recall that fairness as a compromise requires recourse to a fair compromise between disagreeing parties. But by this principle, if there is disagreement about the fairness of the compromise, a higher compromise is necessary to decide which compromise to choose. This leads to an infinite regress under the supposition that agreement will not be secured at any level. Furthermore, if it is wrong to implement one's preferred conception of justice when there is disagreement on it, then it is wrong to impose any controversial conception of fair compromise. Since disagreement is likely, the principle is self-defeating.

Do these problems infect the conception of democracy I have defended? I have argued that conflict over policy grounded in disagreement about civil and economic justice provides reason, grounded in the interests of the parties, for deciding matters democratically. Democratic decisionmaking requires that the interests of each be equally considered. What if there is disagreement on the justice of democratic decisionmaking itself? Does my principle of democracy lead to a regress or does it defeat itself? Let us divide the question a bit here. Three kinds of disagreement are possible here.

First, there is disagreement on whether justice requires the equal consideration of interests at all. Some citizens may think that the equal consideration of interests is unjust and that institutions based on it are unjust. Obviously, equal consideration of interests cannot be advanced by giving them what they want. No one can claim on the basis of the principle of equal consideration of interests that his or her opposition to equal consideration should be given weight. Equal consideration of interests does not automatically require that disagreement be taken into account, as does fairness as a compromise. Yet at the same time, the principle is capable of explaining why some disagreements call for equitable treatment of the parties. It is not self-defeating with regard to this kind of disagreement.

A second kind of disagreement is that some might think that democracy does not embody equal consideration. They might say that equal consideration of interests requires a proper distribution of income and wealth as well as liberty and that democracy is not the best way to ensure such a distribution. They are critics of democracy on the basis of equality. There are two problems here that I want to address. One is whether this conception is self-defeating; the other is what to do when there is apparent conflict between democracy and civil and economic justice. Since there is disagreement on civil and economic justice it is inevitable that in a democratic society policies will be chosen that many regard as unjust. I deal with the self-defeatingness problem here and with the other in the next section.

The question here is, Does the principle behind democracy require us to compromise with those who oppose democracy? The response is that the argument for democratic equality from equal consideration is correct, and that giving any person or group total power to bring about equality will in fact undermine the full realization of equal consideration of interests. If democratic equality does give equal consideration to each person's interests, dissenters' interests are being taken equally into account within the democratic arrangements. And those who oppose democracy cannot in fact promote equal consideration by trying to undermine democracy. Furthermore, the principle of equal consideration of interests requires that citizens' interests be taken equally into account. But it does not require that every interest be taken into account. Whatever interests are advanced by opposing democracy can be consistently ignored if it is true, as I have argued, that democracy best embodies equal consideration of interests. Again, what matters in this argument is the truth of the claim; disagreement does not undermine the justice of implementing the principle.

Third, disagreement about the nature of the democratic equality may arise. Here it is important that the right conception of democratic equality be found. However, there is uncertainty in some aspects of democratic equality, as I will discuss later, and thus there ought to be flexibility and room in a democracy for discussion about the exact principles of democratic equality.[14] Thus, taking interests of individuals in advancing some alternative conceptions of democratic equality is compatible with a principle of equal consideration of interests. We shall see that there is always room for disagreement on the implementation of democratic equality.

The previous considerations suggest that a conception of democracy founded on a principle of equal consideration of interests does not face the same difficulties of self-defeat and infinite regress as does the view of democracy founded on the principle of fair compromise. The former conception avoids these problems because it is grounded on an appeal to the truth, or correctness, of the principles of equal consideration and democratic equality, whereas the latter appeals to consensus and the need to resolve every disagreement fairly. Some may object to the appeal to truth in political theory, but my contention is that such an appeal is essential to any coherent normative political theory.

Democracy and Civil and Economic Justice

So far I have argued that because individuals have interests in the collective properties of society and because those interests conflict, they should be given equal consideration in the choice of the collective properties of society. Furthermore, I argued that, given the facts of ignorance about what exactly our interests are and how to compare them, equality requires the equal distribution of resources, such as votes, for influencing the collective decisionmaking. My arguments have also shown why citizens ought to have an equal say in determining which scheme of property, exchange, and taxation is to be chosen for their society.

But here we come to a difficulty much like the trade-off problem that beset the liberty-based conception of democracy. The principle of equal consideration of interests ought to apply to the distribution of economic resources, such as money and opportunity, since individuals have interests in pursuing their private goals. To the extent that individuals have interests in pursuing private goals and the resources for carrying out these pursuits are scarce, individuals ought to receive equal consideration in the distribution of these resources as a matter of justice. Thus we have a principle of economic justice that is parallel to the principle of democratic equality. The one requires equality of consideration in the distribution of economic resources, whereas the other requires equality of consideration in the distribution of resources for influencing the collective decision procedure.

One question for us is, Why shouldn't people be able to trade off their economic resources for their political resources? Another question is, Why should democratic equality take priority over economic or civil equality when there is an apparent conflict between them? I will answer each question in turn. For example, why shouldn't I be permitted to sell my votes for money or buy votes with my money? Such transactions are forbidden in most democratic states, but why ought they be? Indeed, we might go even further and ask why a person shouldn't be allowed to sell his or her right to vote to another. This suggests a difficulty for our view in that if people make their own distinct trade-offs between economic resources and political resources, it is likely that people will make different trade-offs, and if they do, they are likely to end with different amounts of political resources. And if they have different amounts of political resources, then they will not be political equals and the principle of democratic equality will be undermined in favor of a more global equality.

Neither money nor political power need be distributed equally in this scheme; it is just the bundles of money and power that are equal. Consider this analogy. If we have two piles of apples and pears, one way to distribute them equally would be to distribute equal amounts of apples and pears to each of us. But suppose that you do not like apples and I do not like pears. If the piles are not too different in quality and quantity, it may be reasonable from the point of view of equality to allocate all the apples to me and all the pears to you. Or, if you like apples and pears but you like pears much more than apples whereas I have the reverse preference, it may be reasonable from the point of view of equality to allocate most of the pears and some of the apples to you and most of the apples and some of the pears to me. Here global equality in the distribution of apples and pears does not require equal distribution in each. So why should global equality in economic and political resources require economic and political equality?

The response to this question is that political resources and economic resources are not related in the same way as apples and pears. Political resources are for influencing the collective decision-making procedure of the society, whereas economic resources are primarily geared toward achieving more personal aims through exchange with others. A collective decision procedure plays a unique role in a society. Such a procedure is what makes the pursuit of private aims in a just environment possible. Let us recall the function of the collective decision procedure. In a diverse society, individuals are likely to have not only different interests and aims but different conceptions of justice. In order for any of these aims to be served and even for justice to be served, the members of the society must coordinate on the rules by which they will abide. There are often disagreements among individuals on what the requirements of justice are, so that what one person sees as just treatment of another is thought by that other to be cause for punishment of the first. In the absence of a collective decision procedure these facts lead to distrust, recriminations, and violence, and justice, however construed, is ill served. The chief idea here is that even if economic justice is itself not a conventional matter, the establishment of justice requires coordination among many different actors on a single set of laws coupled with judicial and executive institutions to back them up. Only settled law can help here. And this requires a collective decision-making procedure.[15]

Notice how this applies to the question of trading off between political and economic resources. Even if we were to permit such trade-offs, we would still need a collective decision procedure to decide the rules under which such trade-offs could be made and to establish justice in the system of exchange. A collective decision procedure plays a fundamental and ineliminable role in a society in the establishment of justice.

Why is it necessary that equality be retained in the collective decision procedure? Equality itself is not necessary for the coordinative role of the decisionmaking. The reason, I submit, is that only if people meet each other as equals in the collective decision procedure are they guaranteed that their interests are given equal consideration in a society where there are disagreements about justice. Since there are many such disagreements, many people will not be convinced that equality has been served in the laws that have been made. This is an inevitable fact about complex and diverse societies. On the one hand, if the settled law of the society is thought to be inegalitarian by some and it has been made in an inegalitarian way, then those people have no guarantee that their interests are being given equal consideration. On the other hand, if the settled law is thought to be somewhat inegalitarian but it was made through an egalitarian collective decision process, then even those who think that they have lost out will be able to see that their interests are being given equal consideration in the society at the essential point of choice. Without equality in the collective decision procedure, this guarantee is lost and the equal public status of citizens ceases to hold because there will always be disagreement on economic justice.

The above considerations show that there ought not to be any trade-off between political and economic resources in a society genuinely devoted to equality for all citizens. They also show why democratic procedure ought to be followed even when one is not sure whether the results it has produced are fully just. Each person has a reason, based on equality, to abide by democratically chosen laws even when that person is not convinced that the laws are entirely egalitarian. Democratic equality has priority over economic equality.[16]

There are three limits to these considerations. First, the competing conceptions of justice in society that are subject to democratic decisionmaking ought not to be completely out of line with the principles that underlie democratic equality. The legislative proposals ought to be at least rough attempts at interpreting the idea of equal consideration of interests as it applies to civil and economic justice. Thus the positions of a Nazi party do not deserve the same consideration as do other positions. This does not mean that they must be banned. But it does mean that advancing such a position in democratic decisionmaking need not receive the same protection as other views. And this will make a real difference in a society that is committed to subsidizing political parties as a part of the conception of political equality, as I will argue we ought to do in Chapters 6 and 7. Second, inasmuch as equal consideration of interests has implications for economic and civil equality, the outcomes of democratic decisionmaking can still be unjust even though they have been made in a just manner. The principles of economic and civil justice are to some extent independent sources of evaluation of the society. Therefore, third, the theory described above suggests that democratic equality and economic equality are competing sources of evaluation of the way a society is arranged. Social justice is a complex set of principles that can sometimes conflict. And in general, though democratic equality ought to win out when the outcomes of democratic decisionmaking do not stray too far from social justice in other respects, under some circumstances democratic equality ought to be limited when making decisions democratically leads to profound injustice. Since democratic equality is only a part of a completely just society, there can be conflicts between the different components of justice. If the conflict is so severe that democratically made decisions are likely to severely abridge the other principles of justice, then any reasonable observer will realize that some limits to democracy should be imposed.

For example, if a society is deeply divided between two ethnic groups and the majority ethnic group is for some reason incapable of respecting the equal status of the minority ethnic group, then limits on democracy ought to be imposed if such limits will protect the equal status of the minority. So the defense of democracy I have just given does not make it an absolute requirement for every society. Democracy is the most important virtue of a just society, but it is not unconditionally prior to other aspects of justice.

There are two main nonegalitarian ways to limit severe conflicts between democracy and other elements of justice, such as economic justice and civil liberty. One is to have some of the components of justice embodied in a constitution together with a constitutional court that is legally empowered to strike down legislation when it is deeply unjust. The second is to construct legislative institutions that are themselves nonegalitarian. For instance, one may try to protect a minority by giving it special veto powers over the decisions of the majority. Or one may have legislative institutions that, in effect, require more than a majority to pass legislation, as in the case of bicameral legislatures or in the case of voting rules that require more than a majority vote to pass legislation. Both of these kinds of institutions abridge the principle of democratic equality by empowering minorities to block legislation that might discriminate against them.[17] Whether these countermajoritarian institutions actually block injustice or create even more of it is unclear.[18] I shall not discuss these mechanisms any more since my concern in this book is with democratic institutions alone. The fact that they may need modification on occasion does not in any way undermine my characterization of them. It just shows that we have other values than democracy.

Even without the institutional devices mentioned above, democratic institutions have the resources for dealing with potential sources of severe injustice. Inasmuch as individuals are moved by considerations of justice, and to the extent that democratic institutions provide a forum for discussion where all the different interests and points of view in the society can be heard, those institutions are more likely to moderate tendencies to injustice in the society than any others. As John Stuart Mill argued persuasively, participation in democratic institutions generally provide the basis of moral education for the private citizen: "He is called upon, ... to weigh interests not his own; to be guided, in the case of conflicting claims, by another rule than his private partialities; to apply, at every turn, principles and maxims which have for their reason of existence the common good."[19] Indeed, this is part of the function of public discussion in a democratic society to which we will turn our attention and which it will be the burden of much of the discussion in Parts Two and Three to elaborate. So although there is potential for severe conflict between justice in collective decisionmaking and civil and economic justice, in the long run democratic societies are more likely than any other to produce reasonably just outcomes. Hence, in the long run, the tendency will be towards convergence between the two kinds of principle.

Equality and Democratic Deliberation

Some object to egalitarian views on the ground that they do not adequately account for the importance of deliberation in democratic societies.[20] They observe that deliberation involves a possible change of preferences on the part of the participants, as when I engage in discussion with you, I am prepared to change my mind as a result of listening to your arguments. In democratic discussion, such as in political campaigns and policy debates, individuals are prepared to change their minds when listening to others. The objectors claim that egalitarian views presuppose that individuals' preferences remain fixed throughout the democratic process and that individuals are impervious to discussion with others, as if each citizen were equipped with blinders. They charge that egalitarian theories must say that democratic participation consists merely in voting and bargaining with others when there is deep disagreement. So there is no place for deliberation, they claim.

However, the conception of democratic equality I have defended provides a large space for learning and discussion. The reason why equality of resources (and ultimately democratic equality) is the best interpretation of equal consideration of interests is that individuals do not have full and clear conceptions of their interests and need background conditions for learning about their interests. Democratic institutions provide conditions for this process of education to take place among equals.

Discussion and deliberation play three main roles in the democratic process. First, they play a role in helping individuals learn of their interests and those of others, as well as the extent to which these interests do or can converge. Second, they play a role in deepening citizens' conceptions of justice by informing them of each others' interests and by subjecting their views of justice and the common good to debate. Third, they ensure that the conflicts among citizens are tempered by the strengthened social bond arising from the increased understanding each has of others' interests.

Focusing on the first role, we observed that individuals do not have fully formed understandings of their society and interests; these stand in constant need of improvement. Discussion and deliberation promote greater understanding of the interests of the members of society as well as how the collective properties of the society relate to those interests. They allow us to submit our understandings to the test of critical scrutiny. As Mill says:

> The whole strength and value then of human judgment, depending on the one property, that it can be set right when it is wrong, reliance can be placed on it only, when the means of setting it right are kept constantly at hand. In the case of a person whose judgment is really deserving of confidence, how has it become so? Because he has kept his mind open to criticism on his opinions and conduct. Because it has been his practice to listen to all that could be said against him; to profit by as much of it as was just, and expound to himself, and upon occasion to others, the fallacy of what was fallacious. Because he has felt that the only way in which a human being can make some approach to knowing the whole of a subject, is by hearing what can be said about it by persons of every variety of opinion, and studying all modes in which it can be looked at by every character of mind.[21]

The improved understanding of the collective properties and the interests involved with them is important to actually advancing one's interests in them. Thus, discussion and deliberation are essential to realizing a main concern of democracy: that citizens' interests in collective properties be advanced.

In addition to promoting the overall understanding of collective properties, institutions of discussion and deliberation affect the *distribution* of understanding among the citizens. This is where the principle of political equality comes in. I have argued that each person has a right to an equal share in the resources for deciding the collective properties of society. Egalitarian institutions are charged with the task of disseminating understanding widely so that individuals have the means of informing themselves of how to advance their interests and convictions. Those who do not know what policies will advance their interests or their conception of what is best are not likely to have much real power compared to those who do know. Compare a person at the wheel of an automobile that is ready to drive, who does not know how to drive it with someone who has a car and does know how to drive it. The first person is powerless because of his ignorance in how to use the resources at his command; the second, who has the same resources, does have control. In some ways, this is similar to the comparison between those who vote on the basis of some real understanding of politics and those who have little. There is a considerable differential in power because, although the ignorant might sometimes be able to block the knowledgeable from getting what they prefer, the ignorant will never get what they prefer at all except by accident.

In addition, confused or distorted conceptions of his interests can undermine a person's ability to advance his interests. Thus, compare the person who has a car and knows how to use it but has only confused and contradictory ideas of where he wants to go to the person who knows where she wants to go. The first person is at a considerable disadvantage in power compared to the second. He will drive around aimlessly without achieving any end, whereas the second person will be able to achieve some end that she desires. This is a real difference in power.

Finally, a person whose conception of his interests is more or less arbitrarily arrived at is at a disadvantage in relation to a person who has thought about her aims and has some basis for pursuing the ends she does. He may not always do worse, but in general he is more likely not to pursue aims suitably related to his real interests. This is because a person who has an unthought-out conception of his interests is likely to have a somewhat unstable conception of those interests, especially when he is confronted with many alternative conceptions. Plato's conception of justification and its worth express this well: "True opinions, as long as they remain, are a fine thing and all they do is good, but they are not willing to remain long, and they escape from a man's mind, so that they are not worth much until one ties them down by giving them an account of the reason why."[22] The person who has a poorly reasoned or unreflective conception of his aims is a person who is unlikely to achieve much of worth to himself. He will be easily subject to confusion, arbitrary changes in opinion, and manipulation by others. Since it is important to advance the interests of a person it is important for him to have some reasoned grasp of his interests. A person with unreasoned views is likely to be at a disadvantage in relation to the more sophisticated citizen.

Democratic institutions and in particular institutions of discussion and deliberation have a large impact on whether individuals have the opportunities to reflect on and come to a better understanding of their interests. They can provide resources for learning and reflection. Hence, democratic institutions ought to be structured in such a way as to provide wide and roughly equal access to information relevant to democratic decisionmaking. Discussion and deliberation thus contribute importantly to egalitarian democratic institutions, and the principle of equality provides a rationale for distributing the resources for deliberation equally. Contrary to the objections of critics, these claims are derived entirely from a principle of equal consideration of interests when there is considerable ignorance about the interests that are to be advanced. Institutions of deliberation advance the interests citizens have in the collective properties of society and political equality.

In sum, we have seen the basic argument for political equality from a principle of equal consideration of interests and how the view of democracy defended avoids the problem of self-defeat while providing a solution to the inevitable occurrence of moral disagreement in the society. We have also seen how the view avoids the trade-off problem. Finally, we have seen how the conception of democracy that I have defended gives a large role to social discussion and deliberation in democratic politics. In what follows, we will explore the nature of the ideal of political equality for which I have argued. We will see the implications of the principle of equality for the processes of voting and bargaining among political factions as well as for the process of social discussion.

The Nature of Democratic Equality: From Procedural Equality to Equality in the Process

Justice requires that individuals have political equality, that is, equal resources to influence decisions regarding the collective properties of society. In the next two sections, I will elaborate on the nature of this political equality. This brief discussion will provide the basic standards for evaluating institutions that will be used in the third part of this book. The standards of political equality reflect the two different dimensions in which this equality comes. Political equality involves principles for regulating conflict when there is irresolvable disagreement among the citizens. Voting, agenda setting, and bargaining are the main elements of this first dimension of political equality. People resort to voting and bargaining when they see that there is no more point in trying to secure agreement or when there is no more time to discuss and deliberate about the issues. They make alliances with each other and negotiate terms with people with opposing perspectives. The point of Chapter 1 was to argue that this stage is an ineliminable part of the democratic process. The stage of voting and bargaining represents the end stage of the democratic process. I call this the *adversarial dimension* of democracy.[23] The second dimension of democratic equality is the stage of discussion and deliberation. It is where beliefs and convictions are formed, changed, elaborated, and given final articulation. This is the process wherein individuals learn about their interests and about the interests of others. I have argued that citizens ought to have equal resources for cultivating their understanding of their interests and the relations of these interests to the rest of society. I call this the *deliberative dimension* of democracy.

Equality in the Adversarial Dimension

What are some of the main elements of the adversarial dimension of democratic decisionmaking? First, there is the simple requirement of one-person one-vote. Second, the rule for collective decisionmaking is the majority method. Third, the agenda for decisionmaking must be set up in an egalitarian way. Each must have equal abilities to put items of their choice on the agenda. Fourth, during the voting it is important that individuals be able to make coalitions to enable them to get what they prefer. For this they will need resources to make coalitions as well as information about what other people's preferences are.

All four of these elements play an important role in democratic decisionmaking. Here are some brief remarks on each.[24] The requirement of one-person one-vote seems fairly straightforward so let us pass on to majority rule. What is essential about majority rule is that it gives those who favor measures and those who oppose measures equal power over whether the measure will pass or not. For instance, if there are five people in a group and there are two alternatives x and y to choose from, then majority rule requires that for one alternative to win, at least three people must vote for it. The same is true for the other alternative. Compare this with a rule that requires more than a majority to pass a measure. Unanimity requires that for a measure to pass, everyone must support it. If the measure does not pass, something will nevertheless happen. So a unanimity rule in effect requires that one alternative, say x, receive everyone's vote in order to win, while the alternative, y (the stand against x), need receive just one person's vote in order for it to win. So those who oppose x are given much more power by the procedure than those who support x. Usually the rule requires that a unanimous vote is necessary to pass a measure, whereas one vote is sufficient to keep things the way they are. So unanimity favors those who favor the status quo. By contrast, majority rule puts people on an even playing field in this regard. It is the more egalitarian rule. For the same reason, simple majority is more egalitarian than any rule requiring more than simple majority support for an alternative to be chosen.

Of course, most issues in a complex society such as our own do not have merely two alternative solutions. So simple majority rule will not help us in many of these cases. But the arguments against unanimity still hold. We need more complex rules to handle these situations in an egalitarian way. But let us leave these technical issues aside to discuss the other components of adversarial decisionmaking. One important component of equality is some kind of equal ability to determine what items are to be put on the decision-making agenda. What alternatives are we to choose from when we make a collective decision? How this is done will have a substantial effect on whether the process of decisionmaking is egalitarian or not. If one person has more control than others over what alternatives are on the agenda, that person in effect has considerably more power over the ultimate outcome of the decisionmaking. He or she can exclude items from the agenda that many others favor and so undermine their abilities to bring about alternatives they desire. So it is important that individuals have equal agenda-setting powers if they are to receive equal consideration in the decision-making process. Let us leave more detailed discussion of this to Chapter 6 on electoral and legislative institutions.

When there are many alternatives to choose from and many issues to decide, bargaining and coalition building become very important components of collective decisionmaking. I may not be able to get what I want from the collective decision-making process unless I can make a deal with others to vote together on a number of issues. I make a deal with them to vote with them on issues that are important to them, and they agree to vote with me on issues that are important to me. When decisions have to be made on complex issues and discussion on the merits is over, there is no other way of making decisions except by means of these kinds of compromises.

An egalitarian process of decisionmaking must give individuals equal abilities to make the kinds of compromises favorable to their concerns. Two components enter into these abilities. First, each person must have equal access to information about other people's preferences and the coalitions those others have made. If I do not know what others think or want or what compromises they have already made, then I will be at a severe disadvantage when I try to bring about the outcomes I want. Second, resources like money can be very important to building coalitions with others. Building coalitions requires that one be able to communicate one's views to others, and this may require sophisticated communications technology to do it quickly. To the extent that resources like money are necessary for building coalitions, great inequalities in these resources can lead to serious inequalities in abilities to affect the collective decision-making procedure. Such resources as access to information and money are necessary to participate successfully in a collective decision-making procedure, and political equality requires equality in these resources as well as one-person one-vote.

Commitment to one-person one-vote and majority rule implies commitment to the stronger principle of equality that encompasses all the different kinds of resources for influencing the outcome of collective decisionmaking. One reason for this is that I might be willing to give up some votes on particular items if I am given, in return, resources for building coalitions, such as money or information. These latter resources could easily compensate me for the loss of some procedural resources. To maintain, despite this, that procedural resources (such as votes and voting power) ought to be equal on the basis of equality of citizenship while nonprocedural resources (such as coalition-building resources and access to information) need not be equal, would be arbitrary.[25] Someone who has the right to vote but little influence on the agenda or no resources for building coalitions with others on the basis of common interests cannot but feel that the society ignores him as an equal citizen. Someone who sees the collective decisionmaking never take heed of her interests or point of view because she lacks these nonprocedural resources must experience a sense of inferior citizenship almost as strongly as one who has no vote at all. Also, someone who has no vote but who, because of superior coalition-building resources, is able to influence the political process will not complain as loudly as those who have very few resources but do have the vote. So we ought to evaluate collective decisionmaking with an eye to the equality in the resources for influencing the process overall and not merely equality in the procedure. If equality of citizenship is our rationale for equality in the procedure, then it extends directly to a broader equality in the process. The concerns that lead us to endorse one-person one-vote ought to lead us to endorse the stronger requirement of equality in the process of collective decisionmaking.

In Chapter 6 we will see how equality in the process of decision-making is realized and how one-person one-vote, majority rule, agenda setting, and the process of bargaining are to be integrated into an egalitarian system of electoral and legislative institutions.

Equality in the Deliberative Dimension

To help clarify the nature of equality in deliberation let us make a distinction between *numerical* equality and *qualitative* equality. In numerical equality, persons are treated as equals when resources are distributed equally to persons. When we give individuals the vote we assign equal votes to each person. In qualitative equality, persons are treated as equals when resources are divided equally among certain qualities of persons. For example, if we value two distinct group projects equally, we might distribute monies to them equally regardless of how many persons are involved in each group. This would treat each project equally, even though the larger group would get fewer resources per capita.

Equality in the adversarial process is of the numerical sort. Each person has equal votes and other resources when a decision is to be made. But this is only after deliberation is over, so to speak. The deliberative process ought to be regulated by qualitative equality: Each view ought to receive an equal hearing. Why? First, the deliberative process in a democratic society aims at the truth in the matter discussed. Each person first desires to know the truth in the matter. Participants are concerned primarily with advancing their own views because they think they are *true,* not because they are *their* views. This contrasts with bargaining, wherein each is concerned with advancing his or her own interests. This is part of what is involved in the very notion of social discussion and deliberation.

By way of illustration, consider a case where three persons disagree on two views and two support A while one supports B. If what is really important to each is to assess the truth or falsehood of the views (assuming they are engaged in rational discussion), it is not important to them that more people support A than B, only that some support A and others, B. Suppose John and Jane support A and Joel supports B. For John it matters that A is taken into account and the same goes for Jane. But this mattering does not add up. The fact that two people wish that A be taken into account does not entail that A ought to be taken into account twice in discussion. For each it matters only that A be taken into account. Thus, equal time should be given to opinions A and B. This is because ideas have a certain "jointness of supply." The ideas do not have to be divided up in order for everyone to benefit from them. And the same is true for discussion of the idea. John's view is given as much hearing as Joel's, and Jane's view is also given as much hearing when A is given the same amount of time for a hearing as B. Thus, resources for social discussion ought to be allocated equally to each view, not to each person. Let us call the allocation of resources to discussion of views the deliberative agenda. And let us call a deliberative agenda that satisfies qualitative equality, an egalitarian deliberative agenda.

A second reason for qualitative equality in deliberation is that citizens' interests, or at least their understanding of their interests, are to some extent reflected in the points of view they advance, especially when it comes to the organization of society. Individuals have various reasons to want their views expressed in discussion: One is that preparation for publicly expressing one's views to others stimulates one to serious reflection and learning on what one is about to say. Another is that such expression enables each to hear how others respond to his or her view. If I have no opportunity to raise questions or say what I think to others about some issue, then I will not be able to benefit from hearing what they have to say about what I think. I will not be able to learn from those others on matters that are of importance to me and in particular that relate to my interests. Thus I have a great interest in having my views expressed.

Notice that this value of expression is not based on the intrinsic importance of expressing oneself. There is no such value or at least such a value is of little importance. It is based on the fact that one learns a lot by having one's views responded to. But it is not essential that I do the expressing. What is important is that the view I hold be properly aired by someone and that it be answered by others. Hence, if ten people have the same view, they will all learn from the responses to one single expression of the view. Indeed, if more time is given to their view because there are more of them, the interests in learning of the ten will be much better served than interests of the lesser number. So, a principle that assigns more time for the discussion of a single view merely on the basis of the greater number of believers treats the interests of the greater number with more than equal consideration. This point extends to any resource that facilitates discussion. So, the principle of equal consideration of interests requires a principle of qualitative equality in determining how resources should be allocated to the discussion of views.

To be sure, if John and Jane have different arguments in support of A and Joel has one argument for B, then both John and Jane ought to have a chance to give their arguments, which may mean that more will be said for A than B. But if they have the same argument for A, then only one of them can legitimately speak and Joel will have the same amount of time as they do. The amount of resources given to each view in a debate (time, in our example) depends on the content, not the number of persons who support the idea.

Equality in social discussion requires that different ideas in the community be represented and elaborated in a roughly equal way (or at least in proportion to their significance for the community) in order that the equal consideration of the interests of citizens in the democratic process be realized. We will discuss and elaborate this principle and its institutional implications in detail in Chapters 7 and 8.

A Note on Social Choice Theory and Democracy

These observations on the nature of democratic equality provide the key to answering an important recent critique of democracy. Social choice theorists have argued that democracy suffers from a fundamental problem. In a society where there is a modest diversity of opinion on issues of public concern and where decisions must be made collectively, there is no procedure by which to make these decisions that satisfies certain important normative conditions. This problem is one of how to aggregate the preferences of individuals into a social preference. It has been shown that no aggregation rule can produce a determinate outcome while simultaneously satisfying the following five apparently reasonable conditions for aggregating individual into social preferences: Pareto optimality, nondictatorship, independence of irrelevant alternatives, unlimited domain, and transitivity of preference orderings.[26] Hence, it is impossible to have a general rule satisfying reasonable conditions for constructing a social choice on the basis of sets of individual preferences.

That the conditions are reasonable can be seen from a brief description of them. The condition of Pareto optimality states that if everyone prefers one alternative to another, then the first alternative ought to be the social choice. The condition of nondictatorship states that the social choice ought not to correspond to a particular individual's preference regardless of the preferences of the others. Independence requires that the social choice between two options ought to depend only on the individual preferences between those two options. This is the condition that when citizens have preferences over alternatives, they rank all the alternatives in a way that none of the alternatives are complementary to each other and that there are no interpersonal comparisons that are made that introduce extra information aside from the preference ordering. Unlimited domain requires that the rule produce a social choice no matter what the preferences of the citizens are. Finally, transitivity requires that individual preferences and the social choice ordering be transitive.

A simple example that predates the Impossibility Theorem is the problem of majority cycles. Suppose that three citizens A, B, and C have different preference orderings over three alternatives x, y, and z. They rank the options in the following way: A's preference is for x over y and y over z; B's preference is for y over z and z over x; C's preference is for z over x and x over y. And their orderings are transitive. Of course, none of the alternatives receives a simple majority. Furthermore, we cannot assign numbers to the alternatives and then add up the numbers for each alternative so that the largest number wins; that would violate independence. Indeed, why should we think that we should compare the value of x to A and the value of y to B by giving them the same numbers? Furthermore, the unanimity condition does not help us here since there is no alternative that everyone prefers to every other alternative.

A natural procedure in this context might be to make each alternative compete with each of the others in a pairwise fashion. So instead of making x, y, and z compete together, we shall separate out the pairs x and y, y and z, and z and x and see how each alternative fares when competing with just one other given the citizens' preference orderings. In the pairwise comparisons we shall use majority rule to evaluate which alternative wins. The alternative that beats all the others in the pairwise comparisons wins. This is called the Condorcet method for aggregating preferences.

When x and y compete, A and C prefer x over y and only B prefers y over x; by majority rule, x beats y. When we compare y and z we see that A prefers y over z and B prefers y over z, while only C prefers z over y, so that y beats z. The problem arises when we compare x and z. Here we see that A prefers x over z and B and C prefer z over x. Hence, z beats x. Putting all these results together, we find that x beats y, y beats z, and z beats x. Thus we have an intransitive ordering. Which outcome do we choose? They each beat another and are beaten by another. We cannot select x because it is beaten by z, and we cannot select z because it is beaten by y, and y is beaten by x. So, when the preferences of the citizenry are similar to those mentioned above it appears that we cannot really derive a social choice. And if some alternative is actually selected by the populace we have reason to doubt the legitimacy or significance of the choice. It must be chosen arbitrarily.[27]

Arrow's impossibility theorem shows that this problem is merely a special case of more extensive difficulties with any rule for aggregating preferences in contexts where there are more than two alternatives and more than two citizens or groups of citizens among whom there is disagreement. It appears that democracy is threatened with incoherence.[28]

Some might argue that social discussion and deliberation can alter the preferences of citizens so that at least some of the disagreements between citizens can be resolved and there is more uniformity of preferences than the condition of unlimited domain suggests.[29] But it seems unlikely that, in a society as complex as any modern industrial society with a complex division of labor and a plurality of cultures, there will be sufficient uniformity of views so as to avoid the problems that social choice theorists describe. Although there is considerable consensus on some issues, such as the worth of liberal democracy itself.

Our conception of the democratic process just described shows how we can avoid concluding that democracy is incoherent and still take the findings of social choice theory seriously. What problem does the impossibility theorem raise for democratic theory? Social choice theorists imagine that it is essential to democracy that it aggregate individual preferences into what they call a social preference. The social preference is to be formulated in such a way as to make sense of the idea of maximizing social utility. To maximize social utility is to be as high up on the social preference ordering as is feasible. This is what is undermined by the problem of intransitivity. One cannot get as high up on a preference ordering if the preference ordering is intransitive. So there is a genuine problem pointed out by social choice theory for the idea that society can maximize social utility.

But this problem is really a conceptual one for any utilitarianism that refuses to permit interpersonal comparisons of utility. The social choice theorem states that the idea of maximizing utility cannot be well defined if we accept various reasonable axioms. It is ultimately a criticism of a kind of utilitarianism. Social choice theory analyzes decision-making procedures as ways of aggregating preferences as if they were attempts to maximize utility. It uses what I call an aggregative notion of decision-making procedures.

But democracy is not founded in a concern for maximizing social utility; instead it is based on the ideal of giving citizens equal control over their social world. Democracy distributes resources for controlling the social world, at least with regard to certain issues. On the account argued for in this chapter, democracy is not concerned with aggregating preferences; it is concerned with the distribution of authoritative power. The conception of a procedure is not aggregative; procedures are sets of rules used for distributing power. The equal distribution of authoritative power does not require that utility be maximized; these are two separate concerns. So, that maximizing utility as it is construed by social choice theorists is incoherent and does not imply any incoherence in democratic ideals.

The problem of majority cycles discussed above does not show in and of itself that the individuals are treated as unequal in the process. It merely shows that the outcome of the vote cannot be completely predicted from individuals' equal voting power and their preferences. Presumably something else will come in to determine the outcome of the voting procedure in this case. If that something else is the superior power of one of the participants, say in determining the agenda, then the person who determined the agenda will have been given an unjust advantage in determining the outcome. Democracy in this case requires an equal distribution of power to determine the agenda, to make deals, to persuade, and in general to influence the outcome of the process of which the procedure is merely one part.[30] Arrow's social choice theory has undermined the possibility of formulating a consistent idea of maximizing social utility when interpersonal comparisons of utility have been abandoned; it does not tell us that there is no decision-making procedure that satisfies the principle of equality or that the principle of democracy is incoherent.

Conclusion

I have argued that the principle of equal consideration of interests is the foundation of the intrinsic worth of democracy. I argued that a collective decision-making process is necessary to advance the interests of citizens in the collective properties of society and that in the light of the pervasive disagreements on judgments and conflicts of interests in pluralistic democratic societies, justice demands political equality, or equality in the distribution of resources for influencing the collective decision procedure. Citizens' interests are equally worthy of being taken into account, and political equality is the most important way to embody equal consideration of interests in a political society.

I argued in Chapter 1 that deliberative activities do not have intrinsic value in a pluralistic democratic society. Individuals value social deliberation in different ways, and some do not value participating in democratic deliberation at the level of political institutions. Social discussion and deliberation are important components of democracy however. They enable citizens to become informed about their society and their own interests, as well as how those interests are similar to and different from those of others. The more understanding citizens have of their society, the more the collective decision-making process can advance their interests. Political equality requires that citizens have equal access to the social discussion, which implies qualitative equality in deliberation.

These rather abstract principles will be applied to the evaluation of concrete democratic institutions throughout the rest of this work. In Part Two I will discuss a fundamental challenge to the ideals of democracy that arises in the modern state. In large democracies, the role of ordinary citizens is in danger of being eclipsed by the complex apparatus of the state. Ordinary citizenship appears to be incompatible with the abstract ideals of political equality and rational discussion that I have elaborated in the last two chapters. In Chapter 3 I will lay out the challenge and in 4 and 5 I will discuss different conceptions of citizenship and defend a conception of the role of citizenship in society that reconciles the ideals of democracy with the conditions of the modern state. In Part Three I will elaborate a theory of political institutions for modern society that provides the complement to the role of citizenship I defend. In Chapter 6 I will lay out principles for evaluating institutions for legislative representation. In Chapters 7 and 8 I will discuss principles for evaluating institutions of social discussion and show how the system of interest groups and political parties ought to be evaluated in terms of these principles.

Notes

1. Peter Singer, *Democracy and Disobedience* (Oxford: Oxford University Press, 1974), chapter 5.

2. Singer, *Democracy and Disobedience,* p. 32.

3. See Thomas Christiano, "Freedom, Consensus, and Equality in Collective Decision Making," *Ethics* October (1990): pp. 151–181, especially pp. 171–175.

4. See Robert Dahl, *A Preface to Democratic Theory* (Chicago: University of Chicago Press, 1956), pp. 64–67; Dahl, "Procedural Democracy," in *Philosophy, Politics, and Society,* 5th Ser., ed. James Fishkin and Peter Laslett (New Haven: Yale University Press, 1979), pp. 97–133, especially pp. 99–101 and p. 125; and Peter Jones, "Political Equality and Majority Rule," in *The Nature of Political Theory,* ed. David Miller and Larry Siedentop (Oxford: Oxford University Press, 1983), pp. 155–182, especially p. 166.

5. In Thomas Rainsborough's "The Putney Debates: The Debate on the Franchise (1647)," in *Divine Right and Democracy,* ed. David Wootton (Harmondsworth, Eng.: Penguin Books, 1986), pp. 285–317, especially p. 286.

6. This argument does not require that there be a private realm that is to be protected from paternalistic uses of public power. It merely denies that there is intrinsic justification for democratic decisionmaking in these contexts. The fact that someone does something in his home that I do not like or that I do not approve of is not a reason for me to complain of injustice. Only if his actions impinge on my well-being and that of others in a way that is hard to escape is there a genuine collective property. There may be grounds for criticism and intervention in private actions that are not related to collective properties, but those grounds are not that I or others have been unjustly treated.

7. Those recent thinkers, such as Michael Sandel and Charles Taylor, who agree with me in their emphasis on the importance and value of community in the lives of citizens, have failed to adequately deal with the diversity of people and the lack of consensus on what the community should be like.

8. See Gerald Cohen, "On the Currency of Egalitarian Justice," *Ethics* July (1989): pp. 906–944, for a critical discussion of many of the theories on this subject.

9. See Herbert Simon, *Reason in Human Affairs* (Stanford: Stanford University Press, 1983) for this kind of claim.

10. See Ronald Dworkin, "What Is Equality? Part I: Equality of Welfare," *Philosophy and Public Affairs* 10 (Spring 1981): pp. 185–246, for a similar kind of argument concerning the impossibility of defining an agreed-upon metric for equality of welfare. Of course, he is not concerned with democratic equality where I think this problem is the most severe.

11. See Joshua Cohen, "Deliberation and Democratic Legitimacy," in *The Good Polity: Normative Analysis of the State,* eds. Alan Hamlin and Philip Pettit (New York: Basil Blackwell, 1989), p. 19, for a discussion of this concept.

12. See John Stuart Mill, *On Liberty* (Buffalo, N.Y.: Prometheus Books, 1986), for this principle. See also his *Considerations on Representative Government* (Buffalo, N.Y.: Prometheus Books, 1991), for the application of this principle to democratic theory.

13. Aristotle, *Politics,* trans. Benjamin Jowett, Book 3 of *The Basic Works of Aristotle,* ed. Richard McKeon (New York: Random House, 1941), p. 1282a.

14. We will see the problem of the indeterminacy of political equality in Chapter 8.

15. See John Locke, *Second Treatise on Civil Government* (Buffalo, N.Y.: Prometheus Books, 1986), p. 70, and Immanuel Kant, *The Metaphysical Foundations of Justice,* trans. John Ladd (Indianapolis: Bobbs-Merrill, 1965), p. 76.

16. See Ronald Dworkin, "What Is Equality? Part 4: Political Equality," *University of San Francisco Law Review* Fall (1987): pp. 1–30, for arguments for the opposing position. Richard Arneson also assumes a priority of economic rights over democratic rights on the grounds that democratic rights involve the possession of power of some persons over other persons, which ought only to be exercised when such power promotes the economic rights of those others. The flaw in this argument is that economic rights involve the possession of power of some over others, as when I have the right to tell others to get off my property. So Arneson cannot offer a principled basis for making economic rights prior to democratic rights. See his "Democratic Rights at the National and Workplace Levels," in *The Idea of Democracy,* ed. David Copp, Jean Hampton, and John Roemer (New York: Cambridge University Press, 1993), pp. 118–148, especially p. 120.

17. I discuss these institutions in my paper "Democratic Equality and the Problem of Persistent Minorities," *Philosophical Papers* January (1995): 169–190.

18. For skepticism about the tendency of the Supreme Court to defend justice against majorities, see Robert Dahl, *A Preface to Democratic Theory* (Chicago: University of Chicago Press, 1956). Then Dahl observed: "In only four cases in the entire history of the Court where legislation dealing with [the right to vote, freedom of speech, freedom of assembly, and freedom of the press] has been held unconstitutional, then, the decisions prevented Congress, not from destroying basic rights, but from extending them. Thus, there is not a single case in the history of this nation where the Supreme Court has struck down national legislation designed to curtail, rather than to extend, [the above rights]." p. 59.

19. Mill, *Considerations on Representative Government,* p. 73.

20. See Charles Beitz, *Political Equality* (Princeton: Princeton University Press, 1989), pp. 12–13; and Cohen, "Deliberation and Democratic Legitimacy," p. 19.

21. Mill, *On Liberty,* pp. 26–27. See Philip Kitcher, "The Division of Cognitive Labor," *Journal of Philosophy* January (1990): pp. 5–22 for an epistemic defense of diversity in scientific theorizing.

22. Plato, *Meno,* in *Five Dialogues,* trans. G.M.A. Grube (Indianapolis, Ind.: Hackett Publishing Co., 1981), pp. 59–88, especially p. 86.

23. Following Jane Mansbridge, *Beyond Adversarial Democracy* (Chicago: University of Chicago Press, 1980).

24. My discussion here must be brief and impressionistic. I have discussed these issues in much more detail in my "Political Equality," in *NOMOS XXXII: Majorities and Minorities,* ed. John Chapman and Alan Wertheimer (New York: New York University Press, 1990), pp. 150–183.

25. Charles Beitz, in his *Political Equality,* pp. 109–110, 133, argues that one-person one-vote is sufficient to satisfy each person's interest in recognition as an equal citizen.

26. See Brian Barry and Russell Hardin, eds., *Rational Man and Irrational Society?* (Beverly Hills, Calif.: Sage Publications, 1982) for a good introduction to these issues.

27. For a brilliant and accessible exposition of these and other interesting problems in the theory of democracy, see William Riker, *Liberalism Against Populism: A Confrontation Between the Theory of Democracy and the Theory of Social Choice* (San Francisco, Calif.: W.H. Freeman Co., 1982).

28. See Russell Hardin, "Public Choice Versus Democracy," in *NOMOS XXXII: Majorities and Minorities,* for a statement of this position; see also Riker, *Liberalism Against Populism.*

29. See Cohen, "Deliberation and Democratic Legitimacy," for this kind of argument.

30. I have discussed these issues in detail in my paper "Social Choice and Democracy," in *The Idea of Democracy,* ed. David Copp, Jean Hampton, and John Roemer (New York: Cambridge University Press, 1993), pp. 173–195.

PART TWO

Democracy and the Problem of the Modern State

CHAPTER THREE

The Challenge of the Modern State to the Democratic Ideals

The ideals of democracy require that citizens have equal resources for advancing their interests in the collective properties of society. Political equality demands that individuals understand their interests and that they have roughly equal access to such understanding through the process of social discussion. This is what is implied by giving equal consideration to everyone's interests. But the ideals of democracy defended and elaborated in Chapter 2 face a serious challenge when we turn to the reality of democratic institutions in modern societies. This difficulty is internal to the ideal itself, at least as it applies in modern conditions. This challenge suggests that the ideals of democracy to which many adhere are impossible or even incoherent aspirations under modern conditions.

The basic problem is that ordinary citizens in modern society are not in a position to spend the time and exert the energy to acquire the kind of understanding that is necessary for democratic citizenship. Modern citizens are confronted with a bewildering array of facts and an overwhelmingly complex set of social problems and have little time to contribute to understanding these matters and little power over the outcomes of decisionmaking. If understanding and equal access to it are essential prerequisites for advancing the interests in collective features of society and political equality, then the present difficulty suggests the impossibility of the democratic ideals. A number of scholars have taken note of this problem. Anthony Downs in *An Economic Theory of Democracy* has argued that the problem of information makes political equality an impossible ideal in modern society.[1] Russell Hardin has argued that the problem of ignorance shows that democratic ideals are incoherent.[2] If these authors are right, then we must seriously reconsider the value we attach to democracy or modify our conception of the democratic ideals quite radically.

Two aspects of this difficulty will occupy us in this chapter. First, we will look at the challenge to political equality in the modern state as Downs sees it. Second, we will see how there is a deep difficulty with the idea of rational democratic deliberation in a large population of citizens. In the next chapter, we will survey and assess conceptions of democracy and citizenship that provide solutions to these problems while adhering to Downsian presuppositions about human nature. I conclude that these economic views of democracy are fundamentally flawed, and the conception of human nature on which they are founded has been undermined by empirical evidence. In Chapter 5, I outline and defend a conception of the nature of citizenship that reconciles democratic ideals with the conditions of the modern state. In Part Three, I spell out principles for evaluating democratic institutions implied by the democratic ideals and the conception of citizenship I defend.

The Problem of Participation

Let us start with the perspective of the rationally self-interested person on the problem of voting and the collection of information for voting. Though we will abandon this perspective eventually, this way of thinking about citizens is widespread and it provides an illuminating starting point from which to grasp the problem of democracy.

Consider the case of a group of five people faced with one issue with two possible alternatives. In general, self-interested persons will choose actions that bring the greatest net benefits after a consideration of the costs and benefits to themselves. In deciding whether and how to vote, an agent will consider the costs and benefits of voting. On the benefit side, she will determine which of the two alternatives she *prefers* as well as by how much. She will also consider what the *chances* are that her vote will determine which alternative wins. On the other side, she will consider the *cost of voting* for that alternative. For instance, if Alex believes that he is the only one who prefers x over y and the others know this also and if the cost of voting for everyone is negligible, Alex may not bother to vote since the chance of his making a difference is nil. Alternatively, suppose that Alex knows that two persons favor x and two favor y, and that everyone knows this; in this case, he can cast the deciding vote and he will vote for his preferred alternative.

Usually when people vote, it is *not clear* what the outcome of the voting is going to be. Suppose that Alex does not know what others prefer. In that case, Alex considers the chances that he will prevail in the vote and how strong his preference for x over y is as well as what the cost of voting for x over y is. If the voting rule is majority rule, then Alex has a certain chance of determining the outcome. Since, in this case, the cost of voting is negligible, Alex has a reason to vote for his preferred alternative. Imagine, however, a situation in which Alex's vote is quite costly, namely where he has to travel some distance to cast his vote or where he is likely to make enemies by voting on either side and the ballot is not secret. Here the cost of voting may outweigh the expected benefits of voting. In that case, he may not vote.

In some cases, Alex knows very little about the alternatives. He knows that there are differences between them but not which is best. Consequently, Alex must spend some time learning about the differences and how they matter to him. In a small group, this requires only a bit of reflection. But the time and effort used to analyze and compare the alternatives are a cost to Alex. And the benefit is uncertain since this is what he is trying to figure out. He must decide in advance whether they are worth the trouble. In some cases, it may not be worthwhile for Alex to spend a lot of time thinking about the differences between x and y. In this small group, it may not be worthwhile for him to collect information if he knows that everyone else will vote for one particular alternative anyway, or if there appears to be little difference between x and y of significance to Alex, or if the cost of collecting information is great.

Collecting information and reflecting on it are actions that are separable from voting, so Alex must decide whether to make inquiries even if he has already decided to vote. Consider a case in which Alex and his friends are having a party and they want to choose what kind of ice cream to buy, but he does not like ice cream enough to care much about which flavor to buy. He may have a mild reason to vote for one flavor over another though he has no reason to think hard about what he prefers or inform himself about the options. So even in small groups, one may have a reason to vote on some alternative and not have reason to inform oneself. This holds for many instances of individual decisionmaking. Those who shop for groceries will know the feeling of having wasted their time deliberating over what brand of wheat bread to buy from among the numerous brands on the shelf. Sometimes it is better to make a choice without thinking about it much.

Now consider the situation facing a citizen in a large state. Millions of citizens are affected by the decision and millions participate in the vote. How does this change the way in which a voter will view his or her choices? Decisions often have pervasive effects on persons' lives. Also, there are many *alternatives* proposed in a large society with a diverse citizenry, and many angles from which each decision can be viewed. In addition there is a *massive number* of *complex issues*. Here the problem of understanding issues and making comparisons between various alternative courses of action increases by orders of magnitude. As E. E. Schattschneider observed, "There is no escape from the problem of ignorance, because nobody knows enough to run the government. . . . Even an expert is someone who chooses to be ignorant about many things so that he may know all about one."[3] However, the immense *size of the decision-making group* implies that the chances that one's vote will make a difference to an election or referendum are vanishingly small. In most cases, even when one is uncertain which alternative is going to win, one knows that one of the options will win by thousands of votes. The value of voting, though it is on issues of great significance for one's life and those of one's fellow citizens, must be discounted by the extremely low probability that one will have an impact on the outcomes of these momentous decisions.

Is it rational to vote? The value of the individual vote is nearly zero much of the time. The only question is whether the cost of voting is high or not. It would seem not unreasonable to vote when it is very easy. Sometimes there are benefits to voting: One gets time off from work; one meets friends at the polling booth; there is a mild excitement on election day; and finally, even mostly self-interested voters may have some residual concern for others. In any case, this is what most people do. But the number of voters may decline when one puts any kind of obstacle in their way. Registration requirements, poll taxes, geographical dispersion of polling places, or even lack of clear notice as to where polling places are all have dramatic effects on whether or not persons vote.[4] These costs are relatively small on their own, but in comparison to the expected benefit of voting they loom large and can dissuade large numbers of people from voting. When voters are primarily concerned with determining the outcome of an election in their own interests, it is clear why their voting varies with these kinds of devices.[5] Nevertheless, narrowly self-interested voters often have reasons to go to the polls.[6]

There is a more serious problem, however. In large societies the rationality of an individual collecting information and reflecting seriously on policy alternatives and their relative worth is in serious doubt. Attempts to become well-informed about politics are very costly due to the complexity of the issues. They require a lot of time and energy. In addition, since one's vote makes almost no difference, the information that one collects and the time reflecting on it are all to little or no avail. So most citizens have virtually no reason to inform themselves about the issues they vote on, at least on the self-interest account. This is the problem of rational ignorance.

Citizens, however, are informed to some extent, though poorly. The explanation of self-interest theorists is that people become informed as a by-product of their other activities. That is, while each of us is going about our daily lives, we pick up information about the political situation around us even though we are not actively seeking it out. We overhear others talk about politics and we see things on television and in the newspapers even when we are not particularly interested in finding out about politics.[7] This information is substantially free since we acquire it while pursuing other activities we are already committed to. For example, if I am watching a television show and a news flash about politics comes on, I learn something about politics even though I exerted little or no extra effort to get the information. Indeed, I would have had to deliberately avoid the information in order not to receive it. We do our jobs either for money and power or perhaps for the intrinsic benefits, but we learn about politics through the job since our jobs are affected by the political environment. We may also have friends who are interested in politics as a kind of hobby or sport, and so we hear about politics from them as a part of our friendly interactions.[8]

We also acquire opinions about politics just by following whatever opinions we hear from prominent figures in the society. These people, called "opinion leaders," often serve as sources of expert opinions for citizens. Each citizen need not reflect on the issues on his own, he can simply adopt the opinions of some attractive prominent figure in politics.[9] This is an inexpensive way of collecting information and forming opinions about politics that is at the disposal of citizens. The self-interest account does not say that people will not know anything about politics, it merely says they will not know much and they will not have reflected much on it.

The Challenge of the Modern State to Political Equality

What are the implications of the self-interest account for political equality? It would appear from the observations in the previous section, that everyone will be equally ignorant. But in fact the problems of participation and rational ignorance are not the same for everyone. They do not imply that everyone is poorly informed; they lead to deep inequalities of information and influence on collective decisionmaking. There are four basic sources of inequality that result from the problem of participation and rational ignorance described above. The four sources were discussed fully by Anthony Downs, and they demonstrate how deeply the circumstances of the modern state challenge the democratic ideals of political equality and rational deliberation. Let us review each in turn.

First, some citizens learn a lot about politics in their everyday lives, whereas others learn very little. For instance, a lawyer whose firm deals with government contracts learns a lot about what the government does just from doing her job. She works in order to make money and advance the fortunes of her firm, but she learns about government policy on the way. She learns much more, for example, than a construction worker who is not likely to hear much about politics in his job unless he is a member of an active union. So the lawyer is a lot better informed than the construction worker about politics. Obviously government officials also know a lot more about politics than others. And business persons in large firms who have a lot of contact with the government also know more than others, just as a result of the free information about politics they receive. Thus, occupational status in general should help predict variations in how informed people are, given the problem of rational ignorance. Professionals, members of large business firms, and government officials are in general much better informed than farm laborers, factory workers, service workers, and unemployed people.[10]

Inequality of understanding results, secondly, from differences in peoples' abilities to learn and reason about the information they receive about politics. These variations result from differences in education as well as differences in how much people develop their abilities in their everyday lives. People are more sophisticated in their abilities to reason to the extent that they are better educated, as well as to the extent that they have the incentives to use sophisticated reasoning. Lawyers, managers, and officials who have complex tasks in organizing people as well as the education to perform them develop these abilities more than those who do not. Abilities to learn and reason should vary with differences in occupational status and educational background much as the mere possession of information does. Furthermore, these abilities are helpful in organizing one's thoughts and ensuring consistency and complexity in one's views. They greatly enhance the meaning of any information that persons receive from their free sources of information. An individual who can reason about information in a sophisticated way is more likely than others to make sense of the political news she has heard and relate it to other events and facts in a coherent fashion. Not only does new information add to old information, it often enhances the understanding of the older information, and vice versa. Thus, for someone who has the relevant abilities to reason and learn, information does not merely add up, it multiplies. So some groups of persons in the society are more likely to receive a lot more information than others; they are also likely to be able to do a lot more with that information because of the superior learning and reasoning skills they have acquired.[11]

How do these two systematic inequalities in understanding promote political inequality? Recall the analogy of the drivers in Chapter 2. The person who knows how to drive a car will be able to do much more than the person who does not know. The driver who knows where he or she wants to go will have a greater ability to get there than the person who does not know where to go. These effects of knowledge have analogues in the modern state. In a modern state, the ultimate decisions about law are made by politicians. These politicians have their power by virtue of being elected and reelected. They get reelected by citizens who vote for them. Those citizens vote on the basis of the information they have. Some citizens have some knowledge about what a politician will do or has done, whereas other citizens do not. To appeal to those who do not have much information, a politician will rely on very general and vague promises of action. Since the voter is not likely to be very well informed in the future, the politician does not have to be terribly worried about whether he or she fulfills these promises.[12] And if the voter does have a stand on some issues that is not very well reasoned, the politician will reasonably expect that stand to change or become less salient for the voter in the future. Conversely, those who are informed and have abilities to learn and reason will on some occasions know what the politician has done and can be expected to know some of what the politician will do. To receive their votes the politician must not only make promises that appeal to these persons but must also make good on some of those promises. Thus, the politician is responsive to their concerns more than to the concerns of those who are uninformed. Furthermore, since the more informed are likely to have more reasoned and stable stands on issues, they have a lot more influence on the politicians who make decisions and therefore more influence on what laws are made and the collective features of their society.

Notice that this political inequality is completely unrelated to any special efforts or talents displayed by those who are more powerful. It is merely a systematic effect of the division of labor in society that gives some people greater free access to information and greater ability to reason about that information than others. The greater influence of some is by itself not a reflection of any credit to them, and the lesser influence of others does not reflect any defect in them. And the differences in influence are not explained by any differences in interests either. The factory worker has just as much of an interest in responsive government as does the lawyer. Yet the latter is likely to have a lot more influence on how the society is run.

There are two other important sources of political inequality. They result from a combination of large differences in economic resources and the problem of rational ignorance. The third source is that some citizens or small groups of citizens are affected in highly concentrated ways by particular government actions while other citizens are not. Consider some examples. A firm that employs many workers may be the subject of costly regulation by the government relating to occupational safety. Another firm may benefit from import tariffs that keep foreign competition from digging into their markets. Others receive heavy subsidies from the government. In each of these cases the firm stands to lose or gain a substantial amount from the government action, so it has an incentive to inform itself of the government's plans and to contribute to the election of politicians who favor its interests in the making of policy. If the firm can, by investing resources in the election of a favorable politician, avoid the loss of greater resources from government regulation or gain greater resources from government limits on competitors or subsidies, then the firm has an incentive to invest those resources in that politician.

Firms are likely to be in this kind of position quite often, unlike most ordinary citizens. Most citizens benefit or lose in a very diffuse way from many government policies. I benefit from pollution regulation, but it is a relatively small benefit and it accrues to many other people. However, the cost to those who are regulated is quite high since they are few. I lose as a result of the higher prices of goods because of the tariffs imposed on foreign competitors, but the effect on me is small compared to the immense benefits to the few firms whose products are protected. The overall effects on everyone are very great, but in each case the effects on an ordinary citizen are small. Most citizens have little influence on government action by themselves, thus they have little incentive to make any efforts regarding these matters or even to inform themselves of these issues.

Thus, firms that benefit directly from government action and the citizens who own them are likely to exercise a lot of influence on those decisions, whereas ordinary citizens who are affected by the decisions do not. Concentrated benefits go to those firms while the costs in the form of taxes or higher prices are spread on to inattentive citizens. Since only select groups can benefit in this way, this is a major source of political inequality.[13]

The fourth source of inequality results in part from the third. Citizens or groups of citizens who stand to benefit or lose directly a great deal from particular government actions can influence the government directly by helping politicians to get elected, but they can also influence the government indirectly by influencing those who vote. Recall that most ordinary voters receive their information for free, as a mere by-product of other activities. They receive more-or-less free information from large media, such as television, magazines, and newspapers. Of course, someone must subsidize the transmission of that information. Television must be paid for; newspapers and magazines must be funded. They do not survive merely on the basis of the fees the consumers pay. The groups who have a lot to gain from particular concentrated benefits or the avoidance of large concentrated losses have an incentive to subsidize the transmission of information. Naturally, they tend to subsidize the transmission of information that favors their interests or at least their points of view. And they tend to discourage the transmission of information unfavorable to their interests. They may simply remove their support from one media firm and supply it to another more favorable to their interests.[14]

Thus, most citizens in the society think about politics on the basis of information that they receive indirectly from parties who have special interests in transmitting the information and whose interests may not be similar to the recipients' interests. Yet the recipient rationally relies on this information or some of it since he or she realizes that it is not worthwhile making an independent effort to collect information. Also, politicians must be more responsive to the narrow interests of specially placed groups because of their ability to persuasively advocate policies advantageous to their own interests. Thus, even the basic articulation of the aims of the society is one on which some have a great impact while others have very little impact. This is a major source of political inequality in the society.

These inequalities tend to line up with one another. Those who benefit from the existence of a lot of free information do so because they interact a lot with the government. But this is because they stand to benefit or lose in concentrated ways from government activities and they have incentives and resources with which to inform themselves about governmental policy and to influence processes of mass communication. Thus, the combined effect of these inequalities would appear to be massive political inequality between groups of citizens in the society. Again, these inequalities in political power are related neither to any overall superiority in talents or efforts nor to any greater overall interest in the activities of government. The division of labor in society is such that it produces systematic differences of access in information as well as systematic differences in incentive structure for different citizens.

This picture of political inequality in a large society is an idealization and ought to be qualified in two main ways. First, those who have a lot of power as a consequence of being in a special position in the division of labor do not share all the same interests. They must compete amongst themselves, so their power is by no means monolithic. Indeed, sometimes particular groups have interests in making coalitions with weaker groups in order to win political contests with other stronger groups. This strengthens the weaker groups and thus modifies the political inequality we see in modern society. Also, sometimes groups in more subordinate positions in the division of labor are able to organize and can acquire great power from that organization. Thus, unions and ethnic associations have on occasion been able to modify the extreme inequality at work in society to their own advantage. To be sure, these groups have a difficult time forming since individual members face collective action problems very much like the problem that leads to rational ignorance in politics. I will pursue this more as we go on.

The second main way in which the logic of this inequality can be modified is if we suspend the assumption of self-interested motives that underlies the view. Rational ignorance is rational to the self-interested agent. Different assumptions about motivation may yield different views about the nature and origins of political inequality.

In my view, the assumption of self-interested motivation is not justified, and I will attempt to show this in my discussion of the economic conception of citizenship in the next chapter. Indeed, most economic theorists do not hold to the assumption of self-interested motivation consistently when they discuss political participation.[15] We will see why when we discuss their views in more detail. But first, let us examine another problem for the ideals of democratic equality that might arise in the modern state.

The Challenge of the Modern State to Rational Democratic Deliberation

The processes of social discussion and deliberation are the chief means by which citizens become informed in a democratic society. I have argued that institutions should be structured to contribute to the reasoned understanding of citizens and to the wide distribution of that understanding. These outcomes are important to the promotion of citizens' interests in the collective properties of society and political equality. But in modern democratic states it is hard to see how more than a small minority of citizens can participate in a meaningful way in rational social discussion about politics. The facts of modern life seem to drive a wedge between democracy and the rationality of deliberation.

Here we will need to examine the nature of rational social discussion in order to show how the modern conditions of this discussion seem to be incompatible with democratic equality. In what follows, I rely less on the idea that individuals are self-interested and merely on the idea that a society must have a division of labor in order to perform any of its tasks efficiently.

What Is Rational Social Deliberation?

Rational social deliberation is a communicative process among persons that leads to collective decisionmaking. It results ultimately in the choices of many persons. What are the chief features of this process? How is it distinct from other kinds of persuasion, such as propaganda, indoctrination, manipulation, and bargaining? Like these others it is a communicative process; unlike them it is a process that is animated by a concern for truth and reasoned consensus. When is a process of discussion between various interlocutors rational? There are six conditions under which a process of discussion among persons is a process of rational social deliberation. I shall call these conditions the persuasion, openness, variety, transparency, efficiency, and reason-guidedness conditions. The last is the most difficult to grasp and poses the most serious difficulties for democratic theory.

First, individuals participate in this process by attempting to *rationally persuade* others to support courses of action by giving them reasons for believing that they are best. Those reasons must be independent of the process of discussion.[16] This distinguishes social deliberation from bargaining, which involves the creation of reasons in discussion by the making of threats and offers. When I bargain with another person I give him a reason for acting a certain way by threatening him with unpleasant consequences if he does not or by offering him benefits if he does. In this situation, the reasons the other person acquires depend on and are the result of the process of discussion itself. Conversely, when I engage in rational discussion with another, I appeal to facts, values, or ideas independent of our discussion and over which I have no control. The reasons the other person acquires are not created in the process of discussion; he discovers them through the process.

Second, participants are *open* to persuasion by others in the process. They are guided by a concern for truth and reasoned consensus and think of each other as potential contributors to that pursuit. They participate in the hope of persuading others of the merits of their positions but desire that others change their minds only if they see the reasons involved. And they are prepared to change their minds if they see that the opposing position is better supported by reasons. This helps distinguish the process of rational discussion from mere indoctrination. An indoctrinating agent is merely concerned with inducing some state of belief in another regardless of whether the other sees the reason and with an eye to making the other impervious to subsequent discussions.

Third, a *variety* of views are considered by the group that at least some members reasonably find plausible initially. Of course, the rational social deliberator desires to show that the other alternatives are wrong, but he or she does wish to make sure that they are discussed. This helps separate rational social deliberation from manipulation. This condition is tricky since it does not and ought not require that the rational deliberator include all alternatives. Some alternatives should be excluded on the grounds that consideration of too many alternatives may undermine the process of deliberation and that some alternatives may not be reasonable. It does not seem right to say that every exclusion of alternatives is a case of manipulation. Also, how much effort to include alternatives is necessary is unclear. I shall leave this vague with the understanding that the evaluation of a process of social deliberation may make this more determinate.

Fourth, participants in this process are updated on where the debate is going, and there is a continual concern for making sure that participants understand the arguments that have been given. The process is *transparent*. This also helps distinguish rational social deliberation from manipulation. Though manipulation does not occur merely when a participant has misunderstood an argument, it does seem to occur when the discussant knows that the misunderstanding has occurred, makes no effort to rectify it, and relies on the misunderstanding to persuade the other. Rational social deliberators are unwilling to accept agreement merely on the basis of misunderstanding; thus, they desire that the process be regularly clarified to everyone.

Such a process must also be *efficient* in order for it to be rational. A group of persons acts irrationally when it spends too much time deliberating. The aim of rational social discussion is to produce good choices on a variety of issues. A discussion on one topic that is so thorough and time-consuming that it excludes discussion of other important matters defeats the overall aim. Groups must allocate resources so that they can reach reasonably good and reasoned choices in a timely and energy-conserving manner.

The Reason-Guidedness Condition on Rational Social Deliberation

The first five conditions attempt to exclude nonrational conditions from the process of rational discussion. They contrast rational discussion with other forms of communication. The sixth condition is a more positive condition; it is the most difficult to make clear. It is that a process of rational social deliberation must in some way be *guided by the reasons* that are offered. Some difference in the quality of reasons offered tends to move people to accept one set of views rather than another. In addition to offering and listening to the reasons given for particular views, individuals are capable of discriminating between the quality of reasons and make their decisions between alternatives on that basis. That basis ought to satisfy certain normative requirements on reasoning, so that there is a sense in which the result is based on the better reason.[17]

To say that the result is based on the better reason is to say that at least most people involved in the process tend to come to believe the ultimate view or adopt the ultimate course of action because they see that the best reasons support it. Of course, not everyone need do this for the process to be rational; and the best-supported view does not always emerge victorious. And the best-supported view need not be the true view. In general the best-supported view or choice, if there is one, does emerge from a process of rational social deliberation. The process is reliable in being guided by the best reasons.

The notion of the better reason can be understood in terms of three different standards of evaluation. These standards are a *personal standard*, that is, the standard that an individual holds given her own understanding and information. On this account, individuals might have different standards in a society. Hence, a process of rational deliberation is reason-guided in this particular sense if most individuals come to adopt a view as a consequence of their seeing that it is best by their lights. Each may have separate reasons that accord with separate standards of evaluation. A second standard is a *collective standard*, that is, the standard that evaluates views and the reasons that support them in terms of the best-informed members of the community or those who are experts. A process of deliberation is rational by this standard if most of the participants adopt views because they grasp the reasoning supporting them that is the best by the standard of expertise in the community. Disagreement among the best informed is obviously possible. So, the collective standard need not generate unique outcomes. Finally, there is an *objective standard*, that is, the standard that evaluates views and the reasons that support them on grounds that are independent of what the members of the community think. Thus, a process of social deliberation is rational when most members adopt views that are supported by the objectively best reasons regardless of whether they believe them to be the best reasons. A process could generate beliefs supported by the best reasons even though the members are not aware of the reasons at all. They simply acquire the beliefs.

For the purposes of evaluating a process of rational discussion, the best notion of "better reason" must involve some combination of the personal and collective standards. It cannot be evaluated *merely* in terms of each person's own standards of reasoning. In some cases, many individuals do not have enough understanding to properly evaluate the arguments. Their standards are inappropriate to the task of evaluating the kinds of beliefs under discussion. It is perverse to say that a group's deliberations are rational when most individuals generally adopt views on the basis of reasons far beneath the standards of the acknowledged experts of the group, especially if they disagree with the experts.

One exception to this might be when the less informed adopt views because the better informed have adopted them, as long as the less informed have good reason to believe that the better informed are well informed. We might call this a case of proxy reasoning. But if this generally characterizes the position of the less informed in the process of social deliberation, we ought to say that the less informed are not really participating in the process at all since reasons are not being given to them regarding the subject matter at all. If citizens never form opinions on their own but only follow other persons' opinions, then it is hard to see how they are participating in discussion. Only the experts are deliberating; the rest are simply following along. It may be rational for the uninformed merely to mimic the informed, given limited resources, and it may even be collectively desirable that they do so, but they are not participating in rational social deliberation. Hence, in general, that reasons are evaluated by the personal standard is not *sufficient* for calling a process of social deliberation rational.

The personal standard is not *necessary* either if we adopt the objective standard as a sufficient condition. In my view, though it might be better if the reasoning did satisfy objective standards, satisfaction of the objective standard is not sufficient for calling a process of social deliberation rational. The objective standard view states that the best argument is the one that is in fact based on the best evidence and the best inference. It need not entail that the conclusion is true; indeed, the conclusion supported by the lesser argument may be true. The better argument satisfies objective standards of argumentation better. To be sure, all participants to the debate already think of their own views this way if they are sincere. But inasmuch as the standard is distinct from the standards they apply, this standard will not supply a *guideline* for them in this contest of deliberation. And the satisfaction of the standard will not always consist in reasoned belief since the objectively best inference may not be grasped as such by those who use them. Therefore, even if the better argument were to win, it would not have guided the deliberation. Even if one of the persons is in possession of the better argument, if he or she does not see that it is the better argument, we cannot say that the better reasons guided the adoption of the view. But, we observed above that only if the better reason guides the deliberation is it rational deliberation. The objective standard is devised in a way that is external to the process of thought and choice. It does not guide the making of the choice, beyond telling us that we should conscientiously evaluate the arguments.

One might prefer this standard because it is connected with the aims of the process of deliberation as the participants see them. They aim at reasoning and understanding that satisfies some objective standard, not merely their own standards, though they think that their standards are objectively best. In response to this, one might say that as long as one is choosing an external standard, one might as well choose a standard like the choice should be what is objectively the best choice or it should be based on the understanding that is closest to the truth. Surely it is more important to make a good choice even if it is based on a bad argument than a bad choice based on a good argument, as long as the standards are purely external. Hence, I conclude that the objective standard is not sufficient to call a process of social deliberation rational.

And it is not necessary. Were it necessary, anytime we as external observers see that there is a flaw in an argument or that certain evidence that we can see is germane to the issue is not considered we would have to say that the discussion was not rational discussion. This cannot be right. Rationality must involve doing the best one can do given one's limited resources. If certain modes of thinking are unavailable to a person, it cannot be irrational for them not to use them. Perhaps, however, we must see that certain minimal standards of rationality must be observed before we think of it as rational discussion or deliberation. If the laws of logic are consistently flagrantly violated, if contradictions are consistently accepted as good reasons, we ought to say that the process is not rational, but generally, the personal standard is necessary though not sufficient. It is necessary that deliberation proceed in accordance with reasons that the participants grasp as the best reasons in order for it to be rational.

I submit that the process of social deliberation is rational if the process is guided by reasons that are the best by the standards of the community as a whole. The "better argument" is the one that is most in accordance with the standards of the better-informed members of the group. The discussions must be guided by what are thought to be better reasons by those who are best informed about the subject. Thus, the collective standard is the proper standard for evaluating whether a process of social deliberation is rational.

The bases for this conclusion are that for a process of discussion to be rational, the reasons that guide the process must be grasped by the participants. A purely objective standard does not satisfy this. Yet the standards cannot merely be whatever anyone happens to hold, since then deliberation is rational even when deeply uninformed members determine the choice even when they disagree with the better informed. If someone must be able to grasp the reasons it must be the best-informed members.

These considerations tie in with the idea that it is efficient for a community to invest certain persons with extra time and resources for informing themselves and reflecting on certain matters. They are experts in an intellectual division of labor. Without such a division of labor, the community would waste its intellectual resources and be incapable of handling important issues well. A process of deliberation in a community would be irrational if it failed to use the superior understanding of its experts. It is irrational for a community to invest resources in certain persons for the purpose of developing their understanding and then to ignore them when their expertise becomes relevant.

That a process of discussion is rational only if it satisfies the collective standard has an important consequence. It suggests that some kind of rough parity of understanding on a particular subject is a necessary condition for the participants to engage in rational social deliberation. This is because the personal standard is necessary and the collective standard is necessary. Thus, it is necessary both that the reasons that win out must be reasons that are seen to be the best by the most informed and that most of the participants be able to grasp that these are the best. Therefore everyone who participates must be able to grasp these reasons. Thus, the participants must be on a par in understanding the issues.

This requirement produces a serious difficulty for the idea of *rational democratic deliberation*. The rough parity of understanding required for rational deliberation seems to be absent in a number of ways in a modern democratic society. It is hard to see how rational social deliberation can take place on a societywide level, particularly when it comes to matters concerning the politics of the society. If deliberation is rational then it cannot be democratic, and if it is democratic then it cannot be rational.

Rational Social Deliberation and the Political Division of Labor: Two Problems

That modern society and indeed any society with any degree of complexity requires a division of labor is uncontroversial. Individuals simply cannot carry out all the tasks that are necessary to sustaining their lives. They must rely on others doing their jobs while they do their own. Such a division of labor is necessary in politics as well. And it is necessary in the intellectual labor that politics demands. Specialized knowledge and activity is necessary to maintaining the complicated political process. There must be experts on the environment, on the economy, and many other fields. There must be individuals who specialize in making laws, as well as carrying them out; these are legislators and administrators. If ordinary citizens attempted to carry out these tasks, they would not have the time to carry out all the activities they must perform. A society in which everyone attempted to understand all the complicated issues of politics would be one where nothing else was done and where politics was poorly pursued. In short, such a society would be self-defeating. That is why there is specialization and a political division of labor. Notice that the irrationality of citizens being fully informed is not based on the self-interest axiom. It is based on the limited abilities of each particular person as well as the fact that this deficiency can be made up for with social organization. The problems that follow do not presuppose that citizens are self-interested, only that they are limited in what they can do.

I want to discuss two kinds of difficulty for social deliberation in the context of the political division of labor. First, a problem arises when individuals with different kinds of expertise disagree on a proper course of action because of their different kinds of information. Second, difficulties arise when these individuals wish to persuade some third party who has very little of either kind of information or expertise.

First, let us try an idealized version of the first problem. Suppose that there are two experts who are arguing about what common course of action is best. Further suppose that the disagreement stems from the fact that their areas of expertise are quite different and involve very different factual bases as well as different theoretical commitments. From these opposing bases of expert knowledge, they advance different reasons for pursuing one or another course of action. But since they are restricted to their own expertise, neither can fully appreciate the reasons the other gives. Either they cannot accept each other's factual bases, or they find the methods of reasoning unacceptable.[18]

As an example of this kind of conflict we might think of employers' groups and labor groups deliberating about how to organize production. These groups have different interests to some extent. The workers desire higher pay, greater safety, possibly more control over the process of production, and job security. The employers desire to guarantee the profitability of their firms either because they own the firms or because that is what they are hired to do. Furthermore, suppose that their deliberations are meant to influence certain important pieces of legislation. In short, all participants have some common interests; they desire to ensure the productivity of the economy, they desire that the workforce is well trained and able to work, and they desire that the members of the workforce are sufficiently affluent to consume the products of industry. Finally, they may both be concerned with the justice of the arrangements that are decided. At the same time, however, they disagree on how to achieve these aims and they have opposing interests regarding the solutions.

In this kind of case it is unclear what the collective standard is. There are competing standards that cannot be completely compared. This kind of case does not suggest that there is no rational discussion, only that rational discussion has run out. The opposing views may satisfy very high standards within the different communities of expertise and hence they are the result of rational discussion themselves.

The Citizen and Rational Deliberation with Experts

Citizens in a democracy often experience a sense of bewilderment when experts from these kinds of opposing groups engage in deliberation over the best policies. The groups desire to persuade other citizens as well as each other. And they try to persuade each other in ways that match their interests.

The difficulty described in the previous section helps prepare the ground for the second problem for social deliberation in the context of the political division of labor. Consider the context where two opposed expert deliberators are attempting to persuade a third person who does not have either expertise. In a democratic society, legislators and ultimately the citizens must decide on the relative worth of arguments of the experts. But they are less able to evaluate the relative quality of the arguments than the opposing debaters are. The positions that these groups elaborate and argue for often require full-time attention, that is why experts must often be hired. But the legislators cannot have this kind of knowledge, at least about most of the things they vote on, and the ordinary citizens are even less capable of acquiring this knowledge. These are just descriptions of the political division of labor.

The problem is that when the discussion includes legislators and citizens it is even less likely to be guided by good reasons than in the previous kind of example. In the case of the legislators, they do not specialize in the subjects of debate. They do specialize in the political division of labor, but they are primarily concerned with strategic issues of how, and when, and with whom to form coalitions to produce certain kinds of legislation and to win elections. Some legislators are specialists in particular areas, but it is not true that generally legislators can or even ought to become experts in most of the areas on which they vote. They already have difficult enough tasks of their own. Thus, when they are confronted with opposing arguments from opposing experts who are funded by groups with different positions, interests, and points of view in the larger society, they have a hard time making decisions guided by the best reasons. Their decisions may end up being in accordance with the best argument, but in most cases the legislators are not in a position to grasp that it is the best argument. Hence, the personal standard by which they reason will often not be the same as the collective standard. In this case, the choice of the society (which is usually made by legislators) is not the result of rational deliberation.

Citizens face this problem to an even greater degree. They simply do not generally have the expertise to evaluate these kinds of opposed arguments. And, again, it appears that it would not be desirable for them to make the effort to do this since such effort would take them away from other important tasks. Of course they do listen to experts and form judgments as a result of listening to these experts. But often this process of formation of judgment, though rational for that person, does not satisfy the collective standard. For instance, many citizens form judgments on the basis of what are called opinion leaders' views.[19] Ordinary citizens often accept the views promoted by trusted political leaders or commentators without assessing the evidence themselves. Indeed, the basis of trust itself is unclear in many cases since the citizen has never independently assessed the evidence. Hence, it is not clear why the citizen believes one opinion leader rather than another, but it is not on the basis of a grasp of the better reason.

It appears, therefore, that there are deep difficulties with attempting to establish anything like a process of rational social deliberation on a societywide level in a modern democracy. A process of rational social deliberation in a modern society requires an intellectual division of labor such that only some are capable of making informed judgments on certain matters. For deliberation to be democratic, however, there must be at least rough equality among most of the citizens with regard to understanding the subjects discussed. Only then will citizens be in a position to grasp and assess the arguments so that the force of the better argument prevails. But this possibility seems to be systematically excluded by the need for a division of labor in society.

The Need for a Theory of Democratic Citizenship

The challenge to democratic ideals provided by the four sources of inequality and the asymmetries of understanding is very serious. If a modern state is necessarily inegalitarian and is incapable of democratic rational deliberation, then the ideals defended and elaborated in Chapters 1 and 2 must be deemed incoherent and the ideals of democracy a sham.

In my view, these problems do not present insuperable difficulties to democratic ideals. The basic problem arises from the fact that a modern society must have division of labor, including intellectual tasks. In order to respond to the challenge, therefore, we must elaborate a conception of the role of democratic citizenship in the division of labor that shows how its demands are not so great as to be incompatible with robust ideals of political equality and rational deliberation. We must also show why it is plausible to think that citizens will perform this role. We must answer the questions: What is the appropriate role for the citizen in a democratic state? What are the duties of the citizen? What can we expect from citizens? The problems described in the previous sections arise because we have a certain conception of the citizen and his or her role. We assumed that citizens had to be self-interested in order to elaborate the four inequalities. We assumed that there were no subjects of deliberation that did not admit of an unbridgeable gulf between the knowledge of the ordinary citizen and the experts in society while permitting citizens to be sovereign over their society.

In the next two chapters, I discuss a number of different conceptions of citizenship that attempt to overcome these problems. In Chapter 4 I discuss conceptions of citizenship based on the self-interest view of citizens. Some of these conceptions rest content with a stripped-down conception of democratic citizenship and a very partial realization of the democratic ideals. Others attempt partial reinterpretations of the ideals. I will show that all of these attempts fail to answer in a satisfactory way the questions posed in the previous paragraph. They are self-defeating theories, or so I shall argue. I will defend a conception of citizenship in Chapter 5 that reconciles the conditions of the modern state with full-blooded versions of the democratic ideals. I reject the self-interest axiom and elaborate a conception of the object of concern for democratic citizens, as well as standards for assessing citizen understanding of these objects. The conception of citizenship that I defend will then be used to elaborate principles for the evaluation of particular democratic institutions of representation and deliberation in Part Three.

Notes

1. Anthony Downs, *An Economic Theory of Democracy* (New York: Harper and Row, 1957).

2. In Russell Hardin's "Public Choice Versus Democracy," in *The Idea of Democracy,* ed. David Copp, Jean Hampton, and John Roemer (Cambridge: Cambridge University Press, 1993). There is a voluminous literature on this problem. For two representative collections of essays on the subject see many of the essays in Geoffrey Brennan and Loren Lomasky, eds., *Politics and Process: New Essays in Democratic Thought* (New York: Cambridge University Press, 1989) and John Ferejohn and James Kuklinski, eds., *Information and Democratic Processes* (Champaign: University of Illinois Press, 1991). See also the other works cited in this and the next two chapters.

3. E. E. Schattschneider, *The Semisovereign People: A Realist's View of Democracy in America* (New York: Holt, Rinehart and Winston, 1960).

4. See Francis Fox Piven and Richard Cloward, *Why Americans Don't Vote* (New York: Pantheon, 1988), for how the various formal devices mentioned changed voter turnout. Also, in the United States, those states where voter registration comes virtually automatically with residency, the voter turnout is now much higher than the national average. See also Dennis Thompson, *The Democratic Citizen* (Cambridge: Cambridge University Press, 1970).

5. However, the tendency to vote is not strictly correlated with size. For instance, on average, many more people vote in the presidential elections in the United States than in the state referenda.

6. These points show that self-interested citizens have reason to participate sometimes, but they don't explain why people vote consistently in such large numbers. Let us leave this to the side for the moment in order to discuss the implications of self-interest for the collection of information. See Paul Meehl, "The Selfish Voter Paradox and the Problem of the Wasted Vote," *American Political Science Review* March (1977), pp. 11–30.

7. Downs is at the origin of the by-product theory. See also W. Russell Neuman, *The Paradox of Mass Politics* (Cambridge, Mass.: MIT Press, 1986), and Samuel Popkin, *The Reasoning Voter* (Chicago: University of Chicago Press, 1990) for empirical evidence of the use of the by-product theory.

8. See Morris Fiorina, "Information and Rationality in Elections," in *Information and Democratic Processes*, pp. 329–342, for the spectator sport approach to politics.

9. See John Zaller, *The Nature and Origins of Mass Opinion* (Cambridge: Cambridge University Press, 1992), for a full development of this kind of view. Downs also discusses this in *An Economic Theory of Democracy*, chapter 12.

10. See Neuman, *The Paradox of Mass Democracy*, and Popkin, *The Reasoning Voter*, for statistical evidence for these claims.

11. Downs, *An Economic Theory of Democracy*, p. 223.

12. Downs, *An Economic Theory of Democracy*, p. 248.

13. Downs, *An Economic Theory of Democracy*, p. 230.

14. See Cass Sunstein, *Democracy and the Problem of Free Speech* (New York: Free Press, 1993), pp. 62–66, for good examples of this kind of action. See also Charles Lindblom, *Politics and Markets* (New York: Basic Books, 1977), for a discussion of this problem.

15. For example, see Downs, *An Economic Theory of Democracy*, p. 267, as well as Joseph Schumpeter, *Capitalism, Socialism, and Democracy* (New York: Harper and Row, 1956), p. 270.

16. See Peter Burnell and Andrew Reeves, "Persuasion as a Political Concept," in *British Journal of Political Science* 14 (1984), pp. 393–410, for an explanation of this distinction as well as for descriptions of some of the first four conditions. Some of these conditions are also discussed by Joshua Cohen, "Deliberation and Democratic Legitimacy," in *The Good Polity*, ed. Alan Hamlin and Philip Pettit (New York: Basil Blackwell), pp. 20–21.

17. For the expression of this standard, see Jurgen Habermas, *Legitimation Crisis*, trans. Thomas McCarthy (Boston: Beacon Press, 1975), p. 108, as well as Joshua Cohen, "Deliberation and Democratic Legitimacy," p. 20.

18. In politics, a neutral third person rarely arises for a number of reasons. First, it is hard enough to have the information and training to get any kind of expertise and since decisions must be made in a timely manner,

there is often not the time to develop this kind of expertise before a new set of problems must be handled. Second, different bases of expertise are supported by different sectors of the society, in part because the interests and points of view of those sectors are advanced by these different kinds of expertise. There often is no separate basis for expertise from a neutral point of view. Although presumably university systems in most western countries are partly designed with an eye to this purpose. Even in these systems, however, foundations, fellowships, and grants go towards supporting research that advances more partial interests and points of view.

19. See Samuel Popkin, *The Reasoning Voter*, as well as some of the papers in *Information and Democratic Processes*, ed. John Ferejohn and James Kuklinski, for some views about opinion leadership and its impact.

CHAPTER FOUR

The Economic
Conception of
Citizenship

The Elements of a Theory of Democratic Citizenship

Principles of democracy require, in addition to general standards of evaluation of political institutions, an account of citizenship. We have seen that the Downsian view of citizens poses a deep challenge to the democratic ideals defended in Chapter 2. Indeed, the very idea of egalitarian democracy appears incoherent in the modern state. Thus, a theory of democratic ideals requires a companion conception of democratic citizenship.

A theory of democratic citizenship is a theory about the rights and duties citizens possess in their joint exercise of authority over the society. It is only one part of the total theory of citizenship, which also includes the rights and duties of citizens in their capacities as subjects of the law. There are four main elements of a conception of democratic citizenship. First, the basic *normative principles of democracy* are what give normative force to any conception of citizenship founded on them. The principles defended in Chapter 2 require that all the citizens be sovereign over the society they live in to the extent that their interests are deeply interdependent. A collective decision-making procedure is necessary to advance the interests citizens have in the collective properties of society. Citizens have a right to an equal say in this collective decision process. This political equality requires that citizens have equal resources for participating in the decision as well as the discussion and deliberations that lead up to the decisionmaking. Second, the theory defines the *appropriate role of citizens*. The previous chapter has alerted us to the importance of thinking about modern society as involving a division of labor. Modern society is so complex and the activities required to maintain it and achieve some of its aims are so involved and diverse that specialization in these tasks is necessary. A division of labor implies that different individuals will play different roles in pursuing social aims. Doctors, workers, politicians, engineers, and many others all specialize in tasks that, when put together, realize some social goods. Each of these roles is characterized by the kind of contribution it makes to the social good. Furthermore, these roles entail certain distinctive activities for these contributions. There are also certain standards for assessing the contribution of those activities to the social good. For example, what must a doctor do and know in order to fulfill the role assigned to doctors? Political decisionmaking also requires a division of labor. In addition to ordinary citizens there are politicians, leaders of interest groups, political organizers, policy experts, and many others. These too are roles that make distinctive contributions and that require certain kinds of activities that are evaluated by certain standards. Thus a conception of citizenship must address the questions, What is the appropriate role of citizens in a modern democratic state? What contribution should ordinary citizens make to collective decisionmaking? What should citizens be doing to fulfill their role? and in particular, What are the objects that citizens ought to be thinking about when they reflect on political matters? What standards ought their understanding meet? Given the democratic ideals of Chapter 2 we want to know what assignment of roles enables citizens to exercise their right to an equal say.

If citizens have a right to play a certain role in the making of law and policy and certain activities are required for the adequate exercise of this right, then institutions must be designed with an eye to giving the citizens the opportunities to exercise these rights adequately. So, third, a conception of citizenship must be accompanied by a *complementary conception of the roles of all the other players* in the political system. These roles are to be designed so as to ensure that the role of citizenship can be adequately carried out.

Fourth, we must also determine *what can be expected from citizens*. What are citizens motivated by? Is the kind of role that is required for citizens to have an equal say one that we can expect citizens to assume? Is the role too demanding or unrealistic? Is performance of this role incompatible with all the other roles that citizens play in the society? The Downsian view of citizens as self-interested agents suggests that any role for most citizens that goes beyond mere voting is unrealistic and too demanding. Citizens will simply not perform. The Downsian view of what can be expected from citizens seems to defeat the democratic ideals and any conception of the role of citizens that relies on those ideals. However, perhaps we can and should expect citizens to have a wider variety of concerns than their own self-interest. I will argue that we should think of citizens as being partly motivated by considerations of justice and concern for others. In this case we can expect more from citizens than the Downsian view allows. A more robust conception of the role of citizens in the modern state might then be reasonable.

All of these elements come in a package. If the democratic ideals are too demanding of citizens then they are for that reason deeply flawed. And this is precisely what the Downsian account suggests.

The Economic Models of Citizenship

In this chapter, I will explore conceptions of citizenship that assume that citizens are primarily self-interested and their impact on the ideals of democracy. These I call economic conceptions of citizenship. Though they share a basic commitment to the idea that citizens are self-interested, they differ in the roles they assign to citizens and to the complementary parts of political decisionmaking and in the extent to which they suggest that the democratic ideals can be met. These views claim that we ought not require of citizens that they act in accordance with principles of justice except insofar as such action is compatible with the agent's self-interest. I will discuss three models of citizenship and democracy that are founded on self-interest: the formalist, the interest group pluralist, and the neoliberal accounts.

Before we continue it is important to make a clarification. There are two different approaches to the economic theory of democracy. There are theories that justify basic political principles on the basis of what rational, self-interested individuals would choose in some hypothetical situation. These are contractarian justifications of political principles.[1] And there are critical economic evaluations of political principles. They address the viability of political principles as principles for institutional design on the assumption that citizens are self-interested. Anthony Downs and Joseph Schumpeter, for example, urge a "realistic" approach to democracy and argue for scaling back democratic aspirations on the grounds that only less ambitious institutions can succeed in the light of the self-interest of citizens. Formalist, interest group pluralist, and neoliberal views all defend different democratic institutions and assign distinct roles to citizens. I will discuss the second critical approach only. In general, I will show that these theories are self-defeating in that the institutions they justify are not stable under the assumption of self-interest. These theories cannot succeed on their own terms. Then, I will undermine the argument for self-interest and present evidence that individuals are motivated by moral principles in certain circumstances. In Chapter 5 I will discuss the problem of citizenship as it arises when we think of citizens as morally motivated.

The Formalist Model of Citizenship

The formalist model of citizenship is Joseph Schumpeter's account of the proper operation of a democratic society. He states that "the democratic method is that institutional arrangement for arriving at political decisions in which individuals acquire the power to decide by means of a competitive struggle for the people's vote."[2] This account of the "democratic method" intentionally assigns a very small role to the citizenry of a democratic society. "The role of the people is to produce a government, or else an intermediate body which in turn will produce a national executive or government."[3]

In the political division of labor, Schumpeter assigns a very large role to political parties, legislators, and executives and a rather small role to citizens. Though he does not exclude the possibility of some citizens being well informed and expressing their will in the vote, what is important in his model is that citizens participate in voting and thereby ensure smooth regime transition. What is important for the society at large is how those who are in positions of power rule. Do they rule well? Are they good leaders? We can and ought to expect very little from the great majority of citizens in the way of understanding political issues and sophisticated participation. A society is better off if its citizens participate merely in a formal way by electing leaders. The role of the leaders is correspondingly very large. They have discretion to do what they think is best without regard for what citizens think. The standards that citizen participation are to meet are minimal. Citizens need not know anything about what the leaders think or do; all they have to do is vote.

Schumpeter's view of the ideals we have discussed is that the best we can do is achieve a kind of formal equality wherein everyone may vote. We cannot expect any more robust equality in which citizens have anything like equal resources for determining the outcomes of collective decisionmaking. Furthermore, he suggests that we ought not to expect deliberation to take place in the society as a whole. First of all, there is no common object of deliberation since there is no common good, and, second, the citizens in general can only harm the process of deliberation since they are ignorant of the issues. Only elites can be expected to participate in deliberation, and their deliberation must be focused exclusively on achieving the means to certain ends that they must decide upon. The rest of the population must hope for the best. Thus, a society corresponding to Schumpeter's description will necessarily be profoundly unequal in collective decisionmaking.

The main idea animating this view is that citizens are necessarily irrational and uninformed about politics in modern society. Like Downs, Schumpeter thinks that since individuals are primarily self-interested and the values of votes for advancing their interests are very small, they will tend to be quite uninformed. Schumpeter adds that when individuals do participate without feeling constrained by a sense of self-interest, they will be easily induced to act on the basis of normally dormant irrational motives and swayed by all forms of demagoguery. Hence, he argues that citizens do not participate extensively and that it would be undesirable if they did since they would only act on irrational motives. Extensive participation would produce bad government. The recommendation for extensive citizen involvement in democracy is, he thinks, misguided and even pernicious.

Schumpeter also argues against any greater role for the citizenry for the kinds of reasons elaborated in more detail by social choice theorists.[4] He argues that popular participation is generally considered valuable because it is thought to produce decisions that advance the common good.[5] But, he argues, the common good is a chimera because no such entity can be culled from the diverse and multifarious aims of all the members of the society. Furthermore, he argues that there is no way to rationally argue about issues of justice or morality. "Questions of principle cannot be reconciled by rational argument because ultimate values—our conceptions of what life and what society ought to be—are beyond the range of mere logic."[6] Together these points suggest that there can be no popular will or common good. So the rationale for popular participation is undermined.

A first objection is that Schumpeter's account is incoherent. He criticizes the ideals of democracy in the name of some conception of the common good. It is because he thinks that extensive participation would produce bad outcomes that it is to be eschewed. The badness of these outcomes is surely not the badness for some particular member or sector of the society; it is a common bad to which he is referring, and it is for the common good that he proposes his model of democracy and citizenship. So his claim that there is no common good is very much overstated.

Schumpeter might respond that although the existence of some minimal common good is necessary, the presupposition behind the theory that demands extensive popular participation is that there is a much more extensive common good. Such a good is chimerical and the ideals of democracy must fail because they invoke too ambitious a conception of the common good. It demands a wider and more extensive convergence on some common good than is possible in the modern world. Against this, I have argued in Chapter 2 that an extensive common good is not a necessary condition for being concerned with greater equality in a democratic society. Indeed, equality and rational deliberation stand on their own as ideals of a democratic society.

A second objection is to the assumptions that underlie the view. Schumpeter relies on a view that individuals are motivated virtually exclusively by self-interest in matters that have a direct impact on them, whereas they tend towards infantile and irrational behavior in actions that have only remote and obscure consequences. On this basis, he recommends that one ought to confer a great deal of power on a relatively small group of individuals. But, it may be asked, What interests do the leaders have in the proper use of power? The formalist might say that the leaders have an interest in good rule because this is a necessary condition of reelection. Thus, the leaders have interests in the maintenance of their positions of power and they can only maintain their positions of power by getting reelected by the population. Here we have a kind of analogy to an oligopolistic market with a few competing firms. Each firm has an interest in maintaining the quality and affordability of its products because if it does not, then the consumers will go to one of the other firms. In the same way, each political leader will try to maintain the quality of his or her rule because otherwise voters will shift to another leader or group of leaders. Political competition is thought to be like economic competition.[7] This competition should reveal when the incumbent rulers are making mistakes or the challenger's program is misguided.

But this argument contradicts the Schumpeterian argument for minimal participation. Recall that individuals are not well informed about politics and cannot be entrusted with the task of determining the common good or evaluating the performance of their leaders. To say that the leaders have an interest in being good rulers in order to be reelected is to suggest that citizens know when the rulers are ruling well, but this is what they are not supposed to be able to know in this theory. Contrary to Schumpeter's claim, the rulers must only make sure that they appear to be ruling well to those who are not watching very closely; they do not have to rule well. Given Schumpeter's view of the powers of rulers to manipulate the will and understanding of the citizenry, this should not be such a difficult task for leaders. How can citizens make the necessary discriminations among candidates? Decisions they make between incumbents and challengers are likely to be of a highly dubious quality. Who they side with will depend more on the abilities of the candidates to *appear* worthy than on any fact of the matter. And for the rest, the decision will depend on relatively arbitrary factors. Politicians have interests in assembling powerful campaign war chests and clever handlers but not in good rule itself because the effects of good rule and bad rule can be made to appear the same or at least not the products of whoever is in power and because citizens do not make their decisions on any clear understanding of this anyway. The campaign war chest itself is to be raised from the small class of producers whose interests perhaps will also be taken care of. Overall, it seems the relation between good rule for the people at large and re-election should be quite weak on the Schumpeterian account. Thus, the interest in reelection does not seem to provide the leaders with any incentive to rule well in this view. The market analogy would seem to be particularly inapt in this context since it is precisely the lack of analogy between citizen and consumer that motivates the whole Schumpeterian program.[8] Consumers are likely to be reasonably well informed because the objects they consume have direct effects on them while the voter experiences no such direct effect in most cases of political decisions.[9]

The formalist may respond that rulers are concerned with ruling well because they are deeply affected by the consequences of their own decisions. Since the outcomes of their decisions affect them just as much as they affect others, and their fates are tied with those of all the citizens, we may expect them to treat the citizenry well and be good rulers. Indeed, they are likely to treat the citizens better than if the latter controlled the government themselves since they would individually have little responsibility for outcomes.[10]

Against this we must ask, Why can't the rulers benefit themselves and some small sector of society without benefiting the whole of society? Surely they are in a position to do so and to conceal their actions since the citizenry is not watching closely. In addition, competing elites cannot depend on being able to persuade citizens of the self-servingness of the incumbent's actions, and if they can persuade citizens of the self-servingness of the incumbents, they may be able to do so regardless of whether it is true. Furthermore, there may be gains from trade between elites if they explicitly or implicitly agree to ignore each others' self-serving actions.

This kind of collusion is often alleged against the leaders of political parties in the United States. Perhaps the most famous such case is the charge of collusion against the leaders of the conservative wings of the Democratic and Republican Parties during the period leading up to the election of 1896. These two groups apparently colluded in transforming American politics into one of sectional politics between North and South so as to defeat the movement of Populism. Their actions had the long-run effect of turning back civil and political rights for black Americans for about half a century and defeating the interests of workers and farmers for about the same amount of time. It also had the effect of turning each of the states into one-party states while leaving the national government primarily in the hands of the Republicans.[11] More recently, the charge has been that the scandal of the savings and loan bank collapses and bailouts was covered up by both political parties acting explicitly or implicitly in collusion.[12] Thus the link between their well-being and that of the citizenry provides no clear incentive for elites to be overly concerned with the quality of their rule, especially if we assume that citizens play the passive and formal role assigned to them by this theory.

Finally there is, contrary to Schumpeter's hope, a strong incentive for elites in the system that Schumpeter describes to engage in demagogic and manipulative activity. Schumpeter believes that ordinary citizens are easily manipulable by powerful interests. If this is so, it is hard to see why leaders would not attempt to use this power.[13]

Perhaps the Schumpeterian can attribute a capacity to detect and avoid disaster to citizens, so that in addition to the purely formal role they play, citizens are a fail-safe mechanism. This account requires that individuals are likely to have reasonable beliefs about when a disaster is looming. It also requires that they can achieve consensus on a prediction of disaster as well as its nature. The citizens must also agree that the source of the potential disaster is in a distinct party or candidate to which there is some alternative.

But it is implausible to claim that individuals are more likely to have these kinds of knowledge than other more ordinary forms of knowledge about politics. The view depends on there being some strong salience to information that portends disaster and that this kind of information will leap out at the ordinary citizen, who is otherwise quite unaware of the political situation. To be sure, when a disaster has already occurred, the citizens are likely to know of it.

And this information will be available to all. But the knowledge that a disaster is likely to occur does not seem like the kind of information that the Schumpeterian citizen is likely to have. Furthermore, the knowledge of the source of the disaster or of the way out of the disaster is as remote from the ordinary citizen as any other kind of complex political knowledge.

Perhaps the rulers have an incentive to rule well because they care about the common good. Contrary to what one might expect, Schumpeter does actually invoke this kind of motive in his discussion. He says that it is necessary that citizens and elites practice restraint and be motivated by a concern for the national interest in order for democracy to be stable.[14] But this violates the Schumpeterian motivational assumptions. First of all, individuals are self-interested, and, second, the interests of other people are too remote for them to be properly focused on them. If citizens can be motivated by these considerations, the very foundations of Schumpeter's account are undermined. The point of his theory is to assign a deeply limited role to citizens and a large role to elites because of the self-interest and rational ignorance of citizens. To save the approach however, Schumpeter requires stronger commitments from citizens and politicians.

As a normative conception of democratic method, this view is incoherent. Given the conceptions of the role of citizenship and the springs of motivation, it appears that Schumpeter's model cannot give us on its own terms a plausible picture of a stable democratic order. The trouble is that the very same considerations that lead him to reject the more demanding conceptions of democratic citizenship should also lead him to reject his own model. In my view, any theory that only appeals to predominantly self-interested motives cannot provide a plausible normative account of a stable political order. But let us look at a couple more such accounts before we draw this conclusion.

The Interest Group Pluralist Model of Citizenship

Another conception of democratic citizenship sees citizens as members of interest groups that press their particular claims against the state. The role of citizens is to make their claims known to the state and to attempt to exert pressure on the state with a view to achieving their particular aims. The role of a politician or administrator is to satisfy the claim in return for support in elections. In Robert Dahl's words: "In a rough sense, the essence of all competitive politics is bribery of the electorate by politicians. . . . The farmer . . . supports a candidate committed to high support prices, the businessman . . . supports an advocate of low corporation taxes, . . . the consumer . . . votes for candidates opposed to a sales tax."[15] Citizens are primarily self-interested in this account; they merely press their own sectional needs on the government. In effect the relation of the citizen who is a farmer to a politician need not be much more extensive than that person's relation to her business partners and clients. The farmer does not have to go much out of her way to inform herself about the politician. They are not thought of as aiming at some common good or at any of the collective features of the society. They each bargain for special interests of their own. Dahl has described this kind of democracy as rule by coalitions of minorities as opposed to majority rule.[16] The proponents of this account argue that the common good comes about in this kind of arrangement not by the design of the citizens but rather by a kind of invisible hand that leads to an equilibrium wherein all are better off.

Unlike in the Schumpeterian conception, interest group citizens are more likely to play their roles in an informed way. The problem of understanding is alleviated in three distinct ways. First, the interest group model requires less information gathering and hence it demands less of citizens. Second, it requires that citizens concern themselves only with those matters in which they are directly interested, thus increasing their incentives to gather information. Third, since citizens are to pursue those issues with which they are already concerned, they can use the information they receive as a by-product from their everyday lives and need not use much other information.

The interest group model also makes room for rational social deliberation inasmuch as it ensures that citizens share strengths in understanding particular sectors of the society and that they have incentives to learn from each other about their mutual interests. Insofar as rational social deliberation promotes this understanding it will play an important part in an interest group society. Therefore, the interest group model appears to be able to reconcile the ideals of democracy with the division of labor even while assuming that citizens are essentially self-interested.

The problem of understanding does not of itself pose an especially severe problem for equality since it might be possible to constantly equalize the political power of the various political groups.[17] As long as individuals have access to information and coalition-building resources, they should all be able to promote their aims on a level playing field. There are of course many problems in defining and ensuring equality in an interest group society. But they do not result directly from the fact that there must be a division of intellectual labor in the society. Much of the criticism of interest group theories has been about their neglect of the effects of economic and social inequalities on political equality. These are serious difficulties, but they do not distinguish the interest group approach from other kinds of egalitarian theory that assign a large role in society to private market exchange in the means of production.

The trouble with this model is closely connected with its main strength. The model seems to neglect the question of substantive collective control over the society as a whole. Rather, the overall course of society is determined by an invisible hand. Individuals do not set their sights on the overall collective features of the society. But this leads to a number of difficulties. First, the fact that many different groups are appealing to the legislative and administrative branches of government in an uncoordinated way leads to a kind of incoherence in policymaking. A policy passed for one group might be undermined unwittingly by a policy passed for the benefit of another. Here, a lot of information is necessary to make sure that the different policies do not contradict each other. But in the interest group system there is no agency for coordinating all these interests.[18] Such a role might invite many of the problems these theorists are attempting to avoid. Without such a position, the interest group theorist invites the possibility of no one's interests being fulfilled in any serious way.

A second difficulty with this kind of view is the problem of cost spreading. Each citizen attempts to procure benefits for himself or herself at the expense of the public. In order for the benefits to be procured, taxes must be levied. But this means that there may be overtaxation since each citizen looks only at the cost to himself or herself and measures that cost against the benefit. The citizen does not consider that although he is the only beneficiary, he is not the only benefactor. Thus, he imposes costs on others that they most likely are not willing to bear. This is true of all the different groups, so that almost everyone will be benefiting less than they are taxed. Thus, everyone will be worse off. This seems to be a corollary to the fact that there is no central control.[19]

Finally, the system is unstable overall. This is really a special case of the problems I have just described. No one is looking after the overall justice or efficiency of the political system. It operates as an invisible hand. Or perhaps this metaphor is misleading; there is no guidance at all. Thus, though equality is not ruled out in this system, it is hard to see how it can be preserved. The cumulative effects of the different uncoordinated actions are likely to result in changes in the structure of the political system itself.[20] Thus, the interest group system also seems to fail the test of stability in much the same way as the Schumpeterian system. The expectation that citizens will pursue their self-interest in narrow policy areas makes it possible to think of citizens as knowledgeable about politics, but this limitation undermines the unity and stability of the pluralist society.

The Neoliberal Model of Citizenship

Some have argued, partly on the basis of the previous arguments, that the extent of democratic control ought to be seriously limited and that the state ought to be reasonably small. They argue that a large state can easily be exploited by powerful economic actors who have strong incentives to try to influence policy in a way that benefits themselves and that ordinary citizens do not have sufficient incentives to be informed about state action. They also agree that citizens will tend to concentrate their concerns on small issues of policy, thus guaranteeing inefficiency and loss of control for the whole society. The consequence of these two facts is that powerful actors will seek benefits from the state that are paid for by ordinary citizens. Though equality could in principle be achieved in such a circumstance, it is unlikely that any serious limitations on the power of certain groups will arise because no one is really concerned with the overall character of society or justice. This in turn will lead to deep inefficiencies in state action. In particular, both Downs and

Mancur Olson argued that the policies of the democratic state would be biased in favor of productive interests and against diffuse interests, such as those of consumers as well as the citizenry more generally.[21] Thus, they argue that a large state will be exploitative of most of the population as well as deeply inefficient.

Another argument to this conclusion is offered by some theorists inspired by the results of social choice theory. They argue that in large representative democracies the outcomes of elections are at best meaningless since there is no way to aggregate from individual preferences to collective preferences in a way that satisfies certain properties essential to saying that the collective preference represents a utilitarian outcome or an expression of the popular will. Modern pluralistic societies are most likely to be plagued with the problem of meaninglessness since there is such a wide variety of preferences among the citizens. Since democratic institutions cannot fulfill the function of expressing a utilitarian optimum or the common good, they can be justified only as a means by which citizens protect themselves against potentially abusive government elites.[22] In general, the neoliberal theory is in many ways a pessimistic theory. It argues against large government, not because it opposes the aims of many supporters of large government, but because it does not think these aims can be achieved by government. Indeed, neoliberals think that large government generally defeats the aims it is supposed to advance.

The neoliberal view minimizes the role of citizens in the governance of society by minimizing the role of state institutions. The neoliberal argues that if government plays a small role in the society, then it and its clients will not be able to abuse the population, and the members of the population will have a less daunting task in trying to figure out what the government is trying to do. Furthermore, the neoliberal argues that the ambitions that motivate large government, although not in themselves unworthy, are not aims that can be achieved. Even the pursuit of the ideals of democracy ought to be chastened by the knowledge of the facts of government failure.

The basic difficulty with the view of neoliberals is that they seem to think of government as the only possible source of abuse. They provide no principled distinction between government power and private power that might explain how only the former is likely to be oppressive. I would argue that private power has as much incentive to be oppressive when it faces challenges from those whose interests might sometimes oppose it. There are ample illustrations of this possibility. Labor repression in America derived in large part from private control of towns as well as privately funded armies. Robert Goldstein has noted that at the end of the nineteenth century and at the beginning of the twentieth century: "In 'pure' company towns, the corporations could evict tenants, cut off credit, close meeting halls, arrest strikers with their own police, censor the mails and ban all outside forces from entering the area." In addition, he observed that: "Although supposedly limited in their functions to the protection of company property, private police forces frequently roamed into nearby towns and took the law into their own hands, generally without any legal reprisals."[23] Richard Hofstadter has documented the history of failed efforts on the part of politicians to counter the power of big business in the United States by means of anti-trust law, culminating ultimately in the call to increase the size of government as the only way to curb these powers.[24] The point here is that it is hard to see why we should expect powerful private actors not to engage in repressive and highly costly behavior in a society with few constraints, especially if we assume that all act on their own interests alone.

Furthermore, the arguments neoliberals give suggest that virtually any set of social institutions will be subject to deep instabilities if their only support is the self-interest of the participants. For example, one must wonder how neoliberals who subscribe to the self-interest axiom as well as to the view that the state ought to be small can expect that a small state will be stable. Inasmuch as large private actors can see that the state can benefit them by manipulating elements of the market, such as the flow and distribution of information, the allocation of resources, and the rules for entering the market, they have an incentive to increase the power of the state to their advantage. Even if the neoliberals are right that this would lead to a decrease in welfare for other members, it is hard to see why this should concern those who benefit. Furthermore, the neoliberal view that the market ought to play a much larger role in allocating resources seems not to be of much significance as a motivating factor, and we should not expect it to be. Such views may receive lip service from powerful business interests in society, but in fact it is clear that these interests benefit a great deal from the attentions of the state and they are loathe to change them. As Grant McConnell put it:

> The really effective participants in business politics are those which direct their energies almost wholly to hard, specific matters of imme- diate economic concern to business firms. . . . Thus while a certain fiscal policy or the election of a particular presidential candidate might appear advantageous to a given industry group, much more re- liable and direct benefits may be gained by using available resources of influence to create a governmental administrative agency to care for the industry's interests vis-a-vis the public.

McConnell wryly concludes that "the noisy denunciations of govern- ment from business spokesmen are not to be taken at face value."[25] Surely, this has been borne out by the experience of the Reagan ad- ministration in American politics. It acquired support from an over- whelming majority of business interests apparently on the promise of reducing the size of the government. But government spending did not diminish, it simply shifted towards business interests.[26] Given the benefits these powerful actors receive from the state it is hard to see how the neoliberal ideal could have a chance of being realized or of remaining stable. Also, given these benefits, it is hard to see why large interests wouldn't want to help themselves to substantial state inter- vention. This problem seems to be a general one for normative theo- ries of politics that place so much emphasis on self-interest.[27]

From these observations, I conclude that the neoliberal account of the state suffers from same kind of incoherence as the others. More generally, I conclude that holding to the self-interest axiom is incompatible with the desire to defend any particular set of political institutions. The very axiom that leads Schumpeter, interest group pluralists, and neoliberals to criticize certain institutions and pro- pose new institutions undermines the proposed alternatives. This does not refute the self-interest axiom, it only suggests that such an axiom cannot be reconciled with the normative aims of those who take the axiom as basic. Theories of social reform and political ideals only make sense under different assumptions about human motiva- tion. In what follows, I shall attempt to cast doubt on the self-inter- est axiom independently of its role in political theory.

Participating on the Grounds of Self-Interest

Let us examine the claim that individuals are motivated virtually entirely by self-interest. Is it true? If it were true the implications for normative political theory in general would be quite destructive; for democratic ideals the implications would be disastrous. The evidence suggests that the claim is not true. Individuals are motivated by a variety of considerations, including moral ones.

We must be careful to separate out different notions of interest. Some of these will support the Downsian reasoning whereas others may not. Recall the distinction between preference, desire, and interest given in Chapter 2. A preference is an all-things-considered ranking of alternatives. "A prefers x to y" means that A ranks x over y. A may rank x over y because he judges x to be superior to y in terms of his own interests or because he may desire x or because he judges that it is good and right that x and not y. "A desires x more than y" is different. A may have a very strong desire for x and yet realize that x is not good for him and so may prefer y over x. "X is in A's interest" suggests that x will make A better off. The self-interest doctrine states that people are motivated primarily by their judgment of what will make them better off. People may sometimes be distracted by wayward desires and impulses, but generally they do what they think is best for them. They prefer alternatives in terms of which will serve their interests.

What is an interest on these accounts? Normally when theorists discuss *self-interest* they use the term in a way that suggests that my interest excludes or somehow conflicts with the interests of others. On such a view, my interests connect with someone else's only strategically or otherwise instrumentally, as in the usual interpretation of the variable sum games of game theory. These accounts point to a member of a list of aims that are thought to be the main aims for which people strive. In particular, power, money, pleasure, land, capital, and other divisible kinds of resources are paradigm cases of this kind of aim. It makes sense to say that it is in a person's interests that the distribution of these things be deeply skewed to their advantage and to the disadvantage of others. This kind of account is invoked by such economists as Downs. In these views, politicians maximize their possession of power, firms maximize profits, and citizens want money.[28]

The Assessment of the Self-Interest View
of Voting and Participation

What are the arguments for the self-interest view? There are three basic groups of arguments: metaphysical, empirical, and methodological. The metaphysical argument aims to establish the claim that something about the nature of human action requires that it be self-interested. The crudest version of the argument infers that if I prefer *x*, logically it must be in my interest that *x*. The first premise is that all intentional action is explained by the agent's desire to engage in the action. Second, whatever I want I value. Third, an object has value only *for* an agent who values it. In other words, all value is relative to the evaluator. Fourth, the fact that I value an object cannot imply that it is valuable for another. Fifth, if its value to me has nothing to do with its value to others, then it must follow that my wants are unconcerned with what is valuable for others. Therefore, the fact that it is valuable to me shows that it is in my interest that I pursue it and I am indifferent to the interests of others.

The argument is an obvious howler and relies on many missteps but most crucially on the failure to distinguish two senses of "valuable for me." One sense is that I value the thing; it is good by my lights or in my view. The other sense is that the thing makes me better off. The first interpretation is what matters in the premises of the argument, whereas the second interpretation slips in at the conclusion. To see this, consider the situation in which I desire to help a stalled motorist by the road. In order to do this it must be the case that I value making the other person better off. But from that fact alone it does not follow that I do it because it makes me better off. It is at least possible that I do it just to make the other better off though I do it because I think that it is valuable; hence, valuable for me. This does not settle the question against the self-interest view; it merely debunks a popular argument intended to establish it.[29]

Turn to the empirical arguments. These are meant to establish the truth of egoism as a factual claim about how people are motivated. One kind of empirical argument is the direct one, which establishes what constitutes self-interested behavior under a set of circumstances and experimentally determines whether and to what extent individuals have acted in a self-interested way. The second kind of argument is indirect in the sense that it tests models of social inter-action that assume self-interested agents for whether they predict outcomes as well as or better than models that do not assume self-interested agents. Economic models of markets and politics often assume self-interest in their agents, and some biological models assume self-interest in the organism.

This kind of evidence has proven to be very mixed. First of all, it is generally agreed that the claim that all individuals always act self-interestedly is false. There is some evidence of altruistic and common-interested motivation among human beings that no one contests. Hence, most agree that there are some altruistically and morally motivated actions. The issues are how widespread and how significant for social interaction are the altruistic and moral motives. There are different dimensions along which these can be assessed. First, there is the dimension of context. *Context* refers to the nature of the relationship within which a person is acting. Most believe that parents are altruistically inclined towards their children to some degree that explains a substantial amount of their behavior. There are other contexts, such as relationships of exchange in a market, friendship, citizenship, camaraderie in war, membership in ethnic groups, and so on. A second dimension is the proportion of behavior that is self-interested or not self-interested measured in terms of the costs and benefits that individuals are willing to trade off when self-interest and other motives conflict, as well as the number of situations in which a person is willing to act in a self-interested way or a non-self-interested way. A third dimension is the extent to which one person's acting in one or another of these ways depends on what others do. A fourth issue is how the various kinds of motives and their associated relative significances for explanation of action are distributed throughout the population.[30]

The partial successes of microeconomic theory suggest that self-interest may play a substantial role in market exchange. However, even here the success has not been overwhelming by any means. Economics continues to be a discipline with questionable empirical credentials. This may not be due to a defect in the self-interest view itself, but it does not give very strong indirect support to the general self-interest view. In addition, the theory does not clearly require self-interest in the first place. The theory requires that individual consumers maximize utility, which is a measure of preference, but it does not put clear restrictions on what the contents of preferences are. It assumes that firms maximize profits. But firms are not persons. They are groups of persons organized in such a way that it is not always clear who benefits from the decisions. The manager of a firm does not immediately gain from the making of profits, and he or she is the principal decisionmaker.[31] Furthermore, many other exchanges in markets do not appear to be completely determined by the self-interest of the participants. Bargaining among workers and employers does not always proceed in a way that is easily explained by self-interest.[32] Furthermore, the extent to which economic actors comply with the rules of the market seems to be greater than what is required by self-interest. Also, private charity is certainly much greater than can be predicted by a simple self-interest axiom. Finally, there is evidence that managers of subsidiary firms within larger firms exhibit a kind of allegiance to the decisions of the larger firms, even when it might be against their long-term interests to do so, as long as the decisionmaking proceeded in accordance with accepted norms of procedural justice.[33]

With regard to citizens and politicians, the evidence is quite mixed. Politicians running for election in large democracies almost always appeal to ideals of fairness, morality, and the common good in their attempts to persuade citizens to vote for them. Citizens would not vote for politicians who appealed to their bare self-interest unless the politician could show that everyone would be better off or that the select group of citizens really deserved to receive some benefits. Both of these kinds of appeal are conditioned on the idea that morality or fairness sanctions the special receipt of benefits. The virtually universal appeal to fairness and morality or at least the common good would be utterly bizarre if neither voters nor politicians were concerned with them. Furthermore, the sheer ubiquity of these appeals must have some formative effect on individuals. And politicians, interest groups, and state institutions fund an immense amount of research (including economics) to tell us what policies are for the common good, which are fair, and so on. Even if all this is mere cynicism on the part of elites, a substantial proportion of the population must be consuming all of this. In general, the prevalence of common good and moral rhetoric in the public forum suggests that many are moved to some degree by these concerns. If this is not true, we should surely have been done in by now by our capacities for gullibility and self-deception.

With regard to citizenship, a fair amount of data shows that citizens vote on the basis of considerations of self-interest sometimes and sometimes on the basis of other considerations, such as the common good and fairness. They also vote on the basis of more purely symbolic issues. There does not seem to be a general truth on the matter. Moreover, citizens tend to have opinions about the justice or morality or efficiency of various policies and states of affairs and tend to be concerned with getting them right.[34] It is hard to see how these can be predicted by the pure self-interest view. Finally, party identification among citizens has tended to be the strongest predictor of how citizens vote, at least until recently. But parties identify themselves in a wide variety of ways. They are identified partly in terms of the various groups they favor, but they also identify themselves very strongly on the basis of views of what is fair and for the common good. Motives for participating in interest group activity and party activity are also complex and varied.[35]

The motivations of politicians also appear to be much more complex than the self-interest view suggests. In studies of regulation and deregulation, there is evidence that politicians will make choices based on their assessment of the common good and not their own self-interest. The recent economic theories of economic rent-seeking and regulatory capture by the regulated industries do not predict many politicians' decisions very well and in some cases predict the very opposite of what happens. Some researchers have argued that the key difficulty in these models is the thesis that politicians act only on the basis of their self-interest. They propose that the only explanation of some politicians' behaviors in certain circumstances is that they were moved by ideas of the common good.[36]

This brief survey of some empirical evidence suggests that the view that individuals are motivated entirely or even predominantly by self-interest in areas beyond family and friendship, such as economic exchange and political activity, cannot be sustained. The motivations of politicians and citizens as well as economic actors are more complex and varied than is permitted by such models. And they are complex in a way that has a substantial impact on the expla-

nation of political and economic activity. It remains for us to consider the methodological arguments for the self-interest axiom.

Methodological Arguments for the Self-Interest Axiom

Some scholars use methodological arguments to defend the use of
the self-interest axiom in the analysis and design of large-scale institutions. They openly defend the axiom by saying that despite the
complexity of motivations there is good reason to think of individuals *as if* they were exclusively self-interested in the construction of
models of social institutions or even in the design of these institutions. I will briefly discuss three main arguments.

Symmetry

The first is an argument for symmetry in economic and political
studies. The argument proceeds on the premises that economic theory has succeeded well on the basis of the self-interest axiom and
that political studies do not study a relevantly different object.
Therefore, political studies ought to be grounded on the self-interest axiom as well.

I have given some reason for calling the first premise of this argument into question in the previous section. The second premise is
also problematic. There do seem to be a number of differences between political and economic activity that may be relevant to the
tenability of the self-interest axiom in political studies. First, political activity seeks to impose policy and legislation on dissenting persons, whereas economic activity, ideally, is concerned with interactions that are entirely voluntary. When one engages in market
exchange with another, that other person has in some way agreed to
the exchange. In many circumstances it makes sense to think that
the other has agreed on the basis of a sense of her own interest that
it is unwise to second guess. In politics, conversely, there is always
disagreement with policy proposals and opposition to the policies
that are ultimately implemented. The person who succeeds in having her preferred policy implemented over the opposition of others
will also at times have policies that she opposes imposed on her.

This difference is important. If we accept the standard principle
of justice that one cannot voluntarily do injustice to oneself, then

the standard example of market exchange without external effects will be unproblematic, whereas the case of political decisionmaking with opposition will be crucially different. The possibility of injury exists in the political case, whereas it does not in the economic. Surely this kind of difference is quite relevant if people are motivated at all by considerations of justice and the common good. The symmetry argument merely begs the question on this issue.

A second difference between political and economic activity is relevant. In economic activity, ideally, the outcomes of one's actions are a direct effect of that action. When I buy a car from a dealer, I get a car with all the benefits and costs that car brings. If I do not buy that car and spend my money on something else, my not having the car is a clear opportunity cost for me of my action. The outcome of my action in the exchange relation is dependent on myself alone. In contrast, the same cannot be said for political activity. The policy choices that one makes are not implemented when one has decided in their favor. Whether my preferred policy is implemented depends on the actions of many other people. This is especially true of a voter in a large-scale election. Whether the candidate one prefers is elected or whether the policy one favors is chosen depends on the activities of millions of other people. But this means that my vote for another candidate has very little opportunity cost for me because the outcome does not depend on me. I do not forgo candidate *A*'s being elected president when I vote for candidate *B*. My vote makes almost no difference to my well-being. Again, if motives other than self-interest play a role in human action, this would be a natural place for them.

A similar argument applies to politicians' behaviors. Self-interested politicians attempt to maximize the kind of support they will receive for an upcoming election. Thus, they often do not vote for a policy on the basis of how the policy will affect their interests but on the basis of what support interest groups and their constituencies will provide for reelection given the policies they have voted for. From the previous reasoning, however, the constituency may be voting on the basis of conceptions of justice and the common good. Furthermore, there is often a wide variety of competing interest groups influencing the legislature. A politician will oppose the proposals of some and promote the proposals of others. If there is a

rough balance of groups on different sides of an issue then the opportunity costs to my reelection effort of my voting either way will
be small. This kind of situation may lead politicians to act differently than if there were clear opportunity costs of their actions.
Symmetry ought not to be merely assumed in these contexts.

Hence, the assumption of symmetry is not justified since there
are important relevant differences between political activity and
economic activity. Moreover, there is substantial evidence that there
are differences between individual motivations in the political
sphere and the economic sphere. Individuals tend to think that considerations of fairness are important in assessing their attitudes towards government and the actions of government officials. Conversely, individuals accept self-interested behavior in economic
activity.[37] These differing attitudes are plausibly explained by the
observations described in this section.

Gresham's Law

Another argument for thinking of individuals as self-interested is
appropriately named "a sort of Gresham's Law in social interactions
such that bad behavior drives out the good and that all persons will
be led themselves by the presence of even a few self seekers to adopt
self-interested behavior."[38] Morally motivated individuals face an
assurance problem when the outcomes of their actions depend on
what others do. Even morally motivated persons will cease to act
morally when they see that others get away with selfish and amoral
behavior and where that behavior subverts the ends and interests of
the morally motivated. Moral motivation depends, on this view, on
a kind of reciprocity, and when that reciprocity is disrupted the
moral individual acts in a self-interested way. The moral person
does not want their moral disposition to be exploited.

This argument is often supplemented by two further premises:
that one often does not know who is and who is not self-interested
and that those who seek the powers of political office are precisely
the ones who are most likely to be thoroughly selfish in their action.
And finally there are always, within large-scale institutions, individuals who are willing to take advantage of the ethical behavior of
others to advance their own aims. From these premises many con-

clude that in any large-scale institution, individuals will generally act in a self-interested way.

A couple of points about this argument undermine its general plausibility. First, it rests on a set of assumptions that may not be generally true. Second, the strong form of the argument seems to rest on a false premise. So the conclusion is too strong.

The argument depends on three variables. One, the number of self-interested persons as a proportion of the whole will make a difference. If there are very few self-interested persons, then it is not clear why we should assume that moral persons will resort to entirely self-interested action that exploits other moral persons for a small modicum of protection from exploitation for themselves. It only works if there is a very large proportion of self-interested persons who cannot be detected. The second problematic claim is the undetectability assumption. This assumption is fairly plausible in a large society in which individuals cannot easily determine what a person has done and it is not easy to provide clear interpretations of what a person has done. In large societies individuals can often dress their actions as public-interested simply because the consequences of the actions are obscure and diffuse. Even so, if there are many organizations, such as secondary associations, political parties, and oversight committees, this problem of detection can be reduced. In certain circumstances it will be greatly reduced, whereas in others it will be a larger problem. The third claim is an empirical claim that is questionable. The idea that those who strive for power are likely to pursue their own interests is one that cannot be taken for granted given the mixed evidence we saw in the previous section.

The second general difficulty with the argument is the assumed relationship between moral behavior and reciprocity. The idea that an otherwise moral person would shed their disposition for a more self-interested one merely because a few persons have taken advantage of them is puzzling. If a person is morally disposed and he believes he has been taken advantage of by someone else, it would seem odd for him to turn around and take advantage of all the others who are morally disposed. *Ex hypothesi*, the person will not be willing to do this. If, and this gets back to the first criticism, he has the suspicion that most people will take advantage of his moral disposition, then it might make sense for him to engage in self-protective behavior. Hence, Gresham's Law will not generally or even often hold, even though it is plausible in relatively extreme situations of social breakdown.

The Normative Argument

A third kind of methodological argument for the self-interest axiom is explicitly normative. It states that the harms due to self-interested activity in the midst of social institutions that assume moral or altruistic behavior are greater than the benefits that result from moral behavior in those institutions. From this some conclude that institutions that work best when almost everyone is morally motivated or altruistic are less efficient than institutions wherein each person is "supposed to be a knave and to have no other end, in all his actions, than private interest."[39]

The conclusion, however, does not follow from the premise. The institutions necessary to assure a predominantly moral group of individuals that self-interested persons cannot generally get away with purely self-interested behavior are not going to be the same as institutions that deal with exclusively self-interested persons. The investment in systems of sanctioning is likely to be much smaller in the former. Hence, the claim that in order to ensure themselves against some purely self-interested behavior individuals are rational to set up institutions that are entirely geared towards self-interested individuals is too strong. The educative effects of the institutions ought to be taken into account. If institutions are entirely structured so as to handle exclusively self-interested persons, this may have the effect of inclining people to shed whatever moral or altruistic motives they have. The threat of opportunism would become even greater, and the institutions would have to become more and more detailed and precise in their specification of what is and what is not permitted. The consequence of this would be a drive towards greater reliance on knowledgeable rulemaking by central authorities and less reliance on the willingness of citizens to comply with the spirit of the law. The costs of institution building and maintenance would increase, and generally the institutions would be less likely to succeed. Furthermore, there would be an increasing need for intrusive monitoring and sanctioning.

From these observations, it is clear that the comparative assessment of institutions that are designed for different kinds of motivation cannot be made simply by comparing the local effects of self-interested and moral behavior within a single kind of institution. Hence, I conclude that the last methodological argument fails to establish the superiority of the self-interest axiom in the modeling and construction of social institutions. This completes my review of the methodological arguments for the view that human behavior ought to be thought of as virtually exclusively self-interested.

The Expressivist View of Voting

One strategy by which some theorists have attempted to reconcile the self-interest axiom with the evidence that citizens often vote on bases other than self-interest is to claim that citizens merely express attitudes when they vote. Expressivism is the doctrine that the act of voting is not intended to influence public policy or even to select a candidate. The sole purpose of voting is to express an evaluation. What is the basis of this view? Many argue for this position using some version of the Downsian reasoning. The idea is that a number of factors make self-interested voting virtually meaningless. The expected policy value of a vote for a self-interested reasoner is very low. And the opportunity costs of voting one way or another are nil. So the self-interested agent need not be particularly concerned with the benefits and opportunity costs to herself in this context; indeed, she tends not to evaluate the situation on the same basis that she evaluates actions that have clear consequences for her interests. Since the evaluation has no consequence for her interests, she can express a more impartial evaluation.[40] Hume states the point clearly:

> We may easily remove any contradiction which may appear to be betwixt the extensive sympathy, on which our sentiments of virtue depend, and that limited generosity which I have frequently observed to be natural to men, and which justice and property suppose. . . . My sympathy with another may give me the sentiment of pain and disapprobation, when any object is presented that has a tendency to give him uneasiness; Tho' I may not be willing to sacrifice anything of my own interest, or cross any of my passions, for his satisfaction.[41]

The attitude motivates little or nothing beyond the mere expression; for the self-interested person, it can come into play when little or nothing is at stake for her, such as in voting.

To be sure, the attitude expressed need not be a moral one. Some have feared that dangerous and irrational attitudes might be expressed in this context alongside the more benevolent.[42] In fact utterly frivolous attitudes can be expressed in this context. The fact that voting is merely a form of expression does not imply that a voter must be unsophisticated about the attitudes that are expressed. A person on this account might have very developed views about politics as a by-product of her work or social circumstances or even some intrinsic interest in the subject. She still merely expresses her attitudes towards the alternatives when she votes. Note, however, that people generally express moral attitudes in voting does not defeat the underlying Downsian argument concerning the rationality of ignorance. The attitudes expressed may merely be based on ignorance.

Nevertheless, if this view is true, it might be thought to explain some of the facts that I cited against the self-interest view of citizens in the previous sections. For instance, politicians might be inclined to appeal to moral considerations because they know that citizens are inclined merely to express their moral sentiments in this context. Citizens may vote on the basis of moral attitudes merely because they are expressing those attitudes and without any concern for actually implementing the moral principles. Since the citizen does not really do anything but express an attitude, he will not undertake to make that attitude any more sophisticated by collecting or reflecting on information. The four sources of inequality described in Chapter 3 will still hold as well as the problem of asymmetry in discussion.

Is this a plausible account of the grounds of voting? Empirically there seems to be some clear evidence against the view. Citizens in large-scale elections often vote strategically. They vote for candidates only after they have determined that enough others will vote for them.[43] This behavior makes little sense in the expressivist view. One votes strategically in order to achieve some end that cannot be achieved by voting straightforwardly (i.e., directly reflecting one's preference). If one were to vote merely to express one's attitude about a candidate or alternative, why would one vote only for the one that stood a chance of winning?

Another problem is that the expressivist view does not explain why individuals would choose to express their attitudes in a polling booth. This cannot be explained by reference to the effects of the vote since by hypothesis the expressive voter is not interested in this. So although the expressive view may explain how a person votes, it fails to explain how the person actually arrives in the polling booth. The polling booth seems to be an odd and anonymous place to be trying to express one's attitude about some policy. In fact it appears that citizens are trying to perform some role when they vote. A final difficulty with this view is that it does not explain the many other kinds of participation individual citizens engage in. Though these activities may have expressive value, they also take time, energy, and money. I conclude from these observations that the facts that campaigning and voting often have strongly moral features cannot be reconciled with the self-interest view of citizenship by invoking the expressive view of voting.

Conclusion

The self-interest axiom and the conceptions of citizenship that are founded on it are problematic and cannot serve as a basis for normative political theory. These conceptions of citizenship seem to leave little room for the ideals of democratic citizenship, equality, or rational deliberation, or even for the more austere political ideals economic theorists defend. Thus, the conceptions of citizenship grounded in self-interest alone are self-defeating. Furthermore, the idea that individuals act primarily in their self-interest is not a well-defended view. Much empirical evidence suggests that it is false. In the next chapter, we shall consider a different approach to normative political theory and its relationship to citizenship.

Notes

1. See James Buchanan and Gordon Tullock, *The Calculus of Consent: Logical Foundations of Constitutional Democracy* (Ann Arbor: University of Michigan Press, 1965); James Buchanan and Geoffrey Brennan, *The Rea-*

son of Rules (Cambridge: Cambridge University Press, 1986); as well as Gregory Kavka, *Hobbesian Moral and Political Theory* (Princeton: Princeton University Press, 1987), chapter 5, for contractarian defenses of democratic principles.

2. Joseph Schumpeter, *Capitalism, Socialism, and Democracy*, 3rd edition (New York: Harper and Row, 1975 [1950]), p. 269.

3. Schumpeter, *Capitalism, Socialism, and Democracy*, p. 269.

4. See William Riker, *Liberalism Against Populism: A Confrontation Between the Theory of Social Choice and Democracy* (San Francisco: W. H. Freeman and Co., 1982), for a general argument against the common good based on social choice theory.

5. Schumpeter, *Capitalism, Socialism, and Democracy*, p. 250. I discussed this view in the first chapter in some detail.

6. Schumpeter, *Capitalism, Socialism, and Democracy*, p. 252.

7. Anthony Downs emphasizes this relationship between the market and the political sphere in his discussion of democracy. Though he tries to accommodate the facts of rational ignorance into his model, his discussion suffers from very much the same flaws.

8. For some interesting empirical evidence against what I am saying here see Richard McKelvey and Peter Ordeshook, "Information and Elections: Retrospective Voting and Rational Expectations," *Information and Democratic Processes*, ed. John Ferejohn and James Kuklinski (Chicago: University of Illinois Press, 1990), pp. 281–312. They show that what are called "pocketbook voters," i.e., voters who vote only in response to the effects on their pocketbooks of the previous leadership, are likely to converge on a reasonably accurate view of who will hurt them and who will not after many electoral periods. In my view the environment they describe is vastly simpler than the political environment that citizens operate in and thus the results do not plausibly generalize to actual democratic conditions. Another difficulty is that voters usually take more information into account than the effects on their pocketbooks, see Samuel Popkin, *The Reasoning Voter* (Chicago: University of Chicago Press, 1990), p. 31.

9. Even so, consumers are themselves often not in a particularly good position to know about the objects they consume because of the technical expertise often required to assess the effects of some object of consumption. See Cass Sunstein, *After the Rights Revolution: Reconceiving the Regulatory State* (Cambridge, Mass.: Harvard University Press, 1990).

10. This argument is reminiscent of one of Thomas Hobbes's arguments for monarchy over democracy and aristocracy. See his *Leviathan*, ed. C. B. MacPherson (Harmondsworth, Eng.: Penguin Books, 1975). That there might be some such resemblance should not be surprising since many of the

contemporary arguments against democracy, or at least against a more extensive democracy, are really elaborations of Hobbes's arguments against democracy and in favor of monarchy.

11. See E. E. Schattschneider, *The Semi-Sovereign People: A Realist's View of Democracy in America* (New York: Harper and Row, 1960), and Walter Dean Burnham, "The System of 1896: An Analysis," in *The Evolution of American Electoral Systems,* ed. Paul Kleppner et al. (Westport, Conn.: Greenwood Press, 1981), pp. 147–202.

12. See William Grieder, *Who Will Tell the People? The Betrayal of American Democracy* (New York: Simon and Schuster, 1992). These examples must be used with some care since I am not advocating the view that in general individuals are motivated exclusively by self-interest. These examples seem to be plausible cases of what can happen when individuals who are elites are so motivated.

13. Contemporary theorists argue convincingly that parties play an important role in influencing public opinion. See Patrick Dunleavy, *Democracy, Bureaucracy, and Public Choice* (London: Harvester/Wheatsheaf, 1990). There is evidence that public opinion can be deeply influenced and manipulated by political elites in Benjamin Page, *The Rational Public* (Chicago: University of Chicago Press, 1992), chap. 9. Furthermore, although theorists of the media and public opinion argued many years ago that political messages over the media had little impact on the opinion of ordinary citizens, there is a growing consensus that political leaders, through the media, have a substantial impact on what ordinary citizens think. See John Zaller, *The Nature and Origin of Mass Opinion* (Cambridge: Cambridge University Press, 1992), for the influence of elite discourse on public opinion. See Robert Entman, *Democracy Without Citizens: Media and the Decay of American Politics* (Oxford: Oxford University Press, 1989), for a summary of views of the media and a compelling defense of the view of significant impact.

14. Schumpeter, *Capitalism, Socialism, and Democracy,* p. 270. Here too Downs's view confronts the same kind of problem. He argues that individual citizens will vote in a democracy even though they have no self-interested incentive to do so because they will desire to uphold the democratic system. If no one votes, the system will collapse (Downs, *An Economic Theory of Democracy,* [New York: Harper and Row, 1957], p. 267). But Downs's analysis of what can be expected of citizens does not permit citizens to be motivated by such concerns. His theory seems to suffer from the same kind of incoherence.

15. Robert Dahl, *A Preface to Democratic Theory* (Chicago: University of Chicago Press, 1956), p. 69.

16. Dahl, *A Preface to Democratic Theory,* p. 133.

17. See John Hart Ely, *Democracy and Distrust: A Theory of Judicial Review* (Cambridge, Mass.: Harvard University Press, 1980), for an attempt to defend an egalitarian pluralism. See also Robert Dahl, *Dilemmas of Pluralist Democracy* (New Haven: Yale University Press, 1982), and *Democracy and Its Critics* (New Haven: Yale University Press, 1989), for discussions of the problem of political equality. It should be noted that Dahl steps away from the self-interest axiom in his later works.

18. See Theodore Lowi, *The End of Liberalism* (New York: Norton, 1969), for extensive documentation of this effect.

19. See James Buchanan and Gordon Tullock, *The Calculus of Consent,* for a discussion of this problem. See also Grant McConnell's classic study of this problem in the United States in his *Private Power and American Democracy* (New York: Vintage Books, 1966).

20. See Joshua Cohen and Joel Rogers, "Secondary Associations and Democratic Governance," *Politics and Society* December (1992): pp. 393–472, p. 414 for this criticism.

21. See Downs, *An Economic Theory of Democracy,* p. 254, as well as Mancur Olson, *The Logic of Collective Action* (Cambridge, Mass.: Harvard University Press, 1960). See James Buchanan and Geoffrey Brennan, *The Reason of Rules.*

22. See William Riker, *Liberalism Against Populism.*

23. See Robert Goldstein, *Political Repression in Modern America, 1870 to the Present* (Cambridge, Mass.: Schenkman Publishing Co., 1978), p. 11.

24. Richard Hofstadter, *The Age of Reform: From Bryan to F.D.R.* (New York: Vintage Books, 1955), chapters 6 and 7.

25. Grant McConnell, *Private Power and American Democracy* (New York: Alfred Knopf, 1966), p. 293.

26. See Thomas Ferguson and Joel Rogers, *Right Turn: The Decline of the Democrats and the Future of American Politics* (New York: Hill and Wang, 1986), for evidence of this.

27. See Thomas Christiano, "The Incoherence of Hobbesian Justifications of the State," *American Philosophical Quarterly* January (1994): pp. 23–38, for a discussion of normative public choice theory. See also John Rawls, "The Idea of an Overlapping Consensus," *Oxford Journal of Legal Studies* Spring (1989), for this point.

28. This account comes from Gregory Kavka, *Hobbesian Moral and Political Theory* (Princeton: Princeton University Press, 1986), p. 42. Downs is a little unclear here; he says at one point that voters will select a political party on the grounds of "ideology," which he defines as a "verbal image of the good society"(*An Economic Theory of Democracy,* pp. 98–99). Although it is unclear what role the vision of the good society is playing in the voter's utility function for Downs, he speaks as if this were an ultimate con-

sideration and that the good society is not itself merely an instrument for increasing the stream of benefits from the government. He does not, for most of the theory, say much about what the purpose is of the selection of governments. However, Downs insists on preserving the assumption that "every individual, though rational, is also selfish" (*An Economic Theory of Democracy,* p. 27).

29. Something like this argument can be found in James Buchanan and Geoffrey Brennan, *The Reason of Rules,* pp. 33–45. It is refuted under the name of "Tautological Egoism" in Gregory Kavka's *Hobbesian Moral and Political Theory,* p. 35.

30. See Kavka, *Hobbesian Moral and Political Theory,* pp. 64–65, for a discussion of some of these dimensions.

31. See John Plamenatz, *Democracy and Illusion* (London: Longman Press, 1973), p. 157.

32. See Jon Elster, *The Cement of Society: A Study of Social Order* (Cambridge: Cambridge University Press, 1989), pp. 230–244.

33. W. Chan Kim and Rene Mauborgne, "Implementing Global Strategies: The Role of Procedural Justice," *Strategic Management Journal* 12 (1991): pp. 125–143.

34. See William Gamson, *Talking Politics* (Cambridge: Cambridge University Press, 1992), for evidence of the extent to which citizens engage in and are interested in the moral dimensions of politics.

35. See David O. Sears and Carolyn L. Funk, "Self-Interest in Americans' Political Opinions," and Tom Tyler, "Justice, Self-Interest, and the Legitimacy of Legal and Political Authority," in *Beyond Self-Interest,* ed. Jane J. Mansbridge (Chicago: University of Chicago Press, 1990), pp. 147–170 and pp. 171–179, respectively, for data on self- and other-interested motives in voting. See also Terry Moe, *The Organization of Interests* (Chicago: University of Chicago Press, 1980), for an empirical discussion of the different motives for joining interest groups. See also Paul Sabatier, "Interest Group Membership and Organization: Multiple Theories," in *The Politics of Interests: Interest Groups Transformed,* ed. Mark Petracca (Boulder: Westview Press, 1992): pp. 99–129.

36. For some empirical evidence to this effect, see Paul J. Quirk, "Deregulation and the Politics of Ideas in Congress," in *Beyond Self-Interest,* pp. 183–199. See George Stigler, *The Citizen and the States* (Chicago: University of Chicago Press, 1980), for a model of regulationthat suggests that regulatory agencies must come under the control of the regulated industries; see also Peter Aranson, "The Democratic Order and Public Choice," in *Politics and Process: New Essays in Democratic Thought,* ed. Geoffrey Brennan and Loren Lomasky (Cambridge: Cambridge University Press, 1989), pp. 97–148, especially pp. 110–123.

37. See Mark Isaacs, Debra Mathieu, and Edward Zajac, "Institutional Framing and Perceptions of Fairness," *Constitutional Political Economy* 2, no. 3 (1991): pp. 329–370, especially p. 349, for an elaboration of experimental evidence for these claims.

38. See Brennan and Buchanan, *The Reason of Rules*, p. 60. The methodological arguments I discuss here are summarized in chapter 4 of this book.

39. David Hume, "Of the Independence of Parliament," in *Political Essays,* ed. Charles Hendel (Indianapolis, Ind.: Bobbs-Merrill, 1953), p. 68.

40. Geoffrey Brennan has defended this approach in a number of papers, "Politics with Romance," in *The Good Polity: The Normative Analysis of the State,* ed. Alan Hamlin and Philip Pettit (New York: Basil Blackwell, 1989), pp. 49–66, and (with Loren Lomasky) "Large Numbers, Small Costs: The Uneasy Foundation of Democratic Rule," in *Politics and Process,* pp. 42–59. The idea seems to have first come into the public choice literature in Gordon Tullock's "The Charity of the Uncharitable," *Western Economic Journal* 9 (1971): pp. 379–392. For another account of the expressivist view of voting, see Stanley I. Benn, "The Problematic Rationality of Political Participation," in *Philosophy, Politics, and Society,* 5th ser., ed. James Fishkin and Peter Laslett (New Haven: Yale University Press, 1979): pp. 291–312. His does not proceed from the self-interest view but merely from the political impotence of a particular voter.

41. David Hume, *Treatise of Human Nature,* 2nd edition, ed. L. A. Selby Bigge and P. H. Nidditch (Oxford: Oxford University Press, 1978), p. 586.

42. Joseph Schumpeter in his *Capitalism, Socialism, and Democracy* is the source of this worry; it is also discussed in Brennan and Lomasky, "Large Numbers, Small Costs."

43. See Popkin, *The Reasoning Voter,* for some evidence of strategic voting in American presidential primaries.

CHAPTER FIVE

A Normative Conception of Citizenship

In the last chapter we explored the vicissitudes of the economic conception of citizenship. This view is based on the idea that we cannot expect that citizens will be moved by anything other than self-interest. After reviewing a standard list of these views, our conclusion was that such theories are generally self-defeating and that this conception of what can be expected of citizens is false.

In this chapter we start from a different angle. Instead of defining what can be expected from citizens first and then determining what notion of the role of citizens is compatible with this, I define an appropriate role for citizens that accords with the principles of democratic equality defended in Chapter 2 and then determine whether this role demands too much or too little from citizens. This approach is justified by two key results of the previous chapter. First, citizens are moved by moral principles to some extent, and, second, if citizens are not moved by moral principles there is little reason for engaging in the process of defining the role of citizenship anyway because such theories will tend to be self-defeating. Since citizens are moved by moral principle it is reasonable to attempt to define and defend a set of moral principles before we say what we can expect from citizens. A conception of the role of citizens that accords with the principle of democratic equality outlines the rights and du-

ties of democratic citizenship in a just society. If the view is right
then it ought to be one that can motivate citizens. This is an important implication of claiming that citizens are motivated by moral
principle.

At the same time it is important to determine that the role does
not demand too much of citizens. A role can require too much if it
has one or more of the following implications: It involves citizens
doing things that are not essential from the point of view of the
principles of democratic equality; it requires them to do things that
would seriously impair their abilities to perform other roles in the
society; or it requires them to do things that we cannot reasonably
expect people to do on a regular basis; in other words, it goes beyond what Rawls calls the "strains of commitment."[1] The appropriate conception of citizenship is one that properly takes into account
all of these considerations.

The Role of Citizenship

The normative theory of the role of citizenship includes three components. First, it tells us what *contribution* citizens have a right to
make to the political decision-making process. Second, it tells us
what *distinctive activities* are important to the exercise of this right.
Third, it tells us what *standards* on those distinctive activities citizens ought to be able to satisfy. These three elements define both the
rights and duties of citizenship. They set standards for institutions
by implying what citizens ought to be able to do and what institutions ought to do to promote these abilities. They also say what citizens ought to do if they are to participate as citizens. First, we will
explore the contribution element, which is the core of the conception of the role of citizenship.

The contribution element tells us what citizens have a right to decide on and what the other parts of the political decision-making
process are bound by. A modern democratic society includes a vast
array of tasks that must be performed by people. In our own society, the process of collective decisionmaking includes a variety of
people with different roles. Legislators make laws and policies. Administrators decide how to carry out those laws in particular circumstances. Political parties organize around ideas about what laws

ought to be made by the legislators and attempt to inform legislators and citizens about what are the best laws and policies. Interest groups also organize around ideas and interests and attempt to inform as well as pressure legislators and administrators to adopt certain policies and laws and to carry them out in certain ways. The question we must address here is: What is the role of the ordinary citizen in all this? What is the role of the ordinary voter? Most of these tasks seem to require considerable expertise beyond the abilities of ordinary citizens. Citizens seem to be left out of the process. In democratic societies, citizens vote for legislators, but is this all they ought to do? What else are they supposed to do?[2]

In order to get a better handle on the issue of the role of the citizen, I shall describe collective decisionmaking in terms of a set of basic elements that must be decided upon: the aims of policy, the means for achieving these aims, and the compromises that must be made when there are disagreements on the first two. Recall that the basic purpose of the system of collective decision is the making of law and policy. Laws and policies have separable components. A law is in some ways much like an intention to act. Intentions to act include aims that the intended action is meant to promote as well as a plan by which the aims are realized. When I intend to go to the store to get some ice cream, I have a plan (going to the store) for achieving a certain aim (buying and eating ice cream). When I decide what to do, I settle on an intention to act. I decide first by determining what aims I want to achieve, and then I decide how best to achieve them. Once I have decided on the aims and method for achieving them, I have an intention to act. The laws and policies regulating the society, too, are like intentions, which have certain basic aims, and consist in the means for achieving those aims.

To illustrate these different elements of the decision-making process, suppose that health care reform is under consideration in the United States and there are differences among citizens about what reforms would be best. Two important elements of the issue are the basic aims of health care reform and the means for achieving these aims. A third component includes the compromises that are necessary to reconcile differences among citizens about aims as well as means. Many may have the aim of producing universal quality health care for every citizen at the same time as reducing the cost of health care overall. Some may merely have the aim of reducing the costs of the system. Others may not be as concerned with reduction of costs or the universality of coverage as with the maintenance of choice among physicians and the autonomy of the profession of medicine. These are some competing aims that citizens may have in deciding on health care reform.

There are different means by which these aims can be realized. A system of nationalized health care paid for by the government from tax revenues is one possible means for achieving the ideal of universal coverage and cost reduction. Others may think that a heavily regulated market in medical services would be the most efficient way of achieving the same ends. Similar differences among those who have the other aims can also be found. These choices of ends and means will determine the policy they favor overall. These two components of law and policy are separable, much as they are in the case of individual action.

To be sure, there is an important difference between intention and law. Citizens disagree about the laws and aims that they wish to see brought about. In order for a law to be passed the opposing parties to the disagreement must often reconcile the differences among their preferred plans. Suppose that there is no clear majority for any policy. A compromise must be drawn up between the various opposing parties. Given the complexity of policies, the best compromise will be a matter of controversy even among those who agree on other matters. Some who desire to see the first aim achieved will want compromise with the second group, which prefers merely reduction in cost. But others may think that a compromise with those who desire physician and patient autonomy would more effectively bring about the aim of universal coverage. From the point of view of each citizen, a good compromise is a kind of means for bringing about the aims that he or she wishes to bring about. Without compromise, nothing is achievable; with compromise some aspects of one's aims can be realized. One must find the compromise that most satisfactorily realizes one's aims given the disagreements there are in the society.

The outcome of the decisionmaking will be the result of all of these elements as well as the procedural rules. A political division of labor will assign roles to people associated with these elements of collective decisionmaking. In contemporary democratic societies, some specialize in the role of devising the means for achieving various aims; for example, policy experts in political parties as well as interest groups are knowledgeable in how to bring about certain desirable aims. Legislators are not as knowledgeable in these matters but are experts in the making of compromises by which different aims can be brought together and satisfied. What contribution ought ordinary citizens be able to make in collective decisionmaking? Ought they be able to decide on the aims of the society and the means for achieving them as well as the compromises that must be struck between opposing aims? Where do citizens fit into this complex system of decisionmaking?

In what follows, I will start by sketching what I call the choice of overall aims of society model. Comparisons with the two main alternatives will show that it is the best among conceptions of citizenship. We will then determine what activities citizens ought to be able to carry out to fulfill their roles as well as the standards they ought to live up to in these activities. With the view fully laid out we will see how this conception can help meet the challenge to democratic ideals posed by the conditions of the modern state. We will close this chapter with some difficulties facing this conception of citizenship and a plan for how the theory of democratic institutions of Part Three will answer these problems.

The Choice of Overall Aims Model

Given the framework for analyzing collective decisionmaking outlined above, the role of the citizen is to choose the basic overall aims of the society. There are two components to the choice of overall aims model of citizenship. First, citizenship in a just democratic order entails a standpoint on the whole of the society. Citizens decide the aims of the society overall. Their role is not to organize local areas of policy wherein they are most affected but to put together all the interests and activities in the society in a coherent framework that balances the activities and interests of all. Citizens decide on the collective properties of the whole society. Using our example above, citizens are to choose whether the society is to have universal health care coverage or whether the distribution of coverage is to be left up to a market in health care services. The old and the young, men and women are to contribute to making decisions on the same subject and not on separate decisions relating to their specific interests as the pluralists would have it. Such decisions would be informed by conceptions of their interests as well as the interests of others and a concern for the common good and justice.

Second, the choice of aims model of citizenship is the view that the citizens choose the ultimate ends that the society is to pursue. For example, citizens choose what is fair and what is unfair, they choose how much risk they wish to submit to in foreign relations, and they may choose what the aims of education are as well as the basic features of a system of health care. However, citizens do not choose the means by which to bring about these ends. Though they are to choose what is fair and what is unfair, they are not the choosers of the policies that bring about fairness in economic relations. Though they may choose that there be a certain level of control of environmental damage, they do not choose the means for achieving this control. To turn a common simile on its head, citizens are in the position of passengers on a ship, whereas the government is in the position of the captain. The citizens choose the destination; the captain accepts to take them there and chooses the route and how to navigate it. Once the passengers choose the destination, the captain has the authority to enforce the rules necessary to get there safely.[3]

Two clarifications are in order. First, means and aims need not always be associated with the processes and outcomes of policy respectively. What I mean by the basic aims of society are the aspects of the society that are chosen for their own sakes. Therefore, often citizens will choose the outcomes they want, such as crime control, and officials and experts choose the means for achieving such outcomes. But citizens may also wish to ensure that certain rights of individuals are protected when the government carries out policy. They may have the aim that the government respect the privacy of citizens. Or they may wish to impose restrictions on the government's ability to investigate citizens. To the extent that citizens think that such restrictions on government activity are desirable in themselves, these are among the basic aims of those citizens. So citizens will have things to say about how policy is carried out in some instances. They will choose certain constraints on policymaking.

Second, some means may be opposed to other ends of the citizens. For example, lowering taxes may be incompatible with increasing the quality of the highways and mass transportation in a society. Lowering taxes may be a way to achieve another aim of the citizens, such as temporarily stimulating the economy. Here the means to achieving one aim are in conflict with the achievement of another. The task of choosing ends includes ordering those ends so as to produce a reasonably coherent overall set of aims. Such an ordering would include priorities among the various things that the citizenry desires. In this example, the citizens must specify their preferences between infrastructure repair and economic stimulation. The conflict between some means and some aims is eliminated by requiring that citizens give an overall ordering of aims that specifies priorities and trade-offs among the things citizens want.

The legislative, the administrative, and the informal parts of the political system, such as political parties and interest groups, decide on the necessary means for achieving the citizens' ends. They are completely subservient to the wishes of the electorate with regard to their aims. But they have discretion to choose how to realize the citizens' aims. In this model, the government acts as the citizens' trustee inasmuch as the government chooses means in accordance with its own expert judgments. The citizens do not contribute here; they leave these choices to the government for the most part. Conversely, the government is to act as delegate inasmuch as it is charged with advancing the aims that the citizenry decides upon; the government has no discretion on this matter.

Furthermore, the choices of strategies and means are on a par. Citizens disagree on the aims the society is to pursue, so when they choose aims, there will be a need to reconcile those aims with each other, to compromise and negotiate. These tasks of compromise and negotiation are best carried out not by citizens but by government officials since these tasks are as complex as the determination of means. As long as citizens are reasonably explicit about their priorities and trade-offs among the things they want, the task of compromising and negotiating between opposed conceptions of what citizens want can be carried out by others without any important loss to the citizens.

The argument for this conception of citizenship comes in two stages. First, each of the two components of the conception will be defended by a comparison with a view that denies the component. Second, the conception will be shown to meet the challenges spelled out in Chapter 3.

The Comparison with Normative Pluralism

In defense of the claim that citizens ought to make choices about the society as a whole, we will compare the choice of aims model with the normative pluralist conception of citizenship. Unlike interest group pluralism, normative pluralism is not founded on the premise of self-interest or any merely descriptive claim about people. The basic normative pluralist position is that citizens ought to have decision-making power in those areas where they are directly materially affected.[4] A factory worker ought to have a say in government policy regarding factories; a railway worker ought to have a say in government policy over the railways or at least over working conditions in the industry. Policy is to be made by those most affected, and those who are not affected do not have a say. No one ought to have much of a say in policy regulating what others do. The reasoning behind this kind of view is that individuals have a right to a voice in those areas that affect them and that they are more likely to have reasonable opinions about those areas, whereas those who are not as directly affected neither have the right nor the competence to do so. Policy ought to be the consequence of many different groups making decisions more or less on their own about subjects that concern them most. The different sectors of society have independent authority that they must then coordinate with each other. Since these citizens are not purely self-interested, their activities of local policymaking and of coordination are carried out with an eye to the common good. Nevertheless, citizens or perhaps their chosen representatives have a kind of independent authority to make decisions on policy, and then they coordinate with others.[5]

A number of difficulties undermine this view's account of the appropriate role of citizens in democracy. First, the view is subject to a version of the cost-spreading objection against interest group pluralism. Since each sector has independent authority to make decisions on its own while taxing the whole body of citizens, each group will generally tend to push for greater benefits for themselves while imposing the costs on others. Even if individuals are not merely self-interested, their views on the proper use of tax monies will tend to be interest driven to some extent. They know more about their interests and expertise and know less about others, thus they will often underestimate the importance of the interests of others and overestimate the significance of their own tasks and interests. This kind of bias has been observed when policy-making authority over certain sectors of the society is partly delegated to the interested parties, even when those parties are morally motivated. In his study of boards made up of businessmen for coordinating production of military hardware for the U.S. army in World War II, Grant Mc-Connell found that the businessmen tended to make choices that favored their own firms or interests despite their real concern for promoting the war effort.[6] In these cases, the whole group will consistently make inefficient decisions since each decision benefits a few whereas the cost is borne by many.

A second objection is that political equality may eventually suffer when each citizen is exclusively devoted to a narrow area of policy-making and no one is watching the system overall. Since the society is carved into groups with independent authority, one must ask, What are the relevant independent sectors and groups into which the authority of the state is to be divided? Some groups may outlast their usefulness after a period of time but still hold power. Some groups may become very important in the society and continue to hold no power. How are they to be admitted into the system of decisionmaking and coordination with others? Is there a body to decide on this allocation of authority? If not, then it is hard to see how any reasonable semblance of equality could be maintained in the society in the long run. If there is such an overseeing body, it would have to have a view on the society as a whole, and it would have a say that far outstripped in importance that of the ordinary citizens. And if the citizens were to have this role we would be abandoning the pluralist view in favor of a more holistic view of the contribution of citizens. Citizens would make the basic decisions about the allocation of power and authority in the society overall. They would have to make choices on these allocations on the basis of an assessment of the relative significance of the groups and their contributions to society. So pluralism either gives up political equality or it approaches the choice of aims model.

A third problem is that individuals' membership in one group or another is a matter of controversy in some cases. Many individuals are in more than one group. An Hispanic female construction worker will plausibly be a member of three groups at least. Would they all have independent authority? And who would decide on who is a member of what group? These questions address the very heart of citizenship on the pluralist account. And answers to these questions have great significance for the distribution of political power in the society. The pluralist has no answer or mechanism for making these choices. One fears that the ideals of political equality are just as much at risk in this scheme as in the interest group pluralist view.

Finally, the pluralist underestimates the number of features of the society that are connected to everyone's interests. Pollution control, public schools, defense, distributive justice, and certain cultural features of the society as well as many others are such that the interests of individuals are strongly interdependent and cannot be disentangled. If decisions on these matters are taken by the citizens at large then they have decision-making power over the whole. In general, the activities of individuals in modern society are not as separate from each other as the pluralist suggests. The previous observations on cost spreading and the allocation of authority already imply that interests are interdependent in ways that undermine the idea that there are areas in which only a few are seriously affected. Thus, pluralism threatens the basic requirement that the interests of citizens in the collective properties of society be advanced as well as the requirement of political equality.

To be sure, pluralist institutions have a place in a democratic society, but it must be a subordinate one. Citizens in their capacities as authorities over the whole society may choose to delegate authority to specific groups in specific areas. For instance, groups may be given some independent legal authority if such authority would contribute to the society's pursuit of overall aims.[7] In addition, independent decision-making authority in groups may also be useful on some occasions in promoting democratic character traits in the individuals involved.[8] Finally, even in those areas where citizens have the right to collectively decide, it will sometimes be unwise for them to use that authority to regulate those areas.[9] So although pluralist institutions ought not to define democratic citizenship, they may supplement it. Democratic citizenship ought to involve decision-making power over aspects of the society as a whole.

The Comparison with the Choice of Aims and Means Model

In support of the thesis that citizens ought to choose only the aims of society let us compare this conception with one in which citizens choose aims and means. Notice first, that conceptions of citizens that do not include the role of deciding the aims of society are not plausible models of democratic citizenship. There is inevitably disagreement among citizens about what ends to pursue in modern society. The choice of aims is what gives direction to a person's life, whereas the choice of means is less important. When one person chooses the aims for another, allowing the other only to choose the means for achieving those aims, the former assumes the ruling role in the other person's life. A person who is only permitted to choose means is subservient to those who choose the ends. The same seems to hold for those who are permitted to choose only strategies for realizing ends. Strategies are much like means inasmuch as they are concerned with achieving aims given what others are likely to do or how others are likely to act strategically. Someone who is a mere strategist for another who has chosen the aims is subservient to the chooser of aims. Since a theory of democratic citizenship requires equality among citizens it cannot permit any subservience of this kind among citizens. Therefore, the choice of aims is essential to a conception of democratic citizenship that satisfies the ideals of democracy.

The choice of aims is, with some qualifications, also sufficient. The model of citizenship that includes other elements of decision-making includes more than what ordinary citizens need be concerned with. First, the knowledge of both the necessary means and strategies for achieving the aims of law and policy is inessential as long as the means and strategies are separable from the aims. As long as those who choose the means and strategies do not alter the aims pursued, then it is not clear why citizens should be concerned with means or strategies. For example, compare the choice of aims and means and strategies to the use of a computer word processor. The person who decides on what is written is the ultimate determinant of the outcome as long as the word processor does not change what is written. When I type the text of my book into the word processor, it does many things of which I have no understanding and little interest in understanding. It carries out the means for realizing my aim, which is to have a certain written text at the end. I choose what is to come out; it chooses how to do it. If another person types out my written text on a computer, I am the ultimate determiner of the aims of the whole process whereas he and the computer choose the means for realizing my aims. As long as the typist and the computer do not change my text except in minor ways, I don't care how it is done. Another analogy is to the relation between individual thought and choice and individual behavior. Most of us make choices and act without knowing very much about how the choices are translated into action. We do not understand the functionings of the brain or the operation of the nervous and muscular systems, though these are essential means for realizing our choices in action. Though we know little of these, we nevertheless think of ourselves as autonomous as long as the operations of our bodies do not seriously obstruct our abilities to act.

Similarly, citizens are not essentially concerned with the means that bring about their aims as long as the aims are not interfered with. When members of the government and other political institutions do their best to realize the aims citizens choose without attempting to insert their own aims or interests, citizens have no ground for complaint.

Participating in the choice of means is not a desirable part of the contribution of citizenship either. Inasmuch as the acquisition of expert knowledge is necessary to make even roughly appropriate choices of means in many cases, it is impossible for citizens to choose the means. It is also undesirable since citizens would have to neglect all the other tasks they perform in the society in order to have the requisite knowledge. The political and economic system requires that individuals devote large parts of their lives to specializing in one part or another and that they ignore other activities. A society in which everyone tries to acquire knowledge of means and strategies for accomplishing aims would inevitably undermine itself since food, clothing, art, and other important goods could not be produced. It would also eliminate opportunities to engage in private activities because it would eliminate leisure time. In short, such a view about the contribution of citizenship would be self-defeating in a modern society.

A final objection to the choice of aims and means model is that it is inimical to political equality. Since citizens cannot have all the knowledge to discern the necessary means for achieving ends, the model requires that citizens do as well as possible on this score. But, as noted in Chapter 3, some individuals have greater access to this knowledge than others. And individuals have more knowledge about certain narrow areas of concern to them, whereas others have knowledge of other areas.

The first fact would lead to inequality because certain citizens simply could not, by the same efforts, acquire the same knowledge as others. If the choice of means plays a significant role in the formulation of policy, even to the extent of affecting the aims, then those who are better placed to acquire knowledge will have more power over the society than those who have less. This argument for the inevitability of inequality in a society where citizens choose aims and means is similar to the Downsian argument discussed in Chapter 3, though it does not require the self-interest axiom.

The second fact about the choice of ends and means model is that individuals would know more than others in certain areas whereas others would know more in other areas. This implies that a society that conceives of citizens as determining means and ends will be divided into parts each of which attempts to determine those features relating to its area. But such a society is like the pluralist society we discussed previously. It makes citizens de facto authorities in narrow areas of policy. But, as we saw above, such a society does not have the overall unity necessary for political equality. It also suffers from other ailments of the pluralistic conception, such as lack of coherence in policymaking and cost spreading.

So the choice of aims and means model suffers from a number of serious defects. It fails to explain why citizens should be concerned with means at all if the aims and means are separable, and it imposes impossible and undesirable burdens on citizens. Finally, it undermines the realization of political equality in society. If citizens control the choice of overall aims and their choice of aims is not thwarted by those who choose the means to those aims, citizens are sovereign over the society as well as capable of political equality.[10]

Activities of Citizenship

I have defended three basic claims. First, citizens can be expected to act on the basis of moral considerations and in particular on the basis of considerations of justice. Second, the basic contribution of citizens in a democratic society is to choose the aims of the society, and, third, they are to do so with an eye to the society as a whole. What must they do to make this contribution? The process of choosing aims includes two kinds of activities. Citizens put pressure on the decision-making process to achieve their aims and deliberate to inform themselves of their interests as well as those of others and deepen their understanding of justice and the common good. These two activities correspond to the two basic aspects of democratic decisionmaking described in Chapter 2: the adversarial and the deliberative. The adversarial aspect of democracy is essential since disagreement and opposition are inevitable in a democratic society. At some point, debate, persuasion, and arguments come to an end and decisions must be made despite substantial disagreement among citizens. Here citizens are adversaries to some extent. They put pressure on the decision-making process by voting for alternative policies or political candidates as well as by organizing political parties and interest groups and bargaining with opponents. Up to that point citizens make efforts to improve their understanding of the issues and persuade each other of their points of view. Citizens engage in a mutual learning process of discussion and deliberation. These activities are importantly different and are regulated by different principles. Deliberative activities are regulated by the principle of qualitative equality whereas pressure activities are regulated by the principle of quantitative equality.

Theories of citizenship must strike a balance between these two kinds of activities, giving more weight to one or another. Some theories emphasize only deliberation and do not address pressure; others only emphasize pressure and ignore deliberation. I argued in Chapter 2 that both elements ought to be present. The choice of aims model of citizenship helps us make detailed judgments about what the balance ought to be. I shall defend the claim that the pressure activity of ordinary citizenship ought to be limited to voting on basic aims whereas deliberation on aims ought to be the primary concern of citizens.

Consider briefly the two main alternatives. The purely deliberative view, which states that citizens' exclusive responsibilities are to discuss aims with each other, is only plausible if we assume that they can reach full agreement through discussion. Once we abandon that view it is clear that in order for citizens to contribute to the decision-making process they must vote their opposed views and the outcome must be determined by some kind of decision rule. The ubiquity of disagreement in society requires that citizens engage in pressure if they are to contribute on an egalitarian basis. Conversely, those who advocate an exclusively pressure view of citizens assume that citizens' preferences are fixed and incapable of improvement. Only then does it make sense to say that citizens ought only to be concerned with whatever strategies are necessary for bringing about what they prefer. Once we see that the political process is in part a process of learning and that the conceptions of interests and justice on which our preferences are based are always in need of improvement, we can see that the purely pressure view is not a viable one in democratic societies. It ignores the fundamental importance to political equality of deliberation.

Though both pressure and deliberation are important, the choice of aims view of citizenship implies that the principal focus of citizens ought to be on the improvement of their understanding of their interests and justice. Deliberation and discussion are essential to individuals' acquiring an understanding of their society and to determining what will advance their interests as well as the common good and justice. Citizens must have opportunities to inform themselves, for only then do they have a chance for advancing their interests in the collective features of society. Equal access to the conditions for improving their understanding is required to approximate political equality in the society. However, bargaining and voting can only advance political equality once citizens do have reasonably well-informed bases for choosing aims. The choice of aims model requires that bargaining, since it is a means for achieving aims that requires expertise, ought to be done by experts. The one kind of pressure citizens ought to be able to exert is in the choice of aims they wish to see pursued, which they can do through voting for the aims. We shall explore this aspect of citizenship in great detail in Chapter 6. As long as citizens define the aims for the bargainer, they are in control and the bargainer is a kind of servant.

Here we have a picture of the political division of labor. Citizens are charged with the tasks of thinking about and improving their understanding of the basic aims that society ought to pursue overall and then voting for their preferred conceptions of aims. The complementary parts of the political decision-making process are charged with the tasks of determining the best means for realizing those aims as well as devising reasonable compromises between the citizens' diverse conceptions of aims. If everyone performs their roles as they ought, then the citizens will be sovereign over the society.

The Standards of Citizenship

It is often said that citizens are not sufficiently informed about the issues in politics. But rarely do people define the standard for saying when a person is sufficiently informed. We have seen that citizens ought mainly to be concerned with improving their understanding through discussion and deliberation and that democratic institutions ought to be thought of as contexts in which citizens can learn about their interests and moral concerns. We evaluate electoral campaigns, interest groups, political parties, and the media in terms of whether they enable citizens to educate themselves adequately about important issues and sustain discussion with each other. In order to determine whether institutions adequately educate citizens, we have to know what the standard of adequacy is. What is it that we think citizens ought to know?

The choice of aims model has important implications for how to define the standard of citizen understanding. It tells us that citizens should be primarily concerned with understanding their interests as well as the common good and justice as these affect their choices of aims. It also has implications for how much citizens should understand about politics. In what follows, I will first explain how it is possible to learn something about one's interests as well as justice and the common good; then I will articulate the basic standards for assessing this understanding.

A Brief Note on the Objectivity of Aims

Conceptions of aims include conceptions of the interests of the citizens as well as views about justice and the common good. The reason why it is possible to improve one's understanding of these is that interests, justice, and the common good are objective matters. Some, however, may think that these matters are entirely subjective. They think that the good for each person, what is in his or her interest, is merely what he or she desires or prefers or just what he or she thinks is good. Subjectivist views entail that we have nothing to learn about what is in our interests or that there is no such thing as an improvement in understanding our interests because they deny that there are standards for assessing such understanding. All that is likely to happen from discussion is a change of interest through a change of desire or preference or belief.

All of these purely subjectivist positions are false. And since what follows depends on their falsity I will make some preliminary remarks that show this falsity. Here I shall defend a minimal conception of the objectivity of interests that states only that we can be wrong about our interests. Such a conception is compatible with such diverse views as that our good consists in the satisfaction of fully informed desires, or that our good consists in facts discoverable by scientific or metaphysical analysis. A minimal conception is sufficient for the purposes of defending the possibility and importance of the improvement in one's understanding of one's interests, which underlies the value of social discussion and reflection on interests.

The interests of persons are not the same as what they desire or what they prefer. Desires are mere impulses to action or springs of motivation. Some of the objects of our desires are good for us and some are not. Desires for food, drink, and other things are usually for things that are good for us. We often trust our desires in these matters because we believe they move us to do things that are for our own good. But we do not always trust our desires. Sometimes we are addicted to things, sometimes our desires are neurotic, and we desire many things despite our judgment that they are not good for us. This conflict should not be surprising. If desires are mere impulses or springs of motivation, then some of these impulses will push in the wrong direction. What emerges from these observations is that what we desire is not the standard of what is good for us. Since we desire many things that are not good for us, clearly we have an independent standard for deciding what is good for us. For example, we have an interest in eating when it improves or sustains our health or gives us pleasure. Hunger is usually a good indicator of when we need food or when we will get pleasure from eating. But sometimes it isn't. So desires associated with hunger do not define the good for us; they are at best only indicators of it.

What I believe to be in my interest cannot define what is in my interests. The fact that I believe that something is in my interests implies that I think there is a fact of the matter that makes my belief true or false. To be sure, normally I think my beliefs are true, but I usually am willing to review them and reexamine their relation to the world.

None of this implies that mature persons are not usually the best judges of their own good. Persons can be wrong about their good but still be more likely to know about it than others. That I do not fully understand my own good does not mean that others generally understand it better. And though each person is generally the best judge of his or her interests, he or she can still learn from discussion with others about those interests.

These arguments show that the common good is objective to the extent that the common good is made up of the objective interests of the citizens. Furthermore, since justice concerns the equal consideration of interests, justice is also to that extent an objective notion. Although an extended discussion of the objectivity of considerations of justice is not possible here, two comments are in order. First, individuals often engage in discussion and debates about justice and are willing and able to be persuaded by good reasoning if they see it. This suggests that most people are committed at least to a minimal conception of the objectivity of justice. Second, as we saw in the discussion about Schumpeter's views about democracy and politics, a theory that purports to defend the worth of certain institutions is committed to some claims about the common good and justice that are understood to be at least minimally objective. The premise of writing a such book as this one is that argument and reasoning about issues of justice and the common good are worthwhile and that these are issues on which we can improve our understanding. This is all the objectivity that is required for the claim that social discussion and deliberation are essential components of the tasks of citizens and that institutions ought to be organized so as to enhance such discussion.

Standards of Understanding of Aims

Given that interests and justice are minimally objective notions, what are the standards by which we ought to assess citizens' understanding of them? First, I want to discuss some purely epistemological approaches to assessing our understanding of interests and justice; then we will see to what extent any of these can be transferred to the realm of citizenship. There are three general types of epistemic approach that are relevant for our purposes. The first states that a belief is justified if it coheres with the other beliefs that a person holds on a subject.[11] On the coherentist approach it is possible for a person to a have a justified belief on a subject regardless of the amount or quality of evidence or information they have. As long as the belief is tied in the right way to the other beliefs of the person and they are the result of disinterested reflection. This kind of approach is very demanding on the time and resources of a person in the respect that he or she may have a lot of information and experience to take account of in justifying a belief. As a consequence, the time and effort needed to infer that a belief is justified will be quite large. It is undemanding in the respect that it does not impose any requirements on the quality or amount of information a person has in the first place, except that it be held in a disinterested fashion. So a person may be justified in a belief about a certain subject without having much information on it. If the belief coheres in the right way with other beliefs the person has, it can be justified.

This view does not identify the standards we are looking for. It suggests that citizens can have justified beliefs about politics even if they are almost totally ignorant of it. They may have views about the political system and alternatives to it that cohere with entirely faulty and simplistic beliefs. But inasmuch as the beliefs with which they have started are worthless, the understanding that the citizens have of their political arrangements will not be worth much. This is an intuitive judgment. But it seems clear that any standard that says that a citizen is justified in believing that Donald Duck is the best candidate for president as long as this belief coheres reasonably well with his or her other beliefs is the wrong way to assess the understanding citizens have in modern democracies. The problem is that the coherentist view does not fit with the aims we have when we assess a citizen's understanding of politics. A political system could self-destruct because of the ignorance of its members though they all had justified beliefs about politics on the coherentist view of justification. This is not a criticism of coherentism as a theory of knowledge per se. What my argument suggests is that coherentism is not what we are after when we are attempting to determine the standards by which we ought to evaluate the understanding citizens have of politics.

The second kind of approach is different in that it imposes requirements on evidence gathering as well as reasoning. In this approach, the quality and quantity of the inputs to one's reasoning are crucial factors in assessing the value of one's belief. One such view has been widely adhered to by political scientists: the *full information* view.[12] This approach states that a person is justified in believing a proposition to the extent that he or she has all the available evidence regarding whether the belief is true or false and has reasoned in the right way to the belief in question. Another approach is that one is justified if the information one has guarantees that one's belief is true (though it need not be all the available information). In this *foundationalist* view, beliefs are quite hard to justify because one must have an appropriate set of privileged beliefs from which one can justify the beliefs in question. Furthermore, the beliefs to be justified must be derived in the right way from the privileged beliefs.

These views impose very stringent conditions on the justification of beliefs. It seems unlikely that citizens could have anywhere near the kinds of justification for beliefs that these views recommend. Perhaps it is because they have held these kinds of views about justification of beliefs that many have been quite pessimistic about the quality of political information of ordinary citizens. In any case, this second kind of standard cannot be met by even the most knowledgeable members of the society who spend all of their time attempting to understand political questions. Imagine trying to justify your belief about what a politician is doing on the basis of logical deductions from self-evident beliefs, or only after you have absorbed all the available evidence. The full information condition cannot be met by anyone in politics. And if it could be, it would not be desirable that any more than a tiny minority attempt to do so since the members of the society must concern themselves with other tasks aside from attempting to understand the political system and its defects. All these other tasks would have to be sacrificed for them to live up to the full information or certainty conditions, which would defeat the point of trying to be informed about politics. As with the coherentist view, these claims do not show that foundationalism is false as a theory of knowledge; it is simply not what we are looking for.

The basic problem with these views is that they are not adjusted to the particular requirements of a theory of citizenship. The activities of citizens in deliberating about politics are essential to the maintenance of a democratic society. If the citizens have only silly conceptions of the aims of a society, then a democratic society will lack direction. If some citizens are generally in a position to have a better understanding than others, then such a society will not be egalitarian. A theory of democracy establishes certain desiderata, such as the advancement of the interests of citizens in the collective features of society and political equality, and asks how citizens and the institutional context in which they find themselves can promote these desiderata. The first two approaches were specified entirely independently of the needs of democratic institutions; what we need is an approach that evaluates citizens' activities in terms of how well they promote the ideals of democracy.

A third approach asserts that a belief is justified if it is brought about by processes that are reliable in producing true beliefs.[13] The reliability standard applies not only to the quality of inferences and the initial inputs of those inferential processes but to all the cognitive processes that produce the belief and may include the institutional context in which the beliefs are produced. The issue is whether the processes are reliable in producing, in a causal sense of the term, true beliefs.

This standard is of the right form for a theory of democratic citizenship. It assesses the activities of a person in terms of an external desideratum to be achieved by the activities. And it requires that we consider many influences on the formation of belief, including the context in which beliefs are formed, and asks whether they promote the desired outcomes. This view requires that we evaluate the activities of persons and the background institutions of belief formation in terms of whether they are likely to promote true belief.[14] Clearly, true beliefs about politics promote citizens' interests in collective properties of society.

Though reliabilism is on the right track for our theory of citizenship, it must be supplemented in important ways. First, the reliabilist standard is entirely elaborated in terms of truth. Processes of acquiring understanding that are reliable in producing truths may be deeply inefficient with regard to other ends people have.[15] Political organization is designed with the purpose of making good choices. To some extent, good choices depend on good information, but they also depend on timely and efficient decisionmaking so that all other decisions and tasks can be performed as well. This need for efficiency is why a theory of citizenship limits the object of discussion for citizens in general to a particular subject: the set of overall aims for a society. Only this role is compatible with an efficient division of labor.

The purely epistemic reliabilism also sets aside other important social ideals in its evaluation of the activities of citizens and social institutions. Consider an example: A criminal trial procedure involves the collection of information and understanding concerning the guilt or innocence and the degrees of responsibility of the defendants. We evaluate such a procedure in terms of whether it produces true or false beliefs about the guilt or innocence of defendants. The epistemic reliabilist would stop there. But such a system has other desiderata as well. We want it to protect the rights of the accused as well as the victims of crime and treat all parties as equals. The standard for proving that a person is guilty is much higher than the standard of innocence. Evidence demonstrating the guilt of an accused person that has been acquired in violation of the rights of that person is excluded from the trial for this reason. Indeed, the criminal trial procedure in the United States makes false assessments of the guilt or innocence of defendants more often than necessary. But if this kind of procedure is the best way of defending the rights of citizens, then the price in truths may be well worth paying.

The activities of citizens and the institutions that frame them must be evaluated not only in terms of truth but in terms of other social and political needs. In our theory we are concerned with constructing a conception of citizenship that is part of an efficient decision-making system that advances the interests of citizens and political equality.

The Standards of Citizens' Democratic Activities

The activities that satisfy the basic standard for citizenship are those that are the most reliable in producing true beliefs in citizens regarding their interests and the just accommodation of interests. However, these activities are subject to the constraint that their performance is compatible with the political equality of citizens as well as the preservation of a division of labor in political decisionmaking as well as the society overall. What criteria should these activities satisfy?

The choice of aims model of citizenship along with the conception of deliberation defended in Chapter 2 provides an adequate guide to deciding on these criteria. Participation in a process of discussion in which citizens elaborate articulate, reasonable, and discriminating conceptions of their interests and justice is a reliable method for producing true beliefs regarding their interests and justice subject to the constraints of political equality and efficiency in the division of labor. Let us elaborate on this standard. A set of aims is articulate when it is sufficiently complex and detailed to provide guidance to those who must decide on the means to realizing those aims. For example, a citizen who thinks that the government should pursue social justice but says nothing about what social justice comprises does not have an articulate view, even though she has in some sense chosen an aim for the society overall. Since her position does not discriminate between conceptions of social justice, it provides little or no guidance for policymakers. Compared with those who have more determinate conceptions of justice, she has virtually no impact. Also, to the extent that citizens have only abstract or vague conceptions of aims, they effectively transfer the choice of aims for society to the officials of the government. So political equality will not be possible if some are not able to come up with reasonably articulate views. The standard of articulation requires that citizens provide reasonably detailed schedules of trade-offs of aims to those who would carry out the means; otherwise, when there are conflicts between aims or when compromises must be made, policymakers will have little guidance.

Reasonableness ought to characterize citizens' views as well. Citizens ought to have reasons for preferring their views to others and not simply be driven by emotion in selecting conceptions of aims. They ought to be able to defend their views to themselves as well as to others. If I make an effort to give reasons to myself and others for the beliefs I have, this forces me to consider the basis of my views in general. It compels me to attempt to understand my interests as well as the interests of others in the process. If I must justify my conception of justice or the common good to others, then I will have to be able to show that my conception takes their interests into account and that it is a conception they ought to accept. Furthermore, efforts at public justification invite responses and reasoned criticism from others, sometimes inducing revisions in one's views. This process of trial and error in discussion helps all citizens learn about their own interests as well as the interests of others and the most just way of accommodating them. Participation in this process is surely the most reliable condition that we know of for improving one's understanding of the interests of citizens and justice. In addition, the possession of a reasoned set of beliefs and the habit of rationally assessing my beliefs makes me less susceptible to manipulation by enterprising politicians, whose interests and convictions may well diverge from mine.

The choice of aims must be a discriminating choice. The conception of aims that each citizen defends must be the result of a process wherein a "relevant variety" of conceptions has been entertained. The relevant variety is a broad cross section of conceptions that derive from the different sectors of society. A modern society is highly differentiated in its roles, ethnic groups, economic classes, and other features of citizens. Most of these differences have some significance for the nature of the interests people have as well as their points of view on the society because individuals must develop different talents and character traits to adjust to different parts of the society. They have been molded by the different histories of the groups of which they are members. The effects are not uniform, and they are not easily understood or predicted. Thus, although we can easily be convinced of the truth of the general principle that individuals' interests are affected by the different sectors of the society they inhabit, we often do not know what the different interests are. And when individuals have distinct interests, they may also have distinct points of view on the society overall from which everyone can learn.

A democratic society genuinely committed to equality ought to encourage these different groups to cultivate their understandings of their interests and the society. If the relevant variety condition is satisfied, then it will be possible for all citizens to hear accounts of conceptions of the aims of society that appeal to their interests and that proceed from points of view that make sense to them. They thereby can be in a position to learn about their own interests. They also have a chance to hear responses to those conceptions of their interests and points of view that seem most suitable to them. Under these conditions alone do they have the opportunity to learn from the process of trial and error in discussion. The importance of each group having a voice is very much like the importance of students having a say in a classroom context. Only if a student is able to say what she thinks on the subject will she have the opportunity to hear an account of the material specifically geared to her own concerns. Thus, teachers in classroom contexts attempt to encourage students to speak and express their specific points of view on what they are learning. This opportunity to speak makes an important contribution to the education of the student.

Most important, the audience has interests in hearing these distinctive voices for a variety of reasons. First, some in the audience may actually share the interests of those who are speaking without knowing it and thus may learn about their own interests in the process of discussion. Pursuing the example of the classroom, those who do not ask questions or say what they think often learn when they hear others express the points of view and the questions they have and the ensuing discussion. Second, members of the audience can better formulate their own views of how all the interests in the society fit together once they have a better understanding of those interests. Third, the audience may acquire new points of view against which to test their own views and thus acquire a better understanding and deeper evaluation of their own position. So every citizen need not contribute to this process as long as a relevant variety of views is heard and responded to.

In sum, each citizen ought to form his or her conception of the aims of society as a result of reflection on a deliberative process wherein articulate, reasonable, and discriminating conceptions of interests and justice are debated. This deliberative process is highly likely to promote citizens' interests in collective features of society to the extent that it is reliable in producing true beliefs on these matters; it is egalitarian as long as it is qualitatively equal, that is, all positions are given the time they need; and it is efficient to the degree that it is mainly limited to the basic aims and so is compatible with a political division of labor. One problem that we will have to face is that we do not, in principle, know the relevant variety of alternatives; I will explore this issue in the last chapter.

The Implications of the Role of Citizenship for the Ideals of Democracy

The choice of aims conception of citizenship provides the key to the reconciliation of political equality and democratic deliberation to the conditions of the modern state. It responds to the worries entailed by the Downsian view of democracy described in Chapter 3. First, we have undermined the self-interest axiom that undergirds Downs's arguments. Second, it shows that Downs is mistaken about what citizens need to know in order to be sovereign and equal. They need to be knowledgeable not about everything relating to politics but only about the overall aims of the society. This limits the problem of information collection considerably. Third, since the society actively supports the participation of all sectors of society in deliberation about aims, citizens everywhere have opportunities to become more sophisticated about politics no matter where they are in the division of labor and to learn not only from certain dominant interests but from all groups, including one that might plausibly be their own. Fourth, since the political system is dominated by citizens who choose the aims of the society, the problems of special interest influence are reduced considerably.

We also have the makings of a solution to the problem of rational democratic deliberation in a modern society. Recall that individuals must be on a par with respect to understanding the issues if deliberation amongst them is to proceed rationally. The question arises, Is there any set of issues on which citizens in general can plausibly be thought to have roughly equal understanding? The general answer is that if citizens are concerned with the choice of aims and not with all matters of political concern, the distinction between citizen and expert is greatly narrowed. There are two reasons for this. First, the citizens acquire a great deal of information in their everyday lives about what their interests are as well as about justice and moral constraints. Ordinary persons must deal with these matters every day. I must make decisions about just or fair distributions of benefits in many ordinary circumstances. When friends disagree about what they wish to do or when there are conflicts over wages and salaries, we are confronted in part with issues of justice. Every organization in which a person is a member gives him or her some experience of basic norms of living together and fairness as well as conceptions of how organizations can contribute to the well-being of the members. I am constantly confronted with issues about what my interests comprise, as well as how to order my interests. I am also often confronted with how to compare my interests with those of others and how to find accommodations between them. These are experiences that most people cannot help but have, and these experiences help people in thinking about matters relating to the ultimate ends of society. Thus, each citizen has a very large fund of information and experience with which to reflect on the basic ends of society.

These sources of understanding can be enhanced by giving citizens more power in their everyday lives as well as by a wider distribution of quality education. Thus some elements of workplace democracy would encourage individuals to think more about issues of justice and interests, and these would provide important sources of understanding of political issues. Participation in jury trials can improve individuals' abilities to think through issues of fairness and interests and thus would be helpful in getting individuals to think more about issues relating to politics. In general some participation in such institutions as school boards, day care centers, and the workplace would not add a great burden on citizens, but they would enhance their abilities to think through and appreciate issues that are essentially related to the informed choice of aims for a society.[16]

The second reason why the gap between expert and ordinary citizens need not be great is based on a fundamental article of belief in democratic theory and liberal political philosophy generally. Individuals are, roughly speaking, naturally equally competent on moral matters. That is, individuals have equal natural capacities to discern their interests as well as to understand issues of justice. Our discussion of the arguments for this claim must be very brief. First, we generally acknowledge that individuals are the best judges of their own interests, at least when they reach maturity. No one is more capable of discerning a person's interests than that person, which already introduces an important kind of equality in moral capacity. Second, to the extent that there are differences in capacity for moral insight, these differences seem to be roughly randomly distributed throughout the population. There is no reason to think that differences in capacity are correlated with any of the major categories of interests or points of view. If there are uninsightful people, they are as likely to be left-wing as right-wing, or as likely to be men as women. And this random distribution seems to hold for all the different major interests.[17] In this case, as long as there is qualitative equality in the process of discussion, and generally the more capable end up speaking for the distinct points of view, whatever inequalities in abilities there are should have merely marginal significance. Third, whatever measure we design for determining the relative moral capacities of citizens, it is likely to require adherence to substantive conceptions of interests and morality. A measure relying on one substantive conception of value may imply the superiority of some, whereas a measure relying on another conception of value may suggest the greater capacity of others. And just as there is controversy on the nature of interests and values, there is likely to be controversy on the various measures that rely on them. There may be an objective truth on these matters, but no one has a sufficient claim to knowledge of this truth for it to be the basis of excluding some from participation. This fact about societies is sufficiently deep that any conception of social justice must accommodate it in its basic principles. Fourth, to the extent that there are differences in people's capacities, the social environment is likely to provide a better explanation of those differences than natural differences. That is, the reason why some people tend to have less insight into matters relating to their own interests than others is because those individuals have been in environments that do not encourage the development of thinking about their interests or about justice. In addition, many individuals in society do not have the access to education necessary to develop their basic moral competence.[18] Once individuals are given access to education and opportunities to exercise their judgment regularly, they acquire greater facility in thinking about their own interests as well as about fairness.[19] Thus, the basic article of faith of democratic thought is well founded and ought to serve as part of the basis of our conception of citizenship.

There are of course many differences in what individuals know about politics that are ineliminable. But aside from the differences described above, these consist of one of two kinds. First, many individuals know a lot more than others about the kinds of policies that are in place and their effects as well as how these policies came about. This is important knowledge that a society wants to make use of, but I have argued that this knowledge is not essential for ordinary citizens who are sovereign over their society and politically equal. Citizens must choose the overall aims of the society in order to exercise their rights of sovereignty and political equality. It is not essential for them to know how these aims are being carried out. Second, some individuals may have thought a lot more about interests and justice than others. In my view this gives them greater ability to devise new ways of thinking about interests and justice, but it need not increase their basic moral insight. What they understand is not impossible to grasp for those who have not thought as much about the issue. The writings of moral and political philosophers are not writings that are essentially beyond the abilities of ordinary people to evaluate. Indeed, the common method of evaluating moral and political theories is to determine the extent to which they correspond to our common intuitive judgments on everyday issues. The distinctive task of moral and political thinkers is to attempt to develop new ways of understanding our interests and justice. This task requires a lot of time, discipline, and imagination. It is a useful task, and the ideas that arise from it are among the ones we want to take advantage of in a political society. But it need not increase the basic insight of the moral thinker.

The consequence of these observations is that with respect to the discussion of the overall aims of the society, individuals are roughly on a par with each other with regard to expertise on these subjects. At the very least, each individual is able to grasp the reasons that others advance for their views even if they do not always have the time or energy to actually devise new ideas and reasons for particular conceptions of aims. Thus it seems that rational discussion about the basic overall aims of the society among members of the whole population should, in principle, be possible if other social institutions are organized so as to cultivate the moral insight of citizens.

This concludes my discussion of the choice of aims model of citizenship. In my view, this model presents us with a conception of citizenship that reconciles the apparently conflicting requirements of the democratic ideals and the necessity of the division of labor in modern society. The reconciliation follows from assigning a particular role to citizens in the division of labor that permits them to exercise their rights to advance their interests in collective properties of society and political equality and makes possible a genuinely democratic social deliberation. The question of whether this role demands too much of citizens has been partly answered. I have argued that the choice of aims model limits the type of understanding citizens must have to a more manageable object of thought and discussion. I have also argued that ordinary citizens are well placed to grasp the issues involved with the choice of aims since they are ones citizens must confront in their everyday lives. These issues do not admit of the kind of expertise that differentiates those who understand from those who do not understand. The basic capacity for insight called upon to understand different conceptions of aims is roughly equally distributed throughout the society. Though some specialization in the elaboration of aims is useful, such specialization need not have the effect of separating out those who know from those who do not know.

The Agency Problem

Two problems have been set aside until now: the agency problem and the problem of the complexity of aims. They will provide the starting point for our discussion of the complementary parts of the political system that will occupy us in detail in Part Three. In the choice of aims model, the government has the role of realizing the aims of the citizenry without introducing any of its own. The account relies heavily on the moral motivations of government actors who have the power to take matters into their own hands. It assumes that the members of the legislative and administrative parts of the government as well as interest groups and political parties will generally pursue the aims of the citizens despite the facts that interests conflict and that citizens are not watching closely. The rejection of the self-interest view of motivation clears some ground for this assumption. The worry is, however, that the role assigned to officials may provide too many temptations to deviate from the aims of the citizens. Even without the assumption of self-interest, we cannot assume that individuals will always act in a morally desirable way. They may act from weakness of will in favor of their own interests. They may even question the worth of democracy. Democracy encourages disagreement and may have the effect of producing at least partly antidemocratic opinions among those who are entrusted with power.[20]

Exposing political officials to temptations to supplant citizens' aims with their own is not the same thing as imposing excessive demands on them. The choice of aims model does not demand any special sacrifice from them. It allows that officials be paid more than most other citizens and does not require them to work excessive hours. The choice of aims model and the democratic ideals are compatible with providing strong incentives to attract good government officials, such as high pay and prestige. These incentives would not by themselves undermine political equality. The real threat to political equality is that government officials are exposed to temptations to increase their reward beyond what is sufficient to compensate them for their important contributions. Realism demands that a theory be able to deal with the possible overreaching of government officials. Thus, for a people to have genuine control over the government, it must be able to monitor the extent to which its policies are realized and to make corrections for obstructionist activity.

There are different elements in this monitoring. First, citizens should be able to recognize when the aims they have chosen have been implemented. This ability is part of the main conception of citizenship discussed above. In some contexts this judgment will not be difficult, but in others there may be real disagreements about whether some aim really has been achieved. For example, in the 1960s in the United States a large majority of citizens chose the aim of ending poverty in the United States by greatly expanding the welfare state and empowering poor people. Since then there has been considerable debate as to whether the aims of the war on poverty have been advanced. Some have argued that these aims were set back by the programs offered.[21] Others have argued that social welfare policy was a major success marred only by an eventual loss of political will on the part of the citizenry and political officials.[22] Thus, on some issues there is debate as to whether the aims have been realized.

There are a number of possible reasons for why aims are not realized: (1) The aims are not realizable. (2) Government officials have to compromise among aims because there is a lot of disagreement among citizens. (3) Government officials act incompetently in attempting to bring about the aims. (4) The apparatus of government simply is not structured in the right way to bring about the outcomes. (5) Officials do not wish to bring them about. Which of these explanations accounts for the failure to realize aims has implications for whether we characterize citizens as sovereign and equal or see them as having their authority usurped. The first two explanations do not seem to undermine the equality at all. Citizens may act foolishly when they choose impossible aims, but they do not thereby transfer power to others. And when aims must be accommodated, citizens do not suffer inequality. The last explanation involves a usurpation of the authority of the people since officials simply choose not to realize the aims they are bound to pursue. Here officials or those who influence them assume for themselves the right to choose the aims of the society. The third and fourth explanations are harder to assess. They seem at least to involve some loss of ability to advance the interests of ordinary citizens since citizens cannot expect to have their feasible aims realized. They do not involve any real transfer of authority since it is not the case that any other individuals are assuming the decision-making power. There is also likely to be disagreement as to which of the above explanations really accounts for the lack of realization of the aims of citizens.

In any case, there must be some kind of institutional arrangement for monitoring the operation of government in such a system. But citizens cannot carry out this task for all the reasons given in the criticism of the choice of aims and means model. So, it appears that monitoring the process of the government role of carrying out the means to achieving the aims of the citizens cannot be done by citizens without undermining democratic ideals.

The answer to this problem, which we will explore in later chapters, is twofold. First, it is sufficient for a democratic society that the institutions provide reasonable assurance to citizens that the government is acting on its mandate. As we have seen, the essential role of citizens is to determine the aims of the society. What matters is that the government do its best in choosing means. Second, in addition to the fact that we ought to be able to rely in part on the moral natures of political officials, we shall see that the best way to assure citizens of the good faith efforts of members of the government is to guarantee that a variety of secondary associations, such as interest groups and political parties, have the capacity to monitor the activities of the government. Citizens may then rely on the judgments of these groups for assurance that the government is doing its best to bring about the aims the citizens have chosen. Thus, although citizens engage in genuine deliberation about the aims, with regard to determining whether the government is doing its best in achieving those aims, the citizens engage in proxy judgment.[23] They rely on the judgments of a variety of experts. Genuine deliberation about means is not essential. The only issue is whether this process provides citizens with reasonable assurance that the government is doing its best.

The Problem of the Complexity of Aims

Another problem arises because of the complexity of the aims that the citizens are likely to have. A large part of public policy analysis is concerned with determining the compatibility of social aims with each other. To what extent is pollution control compatible with full employment? Is the maintenance of a high minimum income for everyone compatible with a sufficient degree of liberty? How do unemployment and inflation trade off? In general, what kinds of budgetary outlays are necessary for certain programs, and are they compatible with the priorities that citizens have for these programs? Much of politics consists of deciding between alternative proposals for how all the aims should be packaged together. These issues are of vital concern to citizens. But they are solvable only with a considerable amount of knowledge.

In response to this problem the choice of aims model requires that citizens choose a schedule of trade-offs between all the ends that they have. Each citizen draws up a preference ordering among the possible combinations of aims.[24] For example, in the United States there has been a debate about whether gay men and women ought to be given as much liberty in the military as heterosexual men and women with regard to their sexual preferences. Some have argued that permitting gays these liberties would weaken the morale of the military establishment. Others have argued that the consequences would not be so serious and that they would only be very short-term at worst. The issue here concerns the facts of the matter. My proposal is that citizens ought to be first concerned with what they think is important and how to rank these things. Citizens must decide on how to rank in importance equality among persons of different sexual orientation and morale in the military. Each citizen must choose a schedule of trade-offs between morale in the military and equality. The government chooses the feasible package of aims highest on the preference ordering that emerges after the votes are in. If a majority of citizens are willing to live with a temporary but not disastrous loss of morale in the military in order to uphold the ideal of equality, then the government's task is to determine whether this is feasible and, if so, to implement the policy. If not, then the government must implement a feasible trade-off lower down in the ranking. Citizens do not concern themselves with what the facts are but with what to do with whatever the facts might be. Citizens devise a schedule of trade-offs for all the major aims they wish the society to pursue.

The problem that this method raises is that citizens will be charged with coming up with a very complicated scheme of trade-offs in order to satisfy the standard of articulation defended above.[25] Such a task reintroduces the problems of placing excessive demands on the time and energy of ordinary citizens.

A Division of Labor in the Choice of Aims

This complexity raises problems for the choice model. Deliberation and discussion require a considerable amount of information in many circumstances. To elaborate a sufficiently articulate set of aims as well as to be able to persuade others of the worth of one's aims one must have a great deal of information about what is important to them. One must be able to argue with them in a way that uses forms of reasoning and inferences that make sense to them. And one must be prepared to listen to and understand views and arguments that are unfamiliar and strange at first. This task requires that one not only be able to understand the issues but that one be able to spend the time to theoretically conceive of new approaches to the conceptions of ends and that one be able to conceive of new ways of defending them to those who are not persuaded by other efforts.

As a consequence, there will necessarily be a division of labor in the very formulation of ends since the problems of putting together reasonable packages of ends is itself very complex, as we have seen. We have such a division of labor in our own society. Political parties are charged with the task of putting together packages of aims and trade-offs, and, as a consequence, political parties have the task of setting agendas for decisionmaking even on the general ends that the political society is to pursue. Interest groups are also charged with the tasks of articulating and clarifying aims and interests of large groups of people as well as funding organizations, such as think tanks, to do this.

These facts are hard to fit with the choice of aims model of citizenship. The choice model is organized around the idea that a modern democratic society can be understood as a division of labor that assigns to citizens the role of articulating and choosing the basic aims of society and to the government and informal political groups in the society the role of determining the means for achieving the aims. The fact that the ends are chosen by the citizens is what gives them authority. But our discovery of the necessity of a division of labor in the very formulation of ends suggests the worry that there is no standpoint from which citizens can be thought of as making choices about ends and the rest of the apparatus of government as merely carrying out these ends. The very formulation and dissemination of ends requires a division of labor wherein some will have a lot to say and others will have less to say.

The Need for a Theory of Democratic Institutions

These problems concern the larger institutional context in which the role of citizenship I outlined can be performed. Political officials, parties, and interest groups are the agents that act for citizens. Furthermore, these institutions provide the context for social deliberation. They complement the role of citizens in the political division of labor. Since citizens perform one role in the larger political division of labor, the claim that the division of labor is compatible with the ideals of democracy requires an account of the complementary roles in the political system and how they are appropriately related to the role of citizenship.

We will sketch answers to these problems in Part Three by formulating conceptions of the functions that must be performed by political institutions within the division of labor and then by showing how these functions can be carried out in a way that is compatible with the democratic ideals. The basic functions of institutions are, first, to transmit the citizens' conceptions of aims to government officials in such a way that the agendas for negotiating differences among the aims and for deciding on the means to carrying out these aims are basically determined by the citizens. These institutions ensure that citizens can perform their role in the adversarial aspect of democracy. This function is essentially carried out by the electoral system and the scheme of representation. Second, political institutions must ensure that citizens are able to discuss the basic aims of society in accordance with the standards specified. These institutions ensure that citizens have full and equal access to the deliberative aspect of democracy. This function, I will argue, is carried out primarily by the system of political parties and interest groups. Third, political institutions must ensure some kind of adequate monitoring of public officials in charge of negotiating and implementing the aims of citizens.

The second step is to show how these functions can be carried out by political institutions in a manner that is consistent with the ideals of political equality and democratic deliberation. I will argue in the next chapter that parties in a legislative assembly have the functions of delegates to citizens with regard to the aims of society and trustee to citizens with regard to the means for achieving these aims and the compromises necessary to resolve disagreements over the aims. I will argue that a system of party list proportional representation is the proper institutional mechanism for ensuring that this function is carried out in an egalitarian way. Such a system also helps with the agency problem. In Chapter 7, I argue that the function of providing a context of deliberation for citizens ought to be primarily carried out by a system of informal associations in the society: political parties and interest groups. I will also argue that this is the primary function of these groups in a society that realizes the democratic ideals. And I will argue that despite the division of labor in the formulation of aims, citizens are the basic choosers of aims. In Chapter 8, I will argue that such a system can go a long way towards resolving the agency problem I have described. I will then describe principles for defining an egalitarian deliberative process and discuss the institutions for satisfying those principles.

Notes

1. John Rawls, *A Theory of Justice* (Cambridge, Mass.: Harvard University Press, 1971), p. 145.

2. In case there is any appearance of conspiracy of the experts against the ordinary citizen, it should be noted that each expert in one area is an ordinary citizen in many others. A legislator who is very knowledgeable about how to get laws passed through the United States Congress is not much better off than most other people on the fine points of nuclear policy or environmental law. An expert on one of these latter topics is not likely to be highly knowledgeable about how to get laws through the Congress. Given the size of the system by which laws are made, each expert in one or two

areas is likely to be a nonexpert in most other areas. In short, for most policy areas, each and every citizen is a nonexpert.

3. See Brian Barry, *The Liberal Theory of Justice* (Oxford: Oxford University Press, 1973), p. 145, for something like this use of Socrates's simile of the ship of state.

4. This view is also sometimes called English Pluralism; see G.H.D. Cole, *Social Theory* (London: J. M. Dent, 1925), for a defense of this kind of pluralism, and more recently see Paul Q. Hirst, *Representative Government and Its Limits* (London: St. Martin's Press, 1989), as well as John Burnheim, *Is Democracy Possible?* (Berkeley: University of California Press, 1987).

5. One conception of pluralism recommends a system of functional representation that makes collective decisions by majority rule. I will discuss such a system of representation in Chapters 6 and 7. It is not relevant to the view that the different sectors ought to have independent authority.

6. See Grant McConnell, *Private Power and American Democracy* (New York: Vintage Press, 1966).

7. See Joshua Cohen and Joel Rogers, "Secondary Associations and Democratic Governance," *Politics and Society* December (1992): pp. 393–472, for one among many defenses of granting limited independent decision-making authority to groups.

8. See Carole Pateman, *Participation and Democratic Theory* (Cambridge: Cambridge University Press, 1970), for arguments to this effect.

9. John Stuart Mill gives a great deal of authority to society to decide matters. For example, he argues that all economic transactions come under the jurisdiction of society, which he thinks ought to be democratic. Nevertheless, he argues that the society ought to use this authority sparingly. See his *On Liberty* (Buffalo, N.Y.: Prometheus Books, 1986 [1859]), chapter 5.

10. It appears that there is some empirical evidence that citizens are in fact primarily concerned with deciding on the aims of the society. Those who have noted this fact, such as Popkin and Downs, tend to think of it as merely a shortcut that citizens use so that they do not have to collect more information. In a sense they are right since the amount of information citizens need to collect when they are merely interested in ends is much smaller than it would be if they were interested in the details of policymaking. But Downs goes on and says, "When voters can expertly judge every detail of every stand taken and relate it directly to their own views of a great society, they are interested only in issues, not philosophies." Both Downs and Popkin miss the more important point that what is essential to citizenship is that citizens choose the aims as long as those who are in the government do their best to achieve the citizens' aims. See Samuel Popkin, *The Reasoning Voter* (Chicago: University of Chicago Press, 1990), p. 99, as well as William Gam-

son, *Talking Politics* (Cambridge: Cambridge University Press, 1992), for evidence for these claims. See also Anthony Downs, *An Economic Theory of Democracy* (New York: Harper and Row, 1957), pp. 96–98.

11. Keith Lehrer, "Systematic Justification," in *Essays on Knowledge and Justification,* ed. George C. Pappas and Marshall Swain (Ithaca: Cornell University Press, 1980), p. 300.

12. This is the Berelson standard cited in Edward G. Carmines and James Kuklinski, "Incentives, Opportunities, and the Logic of Public Opinion in American Political Representation," in *Information and Democratic Processes,* ed. John Ferejohn and James Kuklinski (Chicago: University of Illinois Press, 1990), p. 242.

13. See Alvin Goldman, *Epistemology and Cognition* (Cambridge, Mass.: Harvard University Press, 1986).

14. See Alvin Goldman, "Foundations of Social Epistemics," *Synthese* (1987): pp. 109–144, for a discussion of the importance of institutional frameworks in the promotion of true belief.

15. This kind of a limit is fully acknowledged in Alvin Goldman's "Epistemic Paternalism: Communication Control in Law and Politics," *Journal of Philosophy* March (1991): pp. 113–131.

16. See Carole Pateman, *Participation and Democratic Theory,* p. 56, for evidence that most workers desire a greater level of participation in the affairs of the workplace.

17. Consider the following exception to this principle. Conceptually, one might divide the society into morally capable and morally stupid people. If there are important interests that divide them, then the principle does not hold. My sense is that not a lot of interests are associated with these groups.

18. Richard Hernnstein and Charles Murray have argued recently that differences in I.Q. are heritable and that at least a substantial proportion of these differences cannot be remedied by education; see their *The Bell Curve* (New York: Basic Books, 1994), part 1. Their arguments are quite incomplete at best. First, a number of studies suggest that long-term educational intervention can permanently lift the I.Q.s of individuals, even though short-term interventions like Head Start, as they note, have only short-term effects. See Gerald Dworkin and Ned Block, "IQ, Heritability, and Inequality: Part II," *Philosophy and Public Affairs* Fall (1974): pp. 40–99.

19. See Pateman, *Participation and Democratic Theory,* chapters 3 and 4, for evidence of the salutary effects of participation on workers' abilities as well as on their sense of efficacy.

20. Even Plato in *The Republic* designs institutional mechanisms that are meant to control possible wayward temptations of the philosopher rulers.

21. See Charles Murray, *Losing Ground: American Social Policy 1950–1980* (New York: Basic Books, 1984), for a major example of this argument.

22. See John Schwarz, *America's Hidden Success: A Reassessment of Twenty Years of American Social Policy,* 2nd edition (New York: W. W. Norton, 1988).

23. See Stuart Hill, *Democratic Values and Technological Choices* (Stanford: Stanford University Press, 1992), chapter 3, for a full discussion of this process and some measure of its reliability. See also Samuel Popkin, *The Reasoning Voter,* p. 47, for evidence that citizens engage in this kind of reasoning.

24. See Kenneth Arrow, *Social Choice and Individual Values,* 2nd edition (New Haven: Yale University Press, 1963), for an explanation of this; see Russell Hardin, "Difficulties in the Notion of Economic Rationality," *Social Science Information* 23 (1984): pp. 453–467, especially p. 461.

25. See Herbert A. Simon, *Reason in Human Affairs* (Stanford: Stanford University Press, 1983), chapter 1, for a discussion of the incapacity of human beings to elaborate preference orderings of this type. See also Russell Hardin, *Morality Within the Limits of Reason* (Chicago: University of Chicago Press, 1988), chapter 5.

PART THREE

Principles and Problems of Democratic Institutions

CHAPTER SIX

Equality and Legislative Representation

The role of citizens in a democratic society is to choose the overall aims of the society. When citizens play this role they are sovereign over the society they live in and they are plausibly political equals as long as they have equal resources in the process of choosing the aims. But this contribution is not sufficient to make law and policy. Here the issue is to determine the proper roles of the other parts of the political decision-making system. What are the roles of these other parts? How are they related to the contribution of citizens?

Law and policy are the actions of a democratic society whose aims are chosen by the citizens. The citizens do not however choose the means for achieving their aims, nor do they choose the compromises between conceptions of aims necessary to make collective decisions. They have neither the expertise nor the time to concern themselves with the complex tasks of compromise and implementation. The other parts of the political division of labor, made up of persons who specialize in these tasks, make law and policy. The group that chooses the laws and policies that bind citizens is the legislative assembly.

In this chapter I will discuss the role of the legislative assembly in a democratic process regulated by the choice of aims model of citizenship and committed to the advancement of citizens' interests in collective features of society and political equality. I will discuss the methods by which the aims citizens choose are transmitted to the legislature. The electoral system performs this function. Basic principles for evaluating electoral and legislative systems will be elaborated and defended. And I will discuss partial solutions to the agency problem discussed in Chapter 5 as well the problem of the complexity of aims. The main thrust of this chapter is to provide a defense of party list proportional representation as the best system for electing and organizing the legislature.

Political Responsibility

Legislators must attempt to bring about the ends that the citizens choose; in doing so, they encounter two obstacles. First, the aims of citizens do not agree with one another. Usually, these differences must be compromised in order to pass legislation, even when that legislation requires merely majority rule to pass into law. Second, since laws involve concrete solutions to concrete problems, the specification of the aims is not sufficient to make law. Laws are the means by which the aims of citizens are realized. Legislators must decide what the best means are. These tasks are the two functions of the legislative assembly, and they are similar. As long as the aims of citizens are specified in a sufficiently articulate way, finding compromises and discerning the means to achieve aims are mostly technical tasks requiring expertise and skill. They need not interfere with realizing the citizens' aims.

That legislators must determine the means to achieve citizens' aims implies that they have a set of complex responsibilities to citizens. Political responsibility is a relation between a principal and an agent that gives some primacy to the principal. In political responsibility, the citizen is the principal and the legislator is the agent. The citizens have primacy; they are the ones to whom the legislators are responsible. In a democratic society everyone agrees that legislators are responsible to citizens; what they disagree on is the nature of this responsibility. Some think that legislators are responsible to citizens in only a weak sense. Others think that citizens ought to have a large say in what legislators do. We will discuss some different notions of political responsibility so that we can have a clearer idea of the appropriate relation between legislators and citizens. It will not be necessary to decide which one of these notions is the right view of the concept of political responsibility. Our task is ultimately a normative one. We desire to understand the nature of the responsibility of legislators to citizens in a society in which citizens are politically equal and which has a complex division of labor wherein citizens have the role of choosing the aims. Here I will lay out some basic distinctions that are important to the subsequent discussion. These distinctions concern the bases, modes, contents, subjects, and objects of political responsibility.

Formal Accounts of Political Responsibility

The main division in conceptions of political responsibility is between the *formalist* and *substantive* accounts. These two accounts, which are concerned with the *basis of political responsibility,* define the primacy of citizens to legislators differently. Formalist accounts define the primacy of the principal in terms of a set of rules that give the principal the power to initiate, terminate, or merely disassociate the principal from the services of the agent. If I choose someone to do some work for me and I have the power to terminate those services, that person is responsible to me for performing those services. What the formalist account says is that it is merely in virtue of my having chosen the person or merely my being able to terminate the services that makes the person responsible to me. Her responsibility to me does not include any substantive duty on her part to do anything; it merely involves my having the power to hire her or to terminate her service.

Probably the most extreme formalist account of the relation between political leaders and citizens in a democracy has been offered by Schumpeter. His account comes down to the claim that political leaders are responsible to citizens insofar as they are elected and dismissable by means of the electoral vote. The responsibility of legislators to citizens involves nothing more. They may do whatever they think best, and they may pursue whatever course of action and aims they think appropriate. They need not take the citizens' interests or judgments into account. But they are responsible to the citizens inasmuch as the citizens elect them and may dismiss them. The citizens still have a kind of formal primacy in their relation to the legislator even though the legislator is not bound to do anything the citizen desires and the citizen may have no understanding of what the legislator does. This minimal conception of the responsibility of legislators to citizens corresponds with Schumpeter's conception of the minimal role citizens play in a democratic society. Citizens have primacy in such a society only in a technical sense that may not imply that they have much influence over the decisions legislators make.[1]

Formalist accounts need not be as minimal as Schumpeter's. In addition to requiring that the principal have the power to choose or reject the agent, some accounts include a description of the conditions under which these actions of initiation and dismissal must take place. Some have argued that only when the principal is informed about his or her choices can the agent rightfully be said to be responsible to the principal. Others have required that the principal have chosen the agent from among a variety of alternatives in order for the agent to be properly said to be responsible to the principal. They would say that even when a legislator has been chosen by a majority of the citizens, if the citizens had few alternatives and continue to lack significant options, then the legislator is not responsible to the citizens. Some would say that if the citizens did not have the opportunity to inform themselves about the options, then the candidate they voted for is not politically responsible to them. In effect this implies that such a legislator is not a legitimate maker of laws for the citizens. One such stronger account is given by John Plamenatz: "There is political responsibility where two conditions hold: where citizens are free to criticize their rulers and to come together to make demands on them and to win support for the policies they favor and the beliefs they hold; and where the supreme makers of law and policy are elected to their offices in free and periodic elections."[2] For Plamenatz, the first condition is fulfilled only when there is a wide variety of organized groups who reflect the distribution of opinions and interests in the society and who can take demands to the leaders. The second condition implies the existence of significant and intelligible alternatives from which to choose.[3] But Plamenatz rejects a condition of informed choice on the ground that it would make political responsibility impossible.[4] He seems to think that citizens could not be sufficiently informed to meet this requirement. As a consequence, he thinks it is unreasonable to impose the condition of informed choice on the ascription of political responsibility of legislators to citizens. Unfortunately he does not say what this impossible condition of sufficient information is.

It is unclear how the other conditions on political responsibility make any sense when citizens are not informed. In particular, why does it matter that there be intelligible and significantly different alternatives if the main body of citizens do not and are not likely to know about these differences? Surely, there is no reason to insist on significantly different alternatives unless one can be informed about those different alternatives in some substantive way. One must understand the different alternatives as significantly different for oneself or for whomever is the relevant object of the proposed policy. The reason is that the condition of significant alternatives refers to differences in alternatives from the point of view of the citizen, not from the point of view of the leaders themselves. Hence, a condition of a variety of alternatives seems pointless without some kind of condition of informedness.

Plamenatz's worry that citizens cannot have the information necessary to satisfy the informedness condition is legitimate. Our discussion of the problem of information in Part Two bears this out. But this worry seems to undermine the purely formalist account of political responsibility. It gives too much discretion to legislators to do what they desire while citizens remain uninformed about what they do. The conclusion that ought to be drawn from the observation about the problem of information, however, is that the formal conception of political responsibility ought to be supplemented by a more substantive conception of political responsibility because citizens cannot be expected to be fully informed about their legislators' activities. At least we ought to draw this conclusion if we are to hold to the democratic ideals defended above as well as the choice of aims model of citizenship. Or so we shall see.

Substantive Accounts of Political Responsibility

A substantive account of political responsibility imposes duties on the agent. Whereas formal accounts of political responsibility require merely that the agent be chosen in a certain way by the principal, substantive accounts state that the agent is bound to act in certain ways in relation to the principal. The agent may be bound to advance the interests of the principal or to advance the principal's view of the best course of action or even to do what is right for the principal. Examples of cases of substantive responsibility of the agent to the principal are the parent-child relation and the doctor-patient relation. A doctor is responsible to her patient to the extent that she must advance the patient's interests in health even under circumstances where the patient does not have a clear idea of what will advance his interests. The doctor is not merely responsible in the sense that she can be hired or fired, she is under an obligation to advance the patient's interests. Parents are responsible to their children in an even stronger sense. They are charged not only with devising the proper means for achieving the child's interests but also with guiding the child's conception of his interests as well as doing what is right by the child. The parents must perform these duties in accordance with their understanding of what the child's interests are as well as what will advance those interests in a morally desirable way.

Strictly speaking, substantive views of political responsibility do not require any action on the part of the principal. The most extreme version of substantive political responsibility is Plato's conception of the relation between ruler and ruled in *The Republic*. In this account the rulers are responsible to the rest of the population inasmuch as they are charged with discerning the good for the common citizens and determining the means for achieving that good.[5] Often though, substantive and formal elements are combined in a single conception of political responsibility. Indeed, theories that include strong substantive elements also include the requirement of election and dismissal. The relation between citizen and legislator must carry some formal element in a democratic theory insofar as democracy requires that citizens play some kind of active role in organizing society and that legislators are the ultimate makers of law. Only if legislators are subject to election and dismissal by citizens can it be said that citizens are playing an active role in the making of law in a society. As an example of this kind of mixed approach, the mandate theory of political responsibility requires that political parties put forth clear and intelligible programs and that when they are elected to office they follow through with their programs on the assumption that the programs are the reason for which they were elected. Here political responsibility amounts to being selected and dismissable by the electorate as well as being required to follow through with a previously announced substantive program.[6] I will articulate a mixed account as well in what follows.

Trustee and Delegate

Substantive views differ in whether they regard the agent as a trustee or a delegate or both. These are the two *modes of political responsibility*. An account of the political responsibility of political leaders might require that they be delegates for ordinary citizens. Or it might require that they be trustees for the interests of their citizens. The basic difference between the two is that the delegate is under an obligation to act as the principal says, whereas the trustee not only acts in the place of the principal, she thinks for the principal.

As a delegate, an agent has the responsibility of carrying out the express wishes of the principal. A delegate does not have the liberty of making adjustments or substituting his or her own judgment for that of the principal, even concerning those matters where the delegate has a better estimate of the principal's interests or aims or the means to achieving the aims of the principal. The function of a delegate is really to save time and resources for the principal. A delegate is not chosen for his specialization in the collection of information or its processing. There is no need for substitution of judgment.

A trustee, however, is chosen for the purpose of substituting his judgment for that of the principal. The trustee has discretion to choose a course of action within certain limits. It is important that someone have a trustee when they can benefit from the trustee's superior judgment. In this respect, parent and doctor are, to different extents, trustees. The primacy of the principal in this connection is in the fact that it is the principal's interests, moral nature, or point of view that the trustee is entrusted to advance. The principal may not have a clear idea of her interests or of their implications, or she may not have a clear idea of her point of view or its implications in a particular context. The trustee is expected to have or to be able to discern the proper understanding of the matter, whereas the principal is not. This asymmetry may be for reasons of difference in capacity, but it need not be. In a division of labor, it will be useful for the people to entrust others with tasks they could very easily carry out themselves but for the fact that they have other tasks to carry out. This division of labor is true for delegation as well, but trusteeship entails that one person judges for the other as well as acts.

The most crucial implication of this distinction in politics is that a delegate does not deliberate about what to do whereas a trustee is required to deliberate on what the best course of action is. If members of a legislative assembly are delegates for citizens, they are required not to engage in deliberation about those matters for which the citizens have chosen them since this involves the possibility of changing their preferences and thus substituting their judgment for that of the citizen. By contrast, if legislators are thought of as trustees, then the legislative assembly may be a deliberative body, as Edmund Burke saw.[7] The legislators qua trustees discuss amongst themselves the proper course of action without regard to what the citizens think should be done.

Unlike what Burke thought, both trustees and delegates can advance moral concerns as well as the interests of the principal. A delegate can advance the principal's conception of the common good or justice, whereas a trustee may be charged with advancing the interests of the principal. Hence the *content of political responsibility* can vary whether one is a trustee or a delegate. And legislative assemblies can be just as much concerned with the common good and justice whether the legislators are delegates or trustees. Legislative assemblies can be mere forums for bargaining for the interests of citizens whether the legislators are delegates or trustees.

Another issue concerns the *subject of political responsibility*. Who or what is the agent? In some cases an individual is an agent and in others a group of persons can be an agent. In politics, either individual legislators or political parties can be responsible to the citizens. In the latter case, individual legislators would be collectively responsible, as members of parties, to the citizens.

A final important distinction for a theory of political responsibility concerns different views of the *object of responsibility*. In most principal-agent relations, the person to whom the agent is responsible is quite clear. The doctor is responsible to the patient; the parent is responsible to the child. The attorney is responsible to the client. The question is, To whom is the legislator responsible? In democratic politics there seem to be three possible objects of responsibility. A legislator can be responsible to those who voted for her. A legislator can be responsible to all the members of the district or group from which she has been elected. Alternatively, a legislator can be responsible to every citizen of the society of which she is a member.

To illustrate these distinctions in object of responsibility, consider that in single-member district elections, such as elections for the House of Representatives in the United States, a legislator will be elected by a majority of her district. Is she responsible to the minority who voted against her to the same extent as she is to the majority that elected her? Or is she responsible to all the people of the United States, as Edmund Burke might say? The single-member district system allows three different answers. In proportional representation schemes, a legislator is elected in some sense unanimously, but even here we can ask whether he is responsible to all citizens or merely to those who have voted for him?

An Approach to Political Responsibility

We are now in a position to lay out a conception of political responsibility that accords with the democratic ideals and complements the role of citizens as choosers of aims. The political responsibility of members of the government is not to be defended by means of definitions but rather by determining what relations between citizens and political organizations might advance the citizens' interests in collective properties of society, political equality, and rational deliberation overall in a manner consistent with the need for a division of labor wherein citizens have the role of choosers of aims.

Since citizens ought to be choosers of aims, we ought to think of members of the government as delegates of the citizens with respect to the aims that citizens choose. In particular we ought to see legislators as delegates for the different and conflicting aims that citizens have for their society. They are charged with the task of figuring out the means to achieving the aims that the citizens have expressed. Thus, legislators may not substitute their own judgment for those of the citizens with regard to the aims of society. The legislator does not have discretion to choose a new set of aims once in the legislature. Therefore, in this account, with regard to the basic schedule of aims, the legislators' preference ordering ought to be fixed by the citizens and legislators are not to engage in deliberation over the ends themselves. Those preferences over the ends are to remain fixed during the legislative session.

This requirement on legislators results from the fact that those who choose the aims of the society are the ones who hold decision-making authority. When legislators assume authority to set the ends of legislation they substitute their choices of the aims of society for those of the citizens and thus reduce the contribution citizens make to democratic decisionmaking. They usurp citizens' authority and undermine the political equality of citizens.

Someone might object that if the legislator changes her mind about what aims society ought to choose, then she cannot in good conscience pursue the aims the citizens have chosen. In response to this objection, recall that the relations of citizens and legislators are themselves normatively defensible relations. They are relations that are meant to establish political equality in a society in which there must be a division of labor and in which there is considerable disagreement as to what ought to be done. Thus, we ought to see the citizen's relation to the legislator as similar to the relation among persons in which one has legitimate authority and the other must carry out the authoritative directives of the other. The second does not have discretion to make her own choice, and if she disagrees with the authority then she must still comply with the authority as long as the relations are constituted in a just and reasonable way. At the limit, the person charged with carrying out a task she does not believe in may resign her position, but we do not think she ought to decide for herself.

An objection of a different sort is that as long as the legislator is dismissable in periodic elections, the citizens can vote against her for following a different course than they have chosen. This is the formalist account of political responsibility. But clearly dismissability is not sufficient. Recall Plamenatz's worry about the informedness of citizens. In order for citizens to dismiss a legislator on the basis of her failure to pursue an aim they chose, they would have to be informed about this failure. This job is not impossible, but it would impose an extra burden on citizens, making their tasks more difficult. Citizens would have to know whether a legislator had changed aims; there would be a lot of controversy about whether such changes had taken place if such actions were permitted and regularly done. Citizens would have to figure out whether a legislator was likely to change his or her conception of aims in midsession, which would also impose needless burdens on citizens. Since it is important to reduce the cognitive tasks of citizens to whatever extent is consistent with political equality, the relation between citizen and legislator ought to be one of delegation and not merely a formal relation of election and dismissal. Delegation plays an important role in economizing on the cognitive requirements of citizens.

Some may argue that legislators may know more about the aims that a society ought to choose than citizens; therefore, they ought to be able to think independently about those aims and make their own choices. But we have chosen the aims model partly because what aims are desirable is precisely the kind of subject in which the expertise of some is not likely to give them much more insight than others. Legislators are not likely to know much more about the aims that are worthy of pursuing than ordinary citizens, especially after ordinary citizens have been informed by the kind of process of deliberation that we have already discussed and that will be discussed in more detail later. Thus, giving legislators authority to change aims would be an arbitrary infringement on the right of citizens to be equal members of the political community.

A final kind of objection is that if there is a major change in the economic and political environment then legislators must have the ability to adapt and adjust to it. They cannot be inflexibly tied to the aims the citizens have assigned to them because such inflexibility would leave the society incapable of dealing with major crises. But this objection to a large extent confuses the choice of aims and the choice of means. Major crises in the political, social, and economic environment need not affect the choice of aims at all; they most often will affect the choice of means for achieving those aims. Once the aims of society have been chosen, the means must be suited to the particular set of obstacles in the way of realizing the aims. The aims themselves need not change.

Legislators must determine the means for achieving the aims fixed by citizens. They must also determine the best way to compromise between citizens' aims when they conflict. These duties give legislators a great deal of discretion, and they give them discretion in those areas where they are genuinely more likely to have some expertise. At the same time, if the legislature genuinely pursues the aims the citizens choose, the fundamental equality among citizens is not threatened. Thus, legislators ought to be the trustees of citizens with regard to the choice of means and necessary compromises.

Legislators engage in deliberation about the means for achieving the ends, and they may also engage in negotiation and compromise with other legislators in order to pass legislation. Their activities are to be limited to deliberation about means and bargaining with other legislators. Citizens ought to give a suitably articulated idea of the kinds of trade-offs acceptable to them, and the legislators bargain with these in mind to achieve the best possible compromise among citizens' announced schedules of trade-offs.

These claims argue in part against a large group of theorists who have said that the legislative body ought to be primarily deliberative. The civic republican view of representative assemblies is that they ought to engage in deliberation about all matters.[8] They are to deliberate about the common good as well as the means to achieving it. My claim is that the legislative body ought not to be a deliberative assembly with regard to ends, although it may be with regard to means. The deliberative process regarding aims ought to reside in the society among ordinary citizens. If a legislator were to deliberate with other legislators with the intention that the conclusions of these deliberations would be the basis of their voting, then they would be putting their own aims above those of the citizens, even in areas where they cannot claim any special expertise, thus undermining the ideal of equality. Conversely, the legislative assembly ought to be a deliberative assembly with regard to the choice of means to citizens' aims as well as with regard to the best compromises between opposed aims. The legislators ought also to engage in deliberation with the various groups in society that have special expertise in subjects relating to the means legislators are looking for.

It is important here to note that it is only in the position as legislator that the legislator may not engage in deliberation about ends with other legislators. Inasmuch as legislators are citizens or leaders of parties or secondary associations, they are charged with the task of deliberating with an open mind about ends. It is only their voting behavior in the legislature that is to be constrained by the constituency's preferences.

How do the legislators get into the legislature? Inasmuch as citizens are to make an active contribution to political decisionmaking, they ought to elect the legislators in periodic elections. Legislators must campaign for votes on the basis of promises to pursue certain aims. Then citizens in effect choose the aims by choosing legislators who have stated that they will pursue those aims. Legislators attempt to persuade citizens of the superiority of certain aims, and at election time citizens must vote for the legislator who will pursue the aims they think are best. Elections, on this account, are primarily occasions for completing large-scale social deliberation over aims. Political parties, candidate legislators, and interest groups contribute to this process before and during election campaigns. They play crucial roles in the articulation of the points of view and understanding of citizens. The process of an election campaign ideally involves candidate persons or parties articulating overall packages of ends, including some schedule of trade-offs for those ends, and attempting to persuade citizens of the worthiness of those ends. Citizens then choose which among the packages of ends they prefer. Once a legislator is elected, he has the duty to represent the aims of the citizens for which he was elected. He no longer has the discretion to change his conception of the appropriate ends. I will discuss further the kinds of electoral systems that are most appropriate to these purposes.

The Principle of Voluntary Proportionality

So far I have argued that the contribution of legislators is to determine the means for achieving the aims of citizens. Legislators are the delegates of citizens with regard to the aims citizens have chosen. At the same time legislators are the trustees of citizens with regard to the means for achieving those aims. The legislature is a deliberative assembly only with regard to the means for implementing the aims of citizens. Furthermore, the election of legislators to the legislative assembly is the final occasion for large-scale social deliberation about aims among citizens. The election itself is a way for the citizens to convey their conceptions of aims to the legislative assembly. It takes place after deliberation is over and thus is a part of the adversarial part of equality. When individuals who are political equals are unable to convince each other of the superiority of their conceptions of aims and they must make a collective decision, then their influence on the decision-making process ought to be in accord with a principle of numerical equality, giving each person an equal amount of power in the decision-making process. Thus, more power goes to those positions that have more support.

Furthermore, as I argued in Chapter 2, each person ought to have an equal say in the determination of the agenda for making decisions when there is disagreement. The basic choice of the different aims the legislature is to pursue defines the basic agenda for the decisionmaking of the legislature, at least as far as the citizens ought to be concerned. What aims the legislature is to pursue, and how many legislators are assigned to advance each package of basic aims, defines the basic agenda for its decisionmaking.

The electoral process then ought to be in accordance with a principle of numerical equality in which the citizens are the basic agenda setters and the choosers of aims. What does this requirement of political equality entail? In other words, how is the number of legislators representing different views of aims of the citizenry to be related to the number of citizens who hold these different views? In my view, the only principle compatible with a principle of political equality in this context is a principle of voluntary proportionality between the number of citizens who support each of the different overall aims and the number of legislators committed to those aims in the legislature.

Since the legislators are to be occupied with bargaining and making compromises and finally with voting by means of an egalitarian decision-making procedure, they too must decide in accordance with a principle of numerical equality. Bargaining and voting in an egalitarian society are those activities individuals engage in when they have failed to persuade each other. Thus, in an egalitarian society, those processes ought to be regulated by the norm of numerical equality. Those positions that have more support will in effect have more bargaining power on their side and more voting power as well. This method is in accordance with the basic principle of egalitarian justice when there is no longer any time for deliberation among persons. But if citizens are to be the ultimate choosers of aims, then the number of citizens who support each overall package of aims ought to be proportionally represented in the legislature.

The proportionality ought to hold not between merely objective features of the citizenry and the legislature but between those features that the citizens think are salient and thereby choose to make issues of. It ought to be a voluntary proportionality. The idea here is not that the legislature is a reflection of the citizenry in terms of certain social cleavages in the citizenry.[9] The composition of the legislature is in proportion to the composition of the citizenry in terms of what the citizenry chooses to be the salient issues to be decided upon. A society may be divided in terms of ethnic, religious, or linguistic cleavages. But the citizens, or at least some of them, may choose to ignore these cleavages on the grounds that other issues are more important to them. It is the choices of the citizens that ought to be reflected proportionally in the legislature. In this way the citizens' views of the ends of society are not only reflected by the legislature, the composition of the legislature is actively determined by the choices of the citizens. The relation of proportionality is not a mere relation of reflection but one that supposes the active participation of the citizens and the primacy of the citizens' active participation in determining the proportion of the legislators devoted to various aims. This arrangement not only gives the citizens power over the choice of ends, it also assigns them a substantial agenda-setting function. Since the aims are the most important component of the choices legislatures make, citizens are in the driver's seat in the political decision-making process.

The principle of voluntary proportionality ensures equality among citizens in a number of ways. One, when there is in place an effective norm binding legislators to pursuing the aims for which they were elected, citizens are the determiners of the basic package of aims embodied in legislation and thus are sovereign. Two, insofar as the number of legislators who are delegates for each set of aims is proportional with the number of citizens who think those aims ought to be pursued, a basic numerical equality obtains among citizens over the political decision-making process. Three, it ensures that citizens are the ultimate source of the agenda wherein the final collective decisions are made. Thus, it ensures that citizens are the ultimate power in society and politically equal.

This conception of the legislature does, however, require what I call *legislative autonomy*. The legislature is to be insulated from pressures from within the society once it is in place. Thus, legislators are not to make deals with citizens who are not legislators once the assembly is elected. Such deals would greatly increase the power of those citizens. It would also diminish the powers of the other citizens even more since such deals are usually made in secret and thus diminish the relation of delegation between citizens and legislator in ways of which citizens are not aware. The legislature is to negotiate autonomously once it is in session. In order to achieve such autonomy, severe limits on campaign finance, if not a complete ban on private campaign finance, must be imposed. At the same time the legislature need not be autonomous with regard to deliberation about the means for achieving citizen's aims or even with regard to conceptions of how to make good compromises. Here the legislature always needs as much help as it can get, and there is no loss of political equality if the legislators are able to learn new things about how to bring about the aims that citizens have chosen.

Finally, political parties ought to be the main contestants in this process. Individual candidates tend to distract attention from the issues facing citizens. Parties can focus attention on the basic aims that citizens are to be thinking about. There are four reasons political parties ought to be the main contestants: First, when individual candidates become most important, a lot of attention focuses on matters of personality and their personal lives as opposed to substance. But these issues are irrelevant to the basic concerns of citizens. Second, to have individual candidates running independently complicates the issue space in a way that makes choice much more obscure for citizens. It requires that citizens have a lot more information when they are making decisions. Usually, the focus on candidates only apparently complicates the issues. In fact it simply introduces a lot of extra noise into the electoral process since each candidate needs to separate him- or herself out from the others. Third, there is a tendency towards fragmentation when individual candidates are primary. This fragmentation occurs because each candidate is out for himself or herself, which will complicate the bargaining processes immensely. Finally, candidates vary a lot in their abilities to negotiate and compromise. As a consequence, mere competence becomes a much larger issue in campaigns. All of these facts suggest that making individual candidates the focus of the electoral system and the system of representation needlessly complicates the process of choosing the basic aims for the society. Since it is imperative to set up the political system in a way that economizes on the cognitive activities of citizens, a better system is to be preferred.

An electoral system that focuses on parties and a system of representation that has parties representing citizens does economize on the cognitive tasks of citizens. Parties simplify the process of choice to include only basic aims, and they call attention to the issues rather than individual personalities. They contribute to the sovereignty of citizens with regard to aims. Also, parties tend to even out individual differences in abilities to negotiate and compromise since there are many members in each party; therefore, these features do not play as important a role in campaigning. In this way parties can contribute to reducing information costs to citizens since citizens need not be as afraid that their right-thinking candidate is incompetent at the task of negotiating with other legislators. Also, the fundamental equality of citizens with regard to the aims is not undermined by arbitrary differences in negotiating abilities among persons.

Furthermore, political parties can play an important oversight role in guaranteeing that individual candidates actually pursue the aims for which they are elected. Since individual politicians are subordinate to the party and the party is identified by the set of aims that it is bound to pursue, individual politicians are less likely to stray from the pursuit of aims they have been elected to pursue. Thus, parties can help in the process of monitoring and alleviate the agency problem we have described. Finally, parties can have a division of labor in the process of negotiating and discovering the means for achieving aims. The party can afford to have members who are specialists in different areas of expertise. This specialization enhances the abilities of parties to negotiate and find the means for pursuing whole packages of aims. Inasmuch as aims are complementary it is important that packages be pursued in a coherent fashion, and parties can help achieve this coherence. For these reasons, parties ought to play the chief role in electoral and legislative processes.

Proportional Representation

We have established the role that the legislature ought to play in a democratic society. Legislative assemblies are the entities in modern societies that make law and policy binding on all the citizens. Legislatures ought to choose the means for achieving the aims citizens have decided on. A legislator is a delegate for the citizen with regard to the aims and a trustee with regard to the means. Furthermore, the legislature ought to have a distribution of support for different packages of aims that is proportional to the support for those packages among the citizens in the society. The proportional relation ought to be one that is voluntarily chosen by citizens. The chief representatives of the citizens ought to be political parties in the legislative assembly. All of these propositions are supported by the principle of political equality and the choice of aims model of citizenship. Here I will argue for a scheme of representation and elections called party list proportional representation. By way of contrast, I will first describe the electoral systems in the United States and Great Britain, which are schemes of single-member district representation.

In a single-member district system of representation, the society is divided up into geographical districts from which a legislator is elected to the legislative assembly. Each legislator is elected by a majority or a plurality of the citizens in his or her district. These districts are carved up in accordance with one or both of the following principles. First, the districts are usually of equal population. This assures a kind of equality of representation in the legislature; it assures that the principle of one-person one-vote holds in such a system. Not only does each person have a vote but, insofar as districts are of equal size, the strength of a vote in one district is the same as the strength of a vote from any other district. Thus, a kind of elementary equality among citizens is achieved in this system. Second, if any group in the society is salient with respect to the issues but is not well represented by a particular arrangement of districts, then the districts are sometimes reshaped so as to give that group a better chance of electing a member to the legislature. The single-member district method of representation can completely underrepresent minorities in the legislature if the minorities do not have a majority in many districts. In the United States, electoral districts have been changed so as to ensure greater presence of minorities in legislatures. This practice has been, of course, a major source of controversy in American politics.[10]

A number of well-known objections have been made to single-member district representation.[11] I will focus on violations of the principles of voluntary proportionality enumerated above. Proportionality in a single-member district system can easily be lost in a variety of ways. There can be citizens of a certain point of view who are a majority in the society but who are represented in such a legislature by a minority of legislators. These citizens may be a very large majority in a few districts and very large minorities in the rest, making them a majority of the population overall but giving them a minority of representatives in the legislature. Single-member district systems can eliminate majorities.

Consider the following highly simplified example: There are two options, A and B, on a contested policy issue, and there are three districts that have five voters each. In each district two candidates present themselves for election who are concerned to advance either option A or B. Suppose that majority rule is the decision rule for each district, and it is the decision rule for the legislative assembly. In district 1 there are citizens C1–C5; in district 2, C6–C10; and in district 3, C11–C15. Suppose furthermore that citizens C1–C3, C6–C8, and C11 support A and the corresponding candidate in their districts. Citizens C4, C5, C9, C10, C12–C15 support policy B and its corresponding candidates. All the citizens are distributed as in the following table:

Dist. 1	Dist. 2	Dist. 3
A B	A B	A B
C1–C5	C6–C10	C11–C15

With that distribution of citizens and preferences, the candidates favoring A will receive majorities in district 1 and in district 2, whereas the candidate supporting B will be elected in only district 3. Thus supporters of A will be in the majority in the legislature. They will win the ultimate policy contest if this is the only issue involved. This is true despite the fact that a majority of eight citizens support B.[12] This undermining of the principle of proportionality is quite severe since it suggests that the position that would have become law if proportionality had obtained will not become law.

Another violation of proportionality is that if there are substantial minorities that are evenly distributed throughout the society, they may not be able to have any legislators attempting to advance their points of view in the legislature. For example, in the above case, suppose that option B were supported by C4, C5, C9, C10, C14, and C15. A total of six out of fifteen members of the society would support B, and yet no one in the legislature would be supporting B. This outcome does not seem very significant if all the others support A since A would win anyway in the policy conflict. But suppose that three voters support A in district 1 and three voters support C in district 2 and three support D in district 3. In this case, though more voters supported B than any other alternative, B would not even be represented in the legislature, and thus there would not even be a need for compromise on B. This outcome is also a serious violation of proportionality since it means a real diminishment of power over the aims of society for those who support B. Thus, single-member district representation can seriously underrepresent minorities.[13]

One way to solve these problems is by changing the legislative districts from which legislators are elected through reapportionment. Taking the districts in the previous table, we might rearrange district 1 so that it includes voter C9. This way candidates who support option B will win in district 1, although they will lose in 2 and 3. But who will do the reapportioning? The legislature itself is often not given this task because the many legislators have incentives to preserve the current district boundaries since they are elected in them. The task is sometimes entrusted to the courts in the United States for this reason.[14] But giving the task to the courts implies that the courts must determine who the relevant groups are that should be represented in the legislature. The courts must decide what the relevant issues are and who is likely to support which alternatives in those issues. This implies that proportionality, if it arises, is based not on the active choice of the citizens but on features of the citizenry selected by others. The citizenry plays a much smaller role in determining what the issues are and the relevantly different positions on those issues. Therefore, the agenda-setting role of citizens is greatly diminished. Thus, attempts at reapportionment partially solve one problem of equality only by introducing another.

Another problem is that the single-member district system seems to be committed to the salience of geographical districts in determining issues and relevant options. It makes it likely that geographical considerations will become important in campaigns even if citizens are not particularly interested in geographical issues. But why should geography play such a large role in deciding which political issues are important and which are not? The power to decide whether geographical considerations are important is an agenda-setting power that should be held by the citizens. Single-member district representation, however, takes this power out of the hands of citizens.

Someone might object to my arguments by saying that legislators in a single-member district system should be responsible not only to those who vote for them but to their districts as a whole. In that case, there would not be underrepresentation of any sort. In response to this, such a conception of responsibility undermines the delegate function of the legislator in the assembly. For whose point of view will he be a delegate? He will not be a delegate to the majority that elected him or for the minority since he is representing both and their positions diverge. He must independently determine what aims to advance if he is to be thought of as the representative of the whole district. Such a view requires either a trusteeship conception of the relation of the legislator to the citizen, even with regard to the ends the society is to aim for, or a formalistic account of the responsibility of legislator to citizen.

Both of these alternatives entail a loss of equality for the citizens in the society. The trusteeship conception implies that the legislator should substitute his judgment about the proper aims of society for those of the citizens. Again, he would have to rely on his own judgment since the aims of the majority and the minority are to a great extent opposed. This process would undermine the choice of aims model of citizenship and political equality. In the formalistic approach, since the legislator can be dismissed by the citizens, the legislator can be said to be responsible to the citizens. But as we have seen, this account imposes too serious a burden on citizens' information-gathering activities; it requires them to follow extensively the activities of legislators during the legislative session. But this cognitive burden ought not and need not be imposed on ordinary citizens. Finally, it is a burden that citizens will invariably have different abilities to carry. Thus, it reintroduces political inequality. This defense of single-member district representation must fail.

A system of proportional representation is designed to overcome these difficulties. I shall describe a simplified version of this system, the party list system of proportional representation. Proportional representation entails that a number of parties are put up for election to seats in the legislature. In such a system a person can vote for any party he wishes and parties acquire seats in the legislature in proportion to the number of votes they receive throughout the country. Thus, if a party receives 25 percent of the vote in an election, then it gets 25 percent of the seats in the legislative assembly. If the party receives merely 5 percent of the vote, then it receives 5 percent of the seats in the legislature. As a consequence, parties have seats in the assembly roughly in proportion to the number of votes they have received from the citizens.

We can see that the problems of proportionality canvassed in the discussion on single-member district representation simply do not arise from the proportional representation scheme. The scheme of proportional representation guarantees, as much as a scheme of representation can, that the number of legislators representing a particular package of aims is the same proportion of the total number of legislators as that of supporters of that package to the number of citizens in the society at large. Thus, the problems of elimination of majorities, overrepresentation of some minorities, and underrepresentation of other minorities are much smaller in this system of representation.[15]

The proportionality is voluntary. What parties are in the legislature and the proportion of seats they hold is decided by the citizens themselves. The definition of the constituency that is represented is determined by the group itself. A constituency for a representative in a scheme of proportional representation is like a voluntary association in which each person joins only if he or she wants to. If a person prefers another party, then she can join its constituency and increase its vote total. Recall that in single-member district representation, there are occasions when some groups are underrepresented so that the proportion of legislators representing that group to the total number of legislators is smaller than the proportion of that group to the whole society. Attempts at rectifying this problem include altering the size and shape of districts so that more individuals from a certain group can be elected. To do this, a judge must decide on the relevant description of the group by means of criteria that seem appropriate to her. This is not a voluntary constituency. The members of this constituency are in it by virtue of the decision of the judge. Consequently, the judge has a lot of power in defining the agenda for decisionmaking. Proportional representation, conversely, gives agenda-setting power to citizens.

This point can be illustrated by comparing proportional representation to another, less familiar kind of single-member district representation: functional representation. Functional representation is a kind of single-member district representation, but it is distinct from the usual kind in that the districts are not geographical units. The districts from which representatives are elected in a scheme of functional representation are groups in the society. For example, the society may be made up of workers, employers, farmers, and service workers. A scheme of functional representation would make the set of workers an electoral district, and the group of employers another district, and the same for the other groups. Each member of a group would then vote for a representative or a number of representatives of that group to sit in the legislature. The legislative assembly would be made up of representatives of these functionally defined groups just as in the United States the assembly is made up of representatives of geographically defined groups.

Functional representation faces the same difficulty as geographical representation in that the relevant groups have to be defined before the electoral process begins. Every worker is a member of the worker constituency whether he or she desires to be or not, and the same holds for the other citizens. The agenda for legislative decisionmaking will be strongly determined by the fact that the representatives are representatives of these groups that have been defined in advance. Again, this takes a substantial amount of agenda-setting power out of the hands of citizens. Such agenda-setting power is an essential component of political equality, and so functional representation does not satisfy the standards set by the democratic ideals. In proportional representation, by contrast, it is up to each citizen to define how his or her interests and points of view differ from others'.

This point is reinforced by the fact that citizens are encouraged to form parties in order to advocate particular packages of ends. In a single-member district, it is more difficult for new political parties defending new packages of aims to arise than it is in proportional representation systems. Societies governed by legislatures with proportional representation tend to have more parties in the legislative assembly than do societies with single-member district systems. The latter tend to have two-party or two-and-a-half party systems, whereas proportional representation schemes tend to produce three or more strong parties in the legislature.[16] Proportional representation simply has fewer barriers to entry into the political system than does single-member district representation. The latter requires that a party receive a majority or plurality in each district where it runs a candidate. Thus, in each district, the tendency is for there to be two parties. Often, indeed, single-member district representation discourages the formation of more than one party. If one party has a sufficiently strong following and support in a community, other parties will simply not put any serious efforts into contesting elections. Thus, the United States during the period between 1896 and 1932 had mostly one-party dominated districts.[17] There was very little party competition, and many citizens had little or nothing to gain from participation. The one-party system continued in the south until the 1980s and continues today in many large cities in the United States. Thus, it is clear that the single-member district system puts serious obstacles in the way of large numbers of citizens having a say in setting the agenda for legislative decisionmaking whereas proportional representation does not. Therefore, proportional representation gives a lot more choice to citizens in the selection of parties to vote for, thus increasing the power of citizens to define the basic legislative agenda.

In addition, proportional representation and the multiparty system it encourages greatly increase what I call the articulation of packages of aims. Parties tend to develop much more specific and distinctive packages of proposals under this system than under the single-member district system. The latter encourages vagueness and ambiguity on important issues as well as complete neglect of many issues. Each party must attempt to appeal to a much larger base of individuals with a much greater diversity of views in order to win an election. The consequence is not an increase in the complexity of programs but rather an increase in attempts to finesse issues of great importance to constituents so as not to offend other constituents. This practice leads to ambiguity and vagueness in the formulation of all programs. Since no one can escape to another party, except to the other, equally vague challenger, parties do not have an incentive to be very specific in their proposals. They also do not need to take much account of the important needs of minorities who are not likely to defect to the opposite party. Again, what this means for citizens is that the packages of aims that citizens develop are not likely to be highly articulate since the main organizations that specialize in developing such packages have little or no incentive to be precise. Consequently, legislators have little guidance from citizens as to what aims they ought to pursue, so citizens do not play the role of choosers of aims well under these conditions.

Thus, proportional representation ensures a voluntary proportionality between supporters of aims in the legislature and supporters of aims among the citizenry that cannot be ensured by single-member district representation. And it ensures that citizens play a more extensive and pervasive role in the setting of the legislative agenda by making constituencies voluntary and permitting the formation of alternative parties when interests and points of view are genuinely distinct. In addition, proportional representation ensures that the process of articulation of aims goes much further than it might in a system of single-member district representation. Thus, it enables citizens to perform their role as choosers of aims for the society and contributes to political equality in the society. I discuss the impact of party list proportional representation on democratic deliberation in Chapter 7.

Proportional Representation, Equality, Vagueness, and Stability

A number of objections have been made against proportional representation that I will now consider. In my view the arguments and the conception of the political system that I have developed above can help us see that these objections can be answered. The first objection is that proportional representation does not promote political equality as I have suggested; it merely promotes a kind of equality in the success individuals' experience in having their preferred candidates win office. Equality of success is not a part of political equality, it is argued, so political equality does not require proportional representation. The second objection is that though proportional representation does make parties be more specific in their proposals during election campaigns, the vagueness of single-member district systems occurs also in a proportional representation system but simply in a different place. The third objection is that although proportional representation may well be more egalitarian in a way, it tends to produce fragmentation, severe conflict, extremism, and, more generally, instability. Thus, the egalitarian goals are undermined by the instability of the system.

First, Charles Beitz claims that both single-member district representation and proportional representation give equal power to citizens, but proportional representation gives more equal prospects of success to citizens in having their preferred candidate elected to the legislature. In each scheme, each citizen has a vote that is equal to everyone else's, which enables each citizen to overcome as much resistance (i.e., other person's votes) as any other citizen in the voting process. The procedural resources that are assigned to each person are the same, so it appears that they are being given equal power.[18] Beitz argues that proportional representation goes beyond this equal power only to the extent that it gives each person the same chance of success in electing a legislator he or she has voted for. But Beitz argues that such equal prospects of success are not necessary to equality. He says that "even if prospects are unequal, public expression will be given to the equal status of all voters as participants in decisionmaking: each will have procedural opportunities to overcome exactly the same amount of resistance." One-person one-vote,

which is shared by these systems of representation, is egalitarian. All
that proportional representation does is give people equal prospects
of getting the outcomes they want. But democracy is not about getting the outcomes you want. Democracy is concerned with a fair
process for getting those outcomes. If proportional representation is
to be shown to be more egalitarian than single-member district representation it must be shown that the process is more egalitarian independent of the outcomes.

We have seen that democratic equality is an equality in the process
of collective decisionmaking. A society is not nondemocratic because
it fails to give everyone equal success in getting what they want. But
Beitz is mistaken in thinking that proportional representation only
equalizes the chances of success for citizens in getting what they
want. On the contrary, proportional representation ensures equality
in the overall process of collective decisionmaking, which cannot be
assured by single-member district representation. To see this, notice
that equality in the collective decision-making process implies equality in the process of determining the laws and policies of the society,
not the composition of the legislature per se. Democratic citizenship
is not essentially a matter of determining who makes legislation. It is
concerned with the making of legislation itself. Political equality is
not concerned with equality in determining who will be in the legislature but with equality in determining how the society will be
arranged. The electoral process and the legislative system are components of this larger process; they are not the end state of the process.
The legislature ought to be understood as a part of a political division
of labor wherein the citizens choose the aims of the society and the
legislature chooses the means for achieving those aims.

In order to elect a legislator on an equal basis, it is sufficient that
each citizen have an equal vote. But making laws and policies is a
two-stage process involving the election of the legislature and the
decisionmaking of the assembly. Even if each of these stages is egalitarian, it does not follow that the combination of stages is. Members
of the legislative assembly have vastly greater power than ordinary
citizens in the sense that they can do much more than citizens can.
Only if legislators are delegates of citizens with respect to aims can
we have equality with regard to control over the laws and policies of
the society.

The relation of delegation can only hold between the majority in a district and the legislator who is elected in that district in a single-member district. But this means that a fundamental requirement of equality among citizens in the process of decisionmaking will be violated in single-member district representation. Referring to the table in the previous section, recall the first example used with voters C1–C12 and candidates supporting A and B. There is a curious feature of this arrangement. If C1 and C12 were to switch preferences so that C1 now came to support B and C12 came to support A, the candidates preferring B would win a majority of legislative seats and B would be the policy outcome. Therefore, this method of deciding on the policy issue violates the property of anonymity. A voting system is anonymous only when the outcomes of the voting do not change when individuals with opposed preferences switch their votes. But the outcome does change in the case of single-member district representation. Indeed, the problems of underrepresentation of majorities, overrepresentation of minorities, and underrepresentation of minorities all contribute to the failure of single-member district representation to ensure anonymity in the process of determining the basic aims the society is to choose. Thus, they all entail that there is inequality among citizens in the process of making laws and policy.

Anonymity is an elementary requirement of equality in voting and thus in equality in the distribution of voting power. It merely states that the outcome of a vote depends only on the numbers of people voting for each alternative, not on who are among the voters on each side. Furthermore, the notion of voting power here is the ability to overcome resistance to having a say in what the aims of society are to be. This is not an outcome notion; it does not say anything about equality of success or chances for success. Hence, it appears one need not look very far to see how the notion of equality in the process can be used to criticize single-member district representation. Indeed, it can be used to defend proportional representation. It will always satisfy anonymity in the choice of aims. Thus, contrary to Beitz's claim, the ideal of political equality provides strong considerations against single-member district representation and in favor of proportional representation.

The second objection has been brought by Anthony Downs. He argues that the vagueness that is inherent in single-member district representation reappears in proportional representation systems at the level of negotiation in the legislature. This is Downs's conclusion: "The type of political system which seems to offer the voter a more definite choice among policies in fact offers him a less definite one. This system may even make it impossible for him to choose a government at all."[19] In a similar vein, Maurice Duverger asks, "What is the point of guaranteeing that each party's number of deputies will be exactly proportional to that of its voters, if it remains free to ally itself with whomever, whenever, and for whatever purpose it wishes, and to change partners at any moment?"[20]

Downs's argument is that the party one votes for in proportional representation will often not be able to control the government because parties rarely acquire a majority under proportional representation. At best the party one votes for will have to enter into a coalition with other parties in order to become a part of the government. What any party does in government depends on the coalitions it makes with other parties. Thus, in order to know what a party is going to do one must know what other parties will be elected to the legislature as well as how many seats they will get. Therefore, to vote in an informed way for a party requires that one know how everyone else is voting. And since others are voting on the basis of their own predictions of what everyone else is doing, the problem of selecting the best party to vote for becomes an overwhelming information problem. As a consequence, Downs argues, each voter is faced with having to vote on the basis of very little real information about whom they are voting for. So, he argues, it merely appears that proportional representation is superior to single-member district representation on the grounds that it gives voters a more definite choice. In fact, he argues that single-member district representation ultimately does a better job at this task since at least one knows that the party one is voting for will take the reigns of government if it wins. Since citizens are less informed about what they are voting for under proportional representation, they have less control over the society, and differences in opportunities to acquire information make for differences in power.

But Downs's argument suffers from some factual difficulties as well as a basic philosophical problem. First, it is not true that single-member district representation does not produce coalition governments. It often does. Often these societies have two and a half parties such that the large parties must make coalitions with the small party or with the other party. Second, Downs assumes that parties are willing to make coalitions with any other party that will help them produce a majority in the legislature. Indeed, the party will choose that coalition that is the minimum necessary to form a governing coalition. This is the theory of the minimum-winning coalition.[21] In this account, a far right-wing party will make a coalition with a far left-wing party if this will produce the smallest coalition necessary to win a majority. If this were true, it would be quite difficult to figure out what a party will do after it acquires seats in the legislature since it could make a coalition with anyone, depending on the size of the other parties. But this claim is mistaken, and there is a lot of empirical evidence that suggests that parties generally enter into coalitions only with parties that are close to them ideologically.[22] Thus, the level of uncertainty is not nearly as high as Downs or Duverger claim. Furthermore, parties often announce in advance whom they will make coalitions with so that voters can take this information into account without too much difficulty when they vote.

Another more important problem with Downs's and Duverger's arguments is that it is not clear why they think that voters are, or ought to be, concerned with determining exactly what the outcome of all the coalition making will be. I have argued that citizens vote in order to choose the aims of society and that they do so by selecting delegates for those aims. The delegates are committed to the aims and will engage in bargaining and coalition building on the basis of those aims. The choice of the aims is what is most important. The bargaining and coalition building are merely means for achieving the aims to the greatest extent possible given the diversity of conceptions of aims in the society. As long as the conceptions of aims are suitably articulate the legislator has a clear guide with which to conduct the coalition building. It is reasonable to have a division of labor in which the legislator bargains for the aims the citizens choose, if one is committed to political equality. Thus, it is not clear that citizens must know what other people will be in the legislature in order to vote informedly for a legislator. Downs's argument that there is more ambiguity of importance in proportional representation schemes than in single-member district schemes fails on factual grounds, but most important it fails on a basic question of principle. Inasmuch as what is important for citizens is to choose the aims of society, Downs's argument does not touch the rationale for proportional representation that we have explored.

The final objection I will briefly consider is that a system of proportional representation may be ineffective in actually controlling the administrative and executive parts of the government. This problem may occur because of instability generated by constant changes of government. Coalition building and the constant process of making laws may induce a constant change of government, which in turn may make the legislature relatively weak in its dealings with the administrative branch of the government. This weakness is because the administrators may not have an incentive to carry out the laws passed by the ruling coalition since it may not be in existence for long, which might make the representatives ineffective delegates of the people. What such arrangements can amount to sometimes is a transfer of power to the administrative branch of government. In some circumstances, this result might suggest that proportional representation is not the best way of realizing the role of the government as delegate of the people.

The trouble with this argument is that there is only some empirical support for the claim that proportional representation does worse on the stability score than single-member district representation. And it is not clear what this evidence implies. Other evidence suggests that the two are quite similar with respect to stability. First, single-member district representation can and does produce great swings between opposing parties that alternate in controlling the government. Great Britain is a good example; ever since the end of World War II, the country has seen swings back and forth from the Labour Party to the Conservative Party. Second, in general some evidence suggests that coalition governments in proportional representation legislatures are as durable as majority governments in single-member district legislatures. Comparative studies within states between single-member district and proportional representation observe that the durability of ruling coalitions in both kinds of system is roughly the same.[23] However, comparative studies have observed that states in which there is proportional representation see more change in governing coalitions than states in which there is single-member district representation. But even that instability does not always affect the stability of policy since often the new coalitions are very similar to the old. Thus, the transfer of power to the administrative branch need not occur. Finally, such instability is not associated empirically with the instability of the state itself. States ruled by proportional representation are no less stable than states ruled by single-member district representation.[24] Therefore, instability is not a clear consideration showing proportional representation schemes to be inferior to other schemes of representation.

This concludes my discussion of arguments for and against proportional representation. In my view it is clearly the system of representation we ought to have if we are to promote the democratic ideals I have defended in Chapter 2 in the context of a political division of labor wherein citizens have the right to choose the basic aims of society.

The Limits of the Contribution of Proportional Representation

Proportional representation will not bring about political equality on its own however. It has little significance in this respect if citizens are not well informed or if there is no reasonable system for monitoring the behavior of the legislature. Proportional representation can help with both of these tasks, as I will show in later chapters. But the scheme of legislative representation does not solve all of these difficulties. Institutions regulating interest groups and political parties must supplement the salutary effects of proportional representation. These institutions will be discussed in the coming chapters.

Another limit on any reliance on proportional representation as a means of securing equality in the collective decision-making procedure when there is a complex division of labor is the fact that in modern democracies legislatures do not and cannot be expected to control the whole of the policy-making apparatus of the state. The administrative apparatus of the state does not function in a simple hierarchical manner, merely carrying out the orders of the legislature. In this simple hierarchical view, elected politicians have complete authority over the functioning of the administrative state. The administrative state is merely a routinized and rationalized organization for carrying out the orders of the legislative parts of the government. It does not make decisions on its own; it only implements the orders of the legislative branch. This is the classical notion of administration.[25]

The trouble with this picture of legislative control is that the administrative parts of the government are too complex to be completely under the control of the legislature. There is not nearly enough time and information for the legislators to exercise control. Hence, administrators have a considerable amount of discretion in the making of policy. In particular this discretion arises because of the considerable control modern democracies exercise over the economy through regulation, subsidization, and planning. The amount of knowledge required for this control makes expertise necessary, which leads to the possibility of a transfer of power from the legislature to the administration. The irony here is that this potential transfer is the consequence of a great extension of the power of the citizens over the society. It seems to bring with it the threat that citizens lose control over the government.[26] However, giving discretion to branches of government does not entail lack of significant control. As long as the citizens retain the ability to choose the aims of society and the administration is committed to implementing those aims, the citizens are still in control of what matters for democracy. Unfortunately, we cannot pursue this argument further here.

Nevertheless, the principles of political responsibility, voluntary proportionality, and legislative autonomy, which regulate the role of the legislative assembly, reconcile political equality among citizens with the necessity of a division of labor wherein citizens are assigned the role of choosing the aims of society. Proportional representation is the best way to approximate these ideals, but it is not perfect. Furthermore, proportional representation advances these principles only if citizens have reasonably articulate conceptions of the aims they choose. In my account, legislative institutions are not sufficient to ensure fully articulate conceptions of aims. They can only be brought about by a process of deliberation in the society that will determine the basic aims. Chapters 7 and 8 will deal with this process.

Notes

1. Thomas Hobbes had a formalist view of responsibility. He thought that the fact that the members of a commonwealth have authorized the sovereign implies that the sovereign is responsible to the members. But the sovereign has no duties to the members in Hobbes's account. See Thomas Hobbes, *Leviathan*, ed. C. B. MacPherson (Harmondsworth, Eng.: Penguin Press, 1968 [1651]), pp. 228–236. See also Hanna Pitkin, *The Concept of Representation* (Berkeley: University of California Press, 1967), pp. 15–59, for a discussion of a number of formalistic conceptions of representation.

2. John Plamenatz, *Democracy and Illusion* (London: Longman, 1973), pp. 184–185.

3. Plamenatz, *Democracy and Illusion,* pp. 186–187.

4. Plamenatz, *Democracy and Illusion,* p. 190.

5. See Plato, *The Republic,* 2nd edition revised, ed. Desmond Lee (Harmondsworth, Eng.: Penguin Press, 1987), pp. 177–187. Within democratic theory, C. B. MacPherson has articulated a fairly extreme version of substantive political responsibility of rulers to citizens. See his *Real World of Democracy* (Montreal: CBC Enterprises, 1965).

6. See American Political Science Association, *Towards a More Responsible Two Party System* (New York: Rinehart & Co., 1950).

7. See Edmund Burke, "Speech to the Electors of Bristol," in *Burke's Politics,* ed. Ross J. S. Hoffman and Paul Levack (New York: Alfred A. Knopf, 1949).

8. See Cass Sunstein, "Interest Groups in American Public Law," *Stanford Law Review* 38, no. 29 (November 1985): pp. 29–87, p. 46. See also Charles Beitz, *Political Equality* (Princeton: Princeton University Press, 1989), p. 205. This conception of the task of the legislative assembly is attributed by Sunstein to James Madison, but its clearest exponent in the eighteenth century is Edmund Burke in his "Speech to the Electors of Bristol," in which he is very clear on the idea that deliberative assemblies are opposed to democratic equality.

9. See Hannah Pitkin, *The Concept of Representation* (Berkeley: University of California Press, 1967), chapter 4, for this view, which she calls "descriptive representation."

10. See Bernard Grofman and Chandler Davidson, eds., *Controversies in Minority Voting* (Washington, D.C.: Brookings Institution, 1992).

11. See Douglas J. Amy, *Real Choices/New Voices: The Case for Proportional Representation Elections in the United States* (New York: Columbia University Press, 1993), esp. chapters 1–7, for an excellent summary of the standard arguments with supporting empirical evidence.

12. See John Stuart Mill, *Considerations on Representative Government* (Buffalo, N.Y.: Prometheus Books, 1992 [1860]), p. 146–147. An aspect of this problem occurs quite frequently in societies that use this kind of representation. These societies often see legislatures wherein a majority of the legislators have been elected by a minority of voters, as in our example above. Arend Lijphart has observed that problem in his study of elections in six countries during the period of 1945–1980 that use the single-member district system; forty-five percent of elections resulted in the formation of legislatures wherein the party that had won majority in the legislature had been voted in by a minority of the voters. See Arend Lijphart's *Democracies: Patterns of Majoritarian and Consensus Government in Twenty-One Countries* (New Haven: Yale University Press, 1984), pp. 166–168.

13. This problem has been a source of major difficulties in American politics. Blacks and Hispanics have consistently been underrepresented in legislative assemblies.

14. See Richard C. Cortner, *The Apportionment Cases* (New York: W. W. Norton and Co., 1970), for a discussion of the origins of judicial reapportionment in the United States.

15. For evidence of this proposition see Lijphart, *Democracies*, p. 161.

16. Maurice Duverger, "Duverger's Law: Forty Years Later," in *Electoral Laws and Their Political Consequences,* ed. Bernard Grofman and Arend Lijphart (New York: Agathon Press, 1986). See also Lijphart, *Democracies*, p. 161, for evidence for this proposition.

17. See E. E. Schattschneider, *The Semi-Sovereign People: A Realist's View of Democracy in the United States* (New York: Holt, Rinehart and Winston, 1960).

18. Beitz, *Political Equality*, p. 133.

19. Anthony Downs, *An Economic Theory of Democracy* (New York: Harper and Row, 1957), p. 156.

20. Maurice Duverger, "Which Is the Best Electoral System?" in *Choosing an Electoral System,* ed. Bernard Grofman and Arend Lijphart (New York: Praeger, 1984), p. 33.

21. William Riker, *The Theory of Political Coalitions* (New Haven: Yale University Press, 1962), pp. 32–46.

22. See Lijphart, *Democracies,* chapter 4.

23. See Lawrence Dodd, *Coalitions in Parliamentary Government* (Princeton: Princeton University Press, 1976), p. 161, and Vernon Bog-

danor, *What Is Proportional Representation?* (Oxford: Oxford University Press, 1984), p. 147, as well as Amy, *Real Choices/New Voices*, p. 159.

24. See Lijphart, *Democracies*, pp. 111–113, for these claims.

25. See Frank Bealey, *Democracy in the Contemporary State* (Oxford: Oxford University Press, 1988), p. 63, for this term.

26. This is part of the argument of Danilo Zolo, *Democracy and Complexity: A Realist Approach* (College Station: Pennsylvania State University Press, 1992), p. 126.

CHAPTER SEVEN

Interest Groups and Political Parties as Institutions of Deliberation

One aspect of treating citizens as equals in a properly ordered democracy is to give them equal votes in the process of collective decisionmaking. Citizens then have an equal influence on the outcome of the process. We discussed this adversarial equality extensively in the last chapter. Many have thought that this is sufficient to ensure political equality. But there is another element to the distribution of political influence that is perhaps even more important. In politics, citizens must not only be able to exert pressure on the process by which collectively binding decisions are made, they must be able to know what they are making decisions about. They must have some idea about how the decisions are related to their interests as well as the moral worth or the justice of the decisions. They must have some idea about what their interests are as well as what kinds of moral concerns are really important to them. Without any understanding of these issues a citizen would be voting without any clear aim. Thus, it is necessary to include a discussion of the cognitive conditions for meaningful participation in a theory of democracy.

Among the chief cognitive conditions for meaningful participation is the opportunity to engage in rational social discussion with others about one's interests and those of others as well as about justice and the common good. We learn about our lives and our well-being through testing our ideas in discussion with others, as well as through hearing what they have to say about their interests and ours. We also improve our understanding of justice and the common good when we present our conceptions of these to those others who have an opportunity to respond. A robust political equality in the society requires that these conditions be made equal. A vast disparity of knowledge or access to knowledge and the consequent aimlessness, manipulability, and confusion of large numbers of citizens are not compatible with political equality and the principle behind it: equal consideration of interest.

The electoral and legislative institutions that were outlined in the last chapter ensured equality in the adversarial aspect of democracy; in the next two chapters I will discuss the institutions necessary to the deliberative dimension. I will discuss the familiar institutions of political parties and interest groups. First, I will discuss the functions that these groups can play in a properly ordered democracy. Second, we shall see that the primary function of these secondary associations ought to be to promote discussion. Finally, I will discuss some institutional arrangements that can promote the deliberative aspect of interest groups and political parties, such as proportional representation, which promotes deliberation, and public financing of electoral campaigns coupled with severe lobbying restrictions, which insulate the legislature from pressure from interest groups. In the next chapter I will explore the thorny problem of the nature of equality in the process of social discussion and the institutions necessary to ensure it.

The Deliberative Function of Interest Groups and Political Parties

As I argued in Chapter 5, the conceptions of aims citizens have must be fairly complex in order for them to satisfy the standards of citizenship. First, they must be sufficiently articulate in order for them to provide guidance to the legislature. If the aims the citizens choose are very simple or vague, the legislature must assume powers for it-self to define the basic collective features of the society and the soci-ety will fail to realize political equality. The conceptions of aims must also be reasoned as well as based on reflection on alternative conceptions of aims. The cognitive conditions of meaningful partic-ipation must enable citizens to attain the standards of articulation, reasonableness, and discrimination. The complexity of the task of elaborating aims is sufficiently great that not all citizens can fully participate. If everyone participates fully in the elaboration and jus-tification of aims, little time will be left for the other socially useful tasks. It is important that some persons spend a lot of time at it and others spend little time at it in order to do other things. Therefore, a socially useful process of deliberation requires specialization in the task of elaborating and justifying conceptions of aims.

This process requires at least informal associations. Associations are necessary to support the activities of specialists. They provide the material resources and organization that permit some individu-als to pursue these tasks exclusively. For example, even the most ele-mentary discussions about politics among ordinary citizens are car-ried out on the basis of beliefs formed from reading newspapers and watching television. These are organizations that employ armies of specialists at selecting, collecting, processing, and simplifying infor-mation. The participants in these discussions would not have much of interest to say to each other about politics without this massive specialized support system. The newspapers and other media collect most of their information from members of other organizations, such as interest groups, political parties, and government institu-tions.[1] The process of social discussion would not get off the ground without these institutions, which are ultimately the driving force behind it. These institutions are the focus of this chapter.

Political Parties and Interest Groups

Political parties devise reasoned views of the nature and aims of the society *as a whole* and attempt to persuade citizens of their views in competition with other parties. They attempt to accommodate the whole range of interests and concerns in the society, taking stances on most of the issues of relevance facing the political society. They have unified visions of the aims of society. They must have such a stance on the issues since they will have to address them if they take control of the government. For example, in the United States, the words *Democrat* and *Republican* often refer to distinct overall outlooks on how the society ought to be organized that are put into practice when the relevant party comes to power.

Parties are the main participants in the last stage of discussion leading to decisionmaking. A political party is, in part, an organization of persons that attempts to persuade others that a particular, reasoned, overall conception of the aims of society ought to be realized.[2] They put out position papers, their officials give speeches, and they organize conventions and sponsor think tanks. Again, these activities can only be sustained when a number of individuals specialize in the tasks of elaborating platforms, writing speeches, and so on. All of these activities have the purpose of persuading ordinary citizens to adopt or retain certain positions on matters of political concern. The purpose of this persuasion is to win seats in the legislative assembly. Once it has won seats, its members are committed to following the conception of aims for which they have been elected. Thus parties play a role in social discussion during the electoral process, and they play a role in legislative decisionmaking as delegates to their constituencies.

Electoral campaigns are, in part, massive processes of deliberation among citizens with the object of choosing the aims of society.[3] The electoral process functions best as a deliberative process when a number of parties compete to persuade citizens of alternative positions.[4] This process of competitive debate is an essential part of the process of bringing about discriminating and reasoned decisionmaking among the citizens regarding the society as a whole.[5] The debates between opponents and the airing of alternative positions characteristic of electoral campaigns all contribute to enhancing the understanding citizens have about what aims the society ought to pursue. Though we may often dislike the quality of discussion in electoral campaigns, part of the point of this whole system is to enhance the quality of discussion, and it ought to be evaluated in those terms.

Interest groups also play an important role in the process of deliberation. They articulate the interests of groups of citizens as well as the distinctive points of view that might arise in the social division of labor. Unions, women's organizations, and the organizations of business all give voice to distinct interests and points of view of the sectors of society in which they are based. Unlike political parties, their concerns are more narrow. They do not usually attempt to formulate conceptions of aims for the whole society. They articulate in great detail narrower interests and concerns. They fund experts in the research and analysis of these interests and concerns and how they can be met. They are therefore a store of a great deal of in-depth information concerning certain aspects of the society, and they disregard other large areas.

Such groups are essential to the participation of citizens in a democratic society. Citizens must have a conception of how their narrower interests fit into the overall aims. The basic reason for democratic decisionmaking is that it is the embodiment of equal consideration of interests in the society. If, because they lack any such organization, some sectors of the society do not have access to means for understanding these interests, they will be at a disadvantage in the democratic process; they will not be treated as equals.

Interest groups provide citizens with the opportunity to hear developed and articulated views about their interests. They also give citizens opportunities to hear about how others respond to those conceptions of interests. If there is a sufficiently diverse set of interest groups, when one group disseminates a set of views about the interests of a certain group of citizens, other groups may respond to these views with alternative ideas about the interests of the members of that group. The system of interest groups can generate discussion about all the interests in society. In addition, interest groups have uniquely informed perspectives on essential parts of the society. Business organizations have valuable perspectives on the contributions and requirements of business activities. A society that includes a large business sector but in which that sector had no voice would be dangerously uninformed about itself. A society without teachers' organizations would be egregiously ignorant of important parts of the process of education.

It is not necessary that all citizens actively contribute to the discussion as long as their views are expressed and taken seriously. All citizens have an opportunity to join this process of discussion, and most important they have the opportunity to hear it and have it contribute to their own deliberations about their interests and how they will choose the aims of society. Thus, interest groups contribute to the kind of competitive deliberation that parties do. They sponsor informed debate with alternative groups with an eye to persuading citizens about their interests or the justice of the cause of these interests.

Interest groups also support specialization in the understanding of technical matters of policy. For these reasons, these groups often cooperate with each other and government officials in the development of precise policy proposals.[6] They engage in discussion and deliberation on the best way to achieve mutually important goals. It is because of this in-depth information that they are suited for direct contact with legislators and administrators. Indeed, they often play an indispensable role in providing information of even a relatively neutral sort to these officials.[7]

Other Functions of Secondary Associations

To be sure, the deliberative function is not the only one secondary associations carry out in our society. Let us review some of the other functions these groups perform and see why the deliberative function ought to be primary in a society devoted to the ideals of democracy and the choice of aims conception of citizenship.

Many theorists have argued or assumed that interest groups and parties have primarily a *pressure* function.[8] The function of interest groups and political parties on this account is to organize interests and points of view and push for their accommodation in society. Political parties and interest groups are primarily concerned with bargaining and compromise. They perform this task by supporting the election efforts of political parties and candidates for office. Consider the following examples of pressure activity. A businessman contributes a sum of money to the campaign war chest of a politician in return for an explicit or implicit promise that government subsidies for his industry will be maintained or increased. A union threatens to cut off all of its financial backing for a politician's reelection campaign if he fails to support stiffer safety regulations for an industry. Through making offers of support or threats of

withdrawal to politicians, these people bargain in the hope of bringing about policies favorable to their interests. Within the political
system, these are generally thought to be acceptable political activities in the United States, although most ordinary citizens regard
them with considerable dismay.

They also organize pressure on the legislature directly in the society by arranging strikes and other disruptions of social life in
order to force the legislature to act in ways they desire. When all the
groups act in this way, politics as a whole is a search for a kind of
equilibrium of these pressures in the society. Some maintain that
this is not only the best description of the way politics actually
works but also an ideal of politics. They argue that as long as all
these groups are on a level playing field, the equilibrium brought
about by all these groups peacefully exerting pressure for what they
want is the best way to organize politics. A version of this view was
reviewed in Chapter 4 under the rubric of interest group pluralism,
but there are other possible versions, as we will see. In this account
citizens have more or less fixed preferences and the task of interest
groups and political parties is to maximize the satisfaction of these
preferences.

Groups also devise and implement policy in cooperation with the
administrative branch of the state. This is the function of *alternate
governance*.[9] Interest groups are to play a role in making law or
legally binding prescriptions. And they may have a role in making
rules and enforcing them for their members. For example, in many
states in Western Europe labor unions and industry representatives
engage in bargaining over wages and prices for the whole country.
The government participates in this process and the outcomes of the
bargaining are given legally binding status. Specially interested
groups make law in narrow policy areas. Another example is that in
the United States the State Bar Associations of Lawyers have the
power to make rules binding on their members that have the force
of law, and they have some powers to enforce them. Alternate governance is a form of pressure activity since it does not involve
changing or improving preferences but only attempting to satisfy
them whatever they may be.

In addition, interest groups engage in *monitoring* the activities of
the legislature and the administration in the society, making sure

that they are doing their best to do what they are supposed to do. Interest groups and parties can "blow the whistle" on corrupt or incompetent activities of legislators and administrators. This monitoring and the technical discussion that is part of it are primarily undertaken by interest groups and political parties because they require a lot of technical information. Parties monitor the performance of their members that have legislative seats. They make sure that the members actually pursue the party aims that have been chosen. And they monitor the quality of the choices of means and compromises as well as the performance of the administrative branch of government in carrying out the policies chosen by the legislature. They have some of the specialized knowledge necessary to evaluate the actions of the legislature and to understand how the legislative and administrative processes work. Citizens cannot be expected to have the technical expertise to evaluate the effectiveness of alternative policies or understand the strategic contexts in which legislators find themselves when they must make compromises with other legislators. So the legislature must be monitored by people who specialize in monitoring. I will discuss the extent to which parties and interest groups can be relied upon by citizens in their monitoring capacity in the next chapter.[10]

The Primacy of the Deliberative Function of Secondary Associations

In my view, the deliberative function of secondary associations ought to be primary. This has serious implications for how to structure these institutions in a democratic way. For example, if the function of interest groups is primarily deliberative, then the principle of democratic equality recommends a kind of qualitative equality (of the sort I discussed in Chapter 2) among the various groups. If their function is primarily that of exerting pressure on the legislature, then democratic equality requires something closer to numerical equality among the groups; it requires that interest groups have resources in proportion to their size. If the function of alternative governance is an essential part of democracy, then we must revise the conception of legislation proposed in the previous chapter.

Some argue that the pressure function ought to be primary.[11] The arguments for this claim are two: the argument from representation of interests and the argument from realism. The representation argument gives a normative basis for saying that the pressure function of interest groups ought to be primary, whereas the argument from realism gives a factual basis for saying that the primary function of interest groups and parties in society is to exert pressure. Let us examine each in turn.

The representation argument proceeds from the observation that pressure must be exerted somewhere in the political system on the collective decision-making process. Good faith conflicts of interests as well as conflicts of judgment are ubiquitous, even after a great deal of deliberation and discussion. At a certain point decisions have to be made, and egalitarians recommend that they be made by giving each citizen equal resources in deciding. Here, bargaining, negotiation, compromise, and voting among citizens is necessary. Since there must be a division of labor in the society, it is important that the interests and points of view of citizens be represented. The pressure group theorist will argue that a diverse system of secondary associations is the best way to ensure representation of a broad array of interests.[12] For example, an industrial society without labor unions is dominated by the interests of those who own the industries. Unions make sure that the interests of workers and the less well-off are represented by counterbalancing the power of capitalists. Or when a society has only one political party, that party dominates the rest of the society and inevitably represents only a fraction of the interests in the society. Pressure theorists argue that all substantial interests ought to be represented so as to realize equal consideration of interests.

I want to counter this argument in two stages. First, a society in which the main method of resolving conflicts among citizens is through the system of secondary associations is incompatible with the ideal of equality. Second, conflicts of interests and points of view can be adequately handled by the legislative assembly in the way I outlined in the previous chapter, and secondary associations advance the interests of citizens and political equality best by enhancing the quality of public discussion and deliberation.

There are three standard ways in which the system of interest groups can fulfill the representational role: group representation, interest group pluralism, and corporatist governance. Group representation implies that interest groups make collective decisions together in a kind of legislative assembly. Society is divided into groups, such as labor, employer, farmer (in the case of functional representation), ethnic, religious, gender, and other groups. The groups are like legislative districts from which representatives are sent to the legislature. If one is an African American and this is one of the groups that is represented, then one belongs to the group of African Americans that is represented in the legislature. Or if one is a woman and women make up one of the groups to be represented, then one is represented by someone voted in by women. The legislature is made up of representatives of groups of workers, employers, farmers, and other important groups. Each legislator is elected by the group he or she represents. The assembly replaces or exists alongside a territorial system of representation.[13]

We have already seen in Chapter 6 that the problem with such a system is that it strips much of the agenda-setting function necessary for democratic equality from citizens. The division of society into represented groups plays a large role in determining the agenda for legislative decisionmaking since the choice of groups depends on what interests and conflicts between interests are thought to be relevant. And this choice must be made in advance of the citizens' voting in a system of group representation. This approach violates the principle of voluntary proportionality inherent in the ideal of democratic equality.

The interest group pluralist approach, which is the most common in the United States, requires that groups exert pressure on legislators in the form of offers and threats to withhold election campaign contributions. The idea is that if all groups have power to exert pressure, then equal representation is ensured. We have seen how this approach fails in the discussion of the interest group pluralist conception of citizenship. It exposes the whole political system to dangers of incoherence and self-defeat. Associations in this system have reason to focus on narrow policy areas in order to gain influence, and thus different groups try to determine very different aspects of policy. The consequence is often a crazy quilt of policies over which there is little overall control. It also threatens to undermine equality itself. Finally, this method of exerting pressure undermines the kind of relation between citizens and the legislature defended in the previous chapter. It makes the decisions of the legislators regarding the ends that they are to pursue subject to complex bargaining to which ordinary citizens cannot be privy. Thus it undermines a crucial condition of reconciling the system of legislative representation to political equality. A third approach might be that of alternative governance, as in corporatist bargaining by groups on specific areas of policy. There are times when bringing groups into the decision-making process is an important tool for reasonable public policymaking. These groups may on occasion bargain with each other. For example, in Sweden, national organizations of unions and employers bargain on general policies regarding wage restraint, prices, employment security, working conditions, and so on. And the outcomes of the bargaining have a legally binding status.[14] These decision-making arrangements have had the beneficial effects of stabilizing labor relations, inflation, and unemployment in economies where they have been used. If these institutions are implemented, it is important to the establishment of equality that all the significantly affected groups be able to exert pressure on the process.[15]

Though the usefulness of corporatist institutions shows that associations can serve an important function in pressuring the state to act in certain ways, it does not show that this should be the primary function. First, the corporatist arrangements ought to be determined by the territorial legislature if we are to avoid the violation of voluntary proportionality implied by functional representation. What groups are to play a role in corporatist bargaining, and what their roles are, ought to be decided by the legislature. Hence, the territorial legislature ought to be sovereign in these decisions. Second, corporatist institutions are not always useful in solving political problems. Sometimes states adopt them for a while and then abandon them. For example, the Netherlands was for a long time ruled partly by groups representing adherents of the Dutch Reformed and the Catholic Churches. This arrangement proved to be useful because the Protestants and Catholics had very different views about how public education should proceed. But this arrangement faded in importance as Dutch citizens began to lose their strong ties of identification with these churches. The point of these observations is that corporatist arrangements should be chosen on a case-by-case basis depending on the aims and needs of the society. And these decisions should be made by the territorial legislature. Corporatist institutions can at best help achieve the democratically mandated aims of the citizens. But they are not essential to the very process of democratic decisionmaking itself.

Thus, the normative argument for the priority of the pressure function fails because the three ways in which this priority can be conceived are incompatible with the ideal of democratic equality. Furthermore, there is another way to accommodate the facts of disagreement and conflict in a democratic society. We can accommodate these in an orderly and controlled fashion by concentrating them in the legislative assembly after the representatives have been voted into office. Once a representative assembly is seated, the representatives have the job of working out the compromises and coalitions necessary for decisionmaking in the context of disagreement and conflict. Thus, it is in the process of voting for representatives as well as in the representative assembly itself that the adversarial features of democracy must come out. Until the moment when voting for representatives becomes necessary, the democratic process ought to be primarily a process of discussion and rational persuasion. It ought to promote the needs of citizens to become informed about their interests as well as the interests of others and the claims of justice. The function of interest groups and political parties in this process is to contribute to discussion and persuasion.

The argument from realism for the priority of the pressure function of interest groups and parties proceeds differently. It simply claims that it is inevitable that certain groups will attempt to gain power and dominate the rest by whatever means are available. This pursuit of domination is merely a fact of psychology or sociology in this argument. Thus, it is argued, anyone concerned with equality will want there to be countervailing powers exerting pressures in the opposite directions. And the distribution of that power ought to be in accordance with a principle of just distribution of power.

The argument from realism has merit because it recognizes that individuals and groups sometimes pursue their interests or concerns regardless of what others think and to some extent give precedence to their own view over those of others. But the seriousness of the need for countervailing power and the strength of the argument for the primacy of the pressure function of secondary associations depends on the seriousness of the threat of groups exclusively devoted to domination. The degree of seriousness depends on how many groups are devoted to this end as well as how powerful they are. It also depends on how far they are willing to go to achieve dominance and what kind of domination they are interested in. Do some powerful groups wish to overturn the democratic process itself? Or do they merely wish to have their way in such a process? The argument from realism can establish the strong thesis that the primary function of interest groups and political parties is to exert pressure only if the threat of domination is very serious. Otherwise, there may be some need for a variety of interest groups in the society so that no group attempts to take control. But that need may not be so serious as to require that we think of the primary function of each group as exerting countervailing pressure. In what follows we shall see that the strong thesis is overstated.

One argument for the claim that groups generally are only interested in increasing power might be called the genetic argument. Many have argued persuasively that modern democracies were formed as a consequence of organized classes exerting pressure on the state and developing compromises with each other that favored democracy. Democracy, in such a view, is a modus vivendi established because none of the groups were able to dominate the others without severe costs to themselves. In those cases where groups or coalitions of groups were able to control the state without democratic procedures, they did so. Democratic politics is merely the compromise solution to conflict between great landlords, the bourgeoisie, the military class, peasants, and the working classes. Where coalitions could be made that could exclude one or both of the latter two groups, there was no democracy; where coalitions required one or both of the latter two groups, democracy did come into existence.[16]

Democracy may well have come about as the solution to social conflict. From this, however, it does not follow that it must remain a process regulating conflict at every level. From the fact that social institutions come about as a kind of equilibrium of conflicting social forces does not entail that they must remain so. For example, religious toleration arose in the sixteenth and seventeenth centuries as a compromise between different religious groups desirous of domination. Religious toleration has not however remained a mere compromise position; most citizens of modern Western states regard toleration as intrinsically worthwhile, even though there are clearly times when individuals would like to suspend it. Many citizens have a commitment to religious toleration that is now grounded in a sense of the justice of toleration. The same is true for democratic institutions and principles. Though democratic institutions have probably come about as a consequence of compromise and equilibrium among a number of groups, citizens now have an adherence to democratic institutions that is based on a sense of fairness. They do not regard democratic institutions as necessary evils that must be lived with merely because opposed groups cannot be disposed of; their allegiance is founded in a sense of justice.

The argument from realism is a good reminder of an important function of secondary associations in a democratic society. Under certain circumstances, the pressure function will be primary, and it will always be true that individuals' interests are best protected when there are associations concerned with advancing or protecting them in the society. However, this function ought not be primary in modern societies.

The arguments I have just described suggest that there may be different stages of democratic development that are relevant from a normative point of view. There is an initial stage that consists of the balancing of forces in the society and requires that there be sufficient power on all sides for the balance to remain in place. Each group desires, at first, total domination but realizes that it cannot get this much. This stage is one of pacified but boundless conflict. The primary function of associations is to exert pressure in this arrangement. A second stage occurs when generations have grown up and been educated in a democratic society and acquire an allegiance to its basic principles. This stage is one of bounded conflict in which individuals do not agree on everything and they see that they have conflicts of interests but most also have an allegiance to the underlying principles of democracy. At this stage, the pressure function of groups becomes less primary and the deliberative function ought to become foremost.

Legislative Autonomy

The argument for the deliberative functions of interest groups and political parties has a number of important institutional implications that I will discuss in this and the next chapter. The first institutional recommendations derive from the principle of legislative autonomy. The idea is that interest groups are not to be permitted to affect the choice of aims that the legislature makes except insofar as they engage in public deliberation about those aims before the elections. Of course we have seen why legislative autonomy is required by our conception of the function of the legislature, but now we can see why it is required by our conclusions regarding the function of secondary associations. Bargaining and lobbying the legislature are all pressure activities. The point of interest groups and political parties, by contrast, is not to exercise pressure but to enhance the quality of deliberation in the society as a whole. Interest groups are not to act as representatives of citizens, advancing their aims by means of financing campaigns and lobbying the legislature; they are to serve the citizenry by contributing to its understanding of the issues.

There ought to be severe campaign finance restrictions so that in effect the bulk of campaign costs are subsidized by the state. One reason for this arrangement is to ensure that individuals and groups cannot pressure the legislature with offers of support for electoral campaigns and that they concentrate their attentions on promoting public deliberation. In the United States, electoral campaigns have the appearance of deliberative processes, but are largely elaborate processes of deal making accessible to only a small proportion of citizens. It has been widely observed that the costs of elections have increased dramatically over the past forty years. Much of this increase is due to the private financing of campaigns. When candidates win in large part depending on the amounts of money they raise and when interest groups receive special favors when they contribute to campaigns, those who do not contribute to campaigns turn out to be losers. Indeed, those who can afford it contribute to the campaigns of all the main contestants so as to minimize the risk of losing out. The effect of this is to divert massive amounts of time and resources away from the task of public discussion. And though many regard the system as a whole as perverse, no individual group can unilaterally withdraw from this process without losing. Severing the tie between campaign finance and interest groups would enable these groups and the society to spend more resources on deliberation.

Another reason for public subsidization of electoral campaigns is that political parties and candidates for office are freed from the arduous task of constantly raising money from people who expect favors in return. The problem outlined above requires candidates and parties to devote the vast majority of their time to the task of chasing financial support, diverting their energies from the more important business of public discussion and education. Hence, public support for electoral campaigns enables interest groups and political parties to devote themselves to fulfilling their primary responsibilities in the political system. Public support for campaigns is reasonable since the main beneficiaries of electoral campaigns are the citizens themselves. Electoral campaigns ought to be, to a large extent, educational institutions for all. Citizens' interests in collective features of the society and political equality are promoted when they have the opportunity to enhance their understanding of the issues they must vote on.

What democratic equality requires in the distribution of funds to political parties and interest groups and the institutions necessary to ensuring the proper distribution is yet to be determined. These issues will be the subject of the next chapter.

The Contribution of Proportional Representation to Political Deliberation

In Chapter 6 we pointed out the superiority of proportional representation in realizing political equality in voting and representation; here we will elaborate on its merits as a method of organizing discussion and deliberation among parties and citizens in electoral processes. Since electoral campaigns are deliberative, an electoral system that maximizes the quality of social discussion ought to be preferred. Party list proportional representation promotes all three main standards of adequate conceptions of aims that I reviewed in

Chapter 5. It supports greater articulation of aims, greater reasonableness of aims, as well as greater discrimination among aims. Here we shall enlist some of the observations of the last chapter to support the contention that the electoral process involved in party list proportional representation schemes is an optimal way of organizing deliberation.

In general, it has been observed that party list systems of proportional representation and election tend to force parties to be clearer and more articulate about their political platforms than in single-member district systems. The logic of single-member district representation systems requires that a candidate or party must appeal to as many voters as possible, at least enough to get a majority. In a highly heterogeneous population one must appeal to many different and opposed interests and points of view simultaneously. As a consequence, politicians have incentives to say as little as possible in order to avoid offending any group. Candidates are quite vague or ambiguous about their views for the same reasons. These two features tend to militate against substantial discussion of issues during campaigns. They militate against citizens' developing their views with any clarity or articulateness. In proportional representation, the incentives for concealing one's views are less pressing, and parties have reasons to give more articulate and definite views on basic aims and policies. Being clear about what one stands for carries less risk since one need not appeal to everyone in order to get a seat in the legislative assembly. And there are usually more political parties than in single-member district representation so it is necessary to be more articulate about one's aims in order to distinguish oneself from others. In general, empirical evidence supports the contention that campaigns in proportional representation systems are much more centered on issues and on more detailed and substantive alternatives than in those of single-member district representation schemes.

In addition, parties in a proportional representation system are more inclined to persuade citizens in a rational fashion, focusing on the merits of the positions they advance. In single-member district representation, candidates tend to emphasize the appeals of their personalities and images rather than their electoral platforms as a means of avoiding difficult or divisive issues. Conversely, mere candidate appeal does not work as well in a party list system since candidates are less prominent. First, candidates must appeal to issues more. Second, they tend to be more subordinate to the party itself so that the significance of personality is greatly diminished. Much of the emphasis on style and image in the political campaigns in the United States is attributable to its combination of single-member district representation and very weak political parties. This tendency towards issueless and irrational campaigns is diminished in a system of proportional representation. Thus, the second main standard for conceptions of aims, reasonableness, is favored by proportional representation.

Finally, the standard of discrimination is also more likely to be met in proportional representation because proportional representation encourages a proliferation of political parties. It gives citizens much greater opportunities to see the diversity of reasoned and articulate conceptions of overall aims that are held in the society. Acquaintance with such a diversity of views provides the context in which citizens can discriminate between their views and relevant significant alternatives.[17]

Inasmuch as parties play a key role in organizing and leading the process of deliberation, their being forced to give articulate, discriminating, and reasoned accounts of their aims encourages and enables citizens to do the same. The diversity of views in the electoral process encourages citizens to consider a variety of different alternatives to the ones they adhere to. It also encourages those whose views and interests would be less taken into account in other systems to come forth and give clear accounts of their own positions. They then have the opportunity to hear how others respond to their interests or to their conceptions of their interests and the common good.

Defenders of single-member district representation argue that "government by majority is government by persuasion." The reason, as Ferdinand Hermens has argued, is that because majorities must be forged out of heterogeneous populations, "members of a variety of ethnic, religious, economic, and other groups must be brought together. . . . Their leaders must pursue policies acceptable to all."[18] The trouble with these arguments, however, is that they ignore the strong tendency towards vagueness and ambiguity that is generated by these systems. Thus, the persuasion of ordinary citizens is of a superficial sort that leaves much of the decisionmaking to party leaders and leaders of interest groups who are at liberty to bargain with each other in the background. Often this bargaining on the basic points of the legislative agenda is done out of the sight of ordinary citizens and undermines their capacity to control the state. Furthermore, the system of single-member district representation puts a straitjacket on the kinds of issues that are discussed by citizens and parties. In general, the discussion in electoral campaigns tends to take place on a one-dimensional issue space. Discussion in proportional representation elections tends to involve more issues in a number of different dimensions. The single-member district system simplifies unnecessarily the process of social discussion.[19] Some may argue that the multidimensionality of issues for discussion demonstrates that there is greater fragmentation in the public at large than when the issues are very simple. But surely this kind of fragmentation is precisely what we should expect from discussion amongst equals who have very different experiences and roles in the society. And such fragmentation should have the beneficial effect of getting all citizens to understand the diverse interests and points of view that exist in their society and deepening their understanding of how to fairly accommodate these interests.

Overall, a scheme of proportional representation is superior to other electoral schemes in promoting rational social deliberation on the overall aims of society. It encourages citizens to devise articulate, reasoned, and discriminating conceptions of these aims. Not only is proportional representation a more egalitarian method of collective decisionmaking when there are irresolvable disagreements, it is also a superior method for organizing the process of social deliberation in a democratic society.

This completes the picture of the division of labor in democratic decisionmaking among citizens, legislators, interest groups, and political parties. The one element of the view yet to be added is a discussion of the nature and institutional requirements of equality in the process of social deliberation. That discussion will be the task of the next and last chapter.

Notes

1. For the argument that the media are critically dependent on these associations for acquiring information, see Robert Entman, *Democracy Without Citizens* (New York: Oxford University Press, 1989).

2. See Patrick Dunleavy, *Democracy, Bureaucracy, and Public Choice* (London: Harvester/Wheatsheaf, 1990), for a review of the leadership role of parties in generating and encouraging public debate and transforming the preferences of citizens.

3. See Samuel Popkin, *The Reasoning Voter* (Chicago: University of Chicago Press, 1990), for evidence that citizens actually do learn quite a bit during electoral campaigns in the United States.

4. On the importance of party competition, see E. E. Schattschneider, *The Semi-Sovereign People: A Realist's View of Democracy in America* (New York: Holt, Rinehart and Winston, 1960), and Walter Dean Burnham, *The Current Crisis in American Politics* (New York: Oxford University Press, 1982).

5. See Jane Mansbridge, "A Deliberative Theory of Interest Representation," in *The Politics of Interests: Interest Groups Transformed,* ed. Mark Petracca (Boulder: Westview Press, 1992), pp. 32–57, for the concept of "competitive deliberation."

6. See Andrew S. McFarland, "Interest Groups and the Policymaking Process: Sources of Countervailing Power in America," in *The Politics of Interest*, pp. 58–79, especially p. 70, for a discussion of intergroup deliberation. See also Jane Mansbridge, "A Deliberative Theory of Interest Representation."

7. See Graham Wilson, *Interest Groups: A Comparative Perspective* (Oxford: Basil Blackwell, 1991), for a discussion of this role.

8. There are many such theorists. For a sample, see Robert Dahl, *A Preface to Democratic Theory* (Chicago: University of Chicago Press, 1956), and Anthony Downs, *An Economic Theory of Democracy* (New York: Harper and Row, 1957).

9. See Joshua Cohen and Joel Rogers, "Secondary Associations and Democratic Governance," *Politics and Society* 20, no. 4 (December 1992): pp. 393–472, especially pp. 423–425. See Philippe Schmitter, "Democratic Theory and Neo-Corporatist Practice," *Social Research* 50 (1989): 885–928, especially p. 900, for a discussion of the rationale for these kinds of institutions, as well as Mansbridge, "A Deliberative Theory of Interest Representation," pp. 32–57.

10. Groups often have nonpolitical *social* functions as well. Unions have bargaining functions in the economy; they have the function of protecting workers from economic insecurity. Some groups are primarily concerned

with nonpolitical activities, such as religious groups in the United States. Other groups are almost exclusively concerned with politics, such as environmental groups in the United States. Other groups are concerned with both, such as the AFL-CIO union in the United States.

11. Robert Dahl, *Dilemmas of Pluralist Democracy* (New Haven: Yale University Press, 1982), p. 32.

12. Cohen and Rogers state that equal representation is a requirement of the system of secondary associations in "Secondary Associations and Democratic Governance," p. 424. See Hannah Pitkin, *The Concept of Representation* (Berkeley: University of California Press, 1967), p. 142, for this concept of representation.

13. See Paul Hirst, *Representative Democracy and Its Limits* (London: St. Martin's Press, 1989). See also G.H.D. Cole, *Social Theory* (London: J. M. Dent, 1925), for defenses of functional representation. See Iris Marion Young, *Justice and the Politics of Difference* (Princeton: Princeton University Press, 1990), p. 184, for an exposition of some elements of a system of group representation. Young's view is odd because her conception of groups is subjective; it requires a sense of affinity for the other members of the group (p. 46), whereas group representation would appear to require a commitment to groups conceived objectively. This tension in her views about groups shows up in a variety of different places. For example, she advocates affirmative action for minorities and women as well as other forms of special treatment. But surely this requires an objective way of delimiting the groups being helped. One will not limit affirmative action to those who feel an affinity with other members of the minority, and the pregnancy leave she advocates will not be awarded only to those who feel an affinity with women. And yet her subjectivist conception of groups would seem to require these conclusions.

14. See Philippe Schmitter, "Democratic Theory and Neo-Corporatist Practice," p. 900.

15. See Cohen and Rogers, "Secondary Associations and Democratic Governance," pp. 453–464, for an argument to the effect that this kind of institution may be useful in the United States.

16. See Barrington Moore Jr., *The Social Origins of Dictatorship and Democracy* (Boston: Beacon Press, 1966); Adam Przeworski, *Capitalism and Social Democracy* (Cambridge: Cambridge University Press, 1985); Adam Przeworski, *Democracy and the Market* (Cambridge: Cambridge University Press, 1992); and John D. Stephens, "Capitalist Development and Democracy: Empirical Research on the Social Origins of Democracy," in *The Idea of Democracy*, ed. David Copp, Jean Hampton, and John Roemer (New York: Cambridge University Press, 1993), pp. 409–446.

17. Evidence for these propositions is summarized in Douglas Amy's *Real Choices/New Voices* (New York: Columbia University Press, 1993). See John Stuart Mill, *Considerations on Representative Government* (Buffalo, N.Y.: Prometheus Books, 1991), chapter 7, for an understanding of much of the underlying logic of these arguments.

18. Ferdinand Hermens, "Representation and Proportional Representation," in *Choosing an Electoral System,* ed. Bernard Grofman and Arend Lijphart (New York: Preager, 1984), p. 18. See also Charles Beitz, *Political Equality* (Princeton: Princeton University Press, 1989), chapter 6, for an analogous argument.

19. See Arend Lijphart, *Democracies* (New Haven: Yale University Press, 1984), p. 148, for evidence of this.

CHAPTER EIGHT

Equality in the Process of Social Deliberation

The social discussion necessary for full participation in politics must be maintained by a system of interest groups and political parties primarily devoted to deliberation. We saw in the last chapter that social discussion is their primary function in a properly ordered democracy. Here we will ask what this system must be like for it to advance equally the interests of all citizens in society. Recall the example in Chapter 2 of someone who has an automobile but has no idea where to go with the car. Such a person might as well not have a car at all. He is powerless to achieve anything of significance to himself. If one gave him an automobile and did the same for someone else but in addition supplied the other with the means for determining what her interests are and how to achieve them, we would be doing a lot more of significance for her than for the first. Inequality of understanding is as serious as inequality in other means for advancing one's interests.

In democracy, if citizens have the right to vote but lack the means for discovering the purposes to be achieved in voting, then they have little of value. These means are the cognitive conditions of citizenship. And when the conditions for discovering their interests and how to achieve them are available to some and not to others, we have severe political inequality. Political equality, therefore, implies that the conditions for informing themselves about their interests and values ought to be distributed roughly equally among citizens.

The principal cognitive condition for political participation is the process of social discussion sustained by interest groups and political parties. Equality in the cognitive conditions of political participation requires that the system of interest groups and political parties that is necessary to social discussion be an egalitarian one. There are two basic issues concerning equality in the system of associations that we will deal with here.[1] First, I noted in Chapter 5 that social deliberation requires a division of labor wherein some specialize in acquiring knowledge both about basic interests and values and about technical matters and that this division of labor could undermine equality among citizens. I will show how organization in the process of social deliberation is compatible with equality and how the theory defended so far can help alleviate some of these worries. Second, we want to understand how equality in the whole system of deliberation can be established. The principle of qualitative equality articulated in Chapter 2 can help us design a scheme wherein each has equal access to the means for understanding interests and developing ideas about justice and the common good. But there are problems. What points of view should be discussed? How much attention should each point of view receive? In short, I will outline the basic principles and problems for evaluating the agenda of social discussion. I will then discuss three institutional setups for implementing these principles: the free market in ideas, a publicly supported marketplace of ideas, and finally a democratic method for choosing the agenda for deliberation. My consideration of different institutional arrangements for deliberation will show that equality in the deliberative agenda is an elusive and puzzling ideal.

Equality Within Interest Groups and Political Parties

The division of labor within secondary associations takes two forms. There is a division between those who are primarily concerned with elaborating aims and those who specialize in the technical and empirical study of the society and the government's relation to the society and the study of how to implement aims. This division of labor is necessary to the performance of the functions of monitoring as well as technical deliberation about means. And there must be a division of labor in the articulation of the aims of citizens itself.

First, interest groups and political parties are responsible for various kinds of technical deliberation in principle not entirely accessible to ordinary citizens. They must help the government make decisions about the means for pursuing certain aims, and they must be capable of ascertaining that the government is actually doing what it is supposed to do. These activities require specialized social scientific knowledge about the effects of government action on the society. How can we be reasonably sure that the technical experts as well as the leaders in secondary associations will not advance their own interests and points of view to the detriment of those of ordinary citizens? This is an agency problem since most citizens cannot have the understanding necessary to evaluate these activities that are supposed to advance their interests and points of view.

Two factors mitigate against the potentially antidemocratic character of the first kind of division of labor. First, the interests and points of view of the members of associations are closely bound to each other. These organizations are voluntary so that members will join when they are in favor of their goals. Hence, there is some similarity of interest and point of view, which produces solidarity among the members. Generally, experts and specialists are among the most strongly motivated by these concerns and by a professional ethic.

The leadership, however, is more often in danger of abusing its power and straying from the aims of the association for the sake of political or even pecuniary gain. And since the leaders are placed in a unique position of authority to make decisions for the group in contexts that are strategically complex, they are potentially able to run the group for their own purposes. The "iron law of oligarchy" for which some have argued suggests that even institutions with the most egalitarian aims are often deeply hierarchical and in the control of their leaders.[2] Against this claim many have argued that the leadership of organizations like parties and interest groups is constrained by the fact that many of the members of the group are members because of their commitments to the aims of the group. They are ideologically committed and not willing to sacrifice the aims of the group for greater political power.[3] And leaders depend on their commitment to achieve their aims.

A second factor mitigating the potentially antidemocratic character of groups with divisions of labor is that there is overlap between the different kinds of expertise so that those who are charged with in-depth empirical analysis of some issues are accountable in part to those who are charged with the study of another aspect of the society. They in turn are partly monitored by those who are more concerned with the articulation of aims. And these are accountable to ordinary members and citizens. When there are a number of different kinds of experts in different areas who have some understanding of what the others are doing, they can check on each other to make sure that they are in fact pursuing the interests and points of view that they are supposed to be pursuing. Leaders are accountable also because their activities are understood by other members of the association who are able to evaluate them and who are likely to be committed to the aims of the group.

Four institutional factors also temper the threat of oligarchy. First, as we saw above, in a properly ordered democracy the function of interest groups and parties is primarily deliberative and only secondarily concerned with pressure; thus, the ability to acquire power will be significantly lessened, and the temptations of power will consequently be less prominent. Second, the party list proportional representation system defended in Chapter 6 should strengthen party discipline in party politics. The consequence of this system is to diminish incentives for individuals to attempt to pursue personal gain or idiosyncratic aims while increasing the ability and incentives of the party to monitor members who are running for office and those seated in the assembly. The system should reinforce the commitment of each member of the party to pursue the aims to which the party is dedicated. Third, public subsidies of electoral campaigns relieve leaders of political parties of the need to make backroom bargains in order to secure the necessary resources to support election efforts. Such needs often separate the interests and points of view of the leaders of parties from those of ordinary members. I will argue that interest groups ought to receive public subsidies as well, which should have similar benefits. Fourth, the leaders of groups can be made democratically accountable to the more ideologically committed members so that they genuinely are tied to articulating and advancing the points of view of the group. It is certainly true that the groups do not have to be democratic in order to articulate and advance, through persuasion, the interests and points of view of their members as well as the citizens in the society.[4] But since these groups require a division of labor and must be supported by funds, there is temptation for collusion among their leaders for the purpose of mutual support. Such collusion undermines the democratic process inasmuch as the colluders are able to conceal it. One way to avoid such collusion is to make leaders democratically accountable to members, who may be more committed to the basic aims of the group. Therefore, each group has the resources for policing itself and making sure that the group continues to serve its deliberative function more or less honestly.

These remarks suggest that properly structured groups can be relied upon to monitor the process of legislative decisionmaking. Groups have the capacity to monitor the legislative process because of their support for specialized knowledge; they are capable of detecting when the legislature is or is not doing what it is supposed to be doing and evaluating these activities. And they are reliable monitors of this process to the extent that they are capable of ensuring that members within the group are acting in accordance with the concerns of the ordinary citizens. Citizens can reasonably rely on the opinions of members of various groups to help them decide whether politicians and administrators are doing the job for which they have been chosen, and they can be confident that the judgments they express are at least the most reasonable the society can expect.[5] Furthermore, insofar as citizens know that interest groups and political parties have the capacity to blow the whistle on wayward legislators and administrators, they can be confident that the latter will not often stray from their assigned tasks. So although citizens cannot be expected to know a lot about the process of technical deliberation, they are in a position to indirectly oversee the process of legislative decisionmaking to a degree that is sufficient to give them confidence that their aims are being realized when possible. To be sure, this process of interest group and party supervision of the legislative process can only give confidence to all citizens that the means to their aims are being pursued, if the system of associations reflects the broad array of interests and points of view in the society in a roughly egalitarian way.

The second kind of division of labor constitutes a different kind of problem. If some are in charge of and specialize in clarifying and elaborating the conceptions of aims, they will have substantially greater understanding of the aims and issues. This greater understanding seems to threaten the political equality of citizens. The government might have more reason to be responsive to these better-informed individuals than to the ordinary citizens. But this need not be so serious a problem for democratic ideals. Though not every citizen is an expert at articulating and developing conceptions of interests and aims it does not follow that the citizens are not in a position to understand and discuss the ideas that have been articulated. They do not have the time to discover values and interests, but they are able to understand what has been discovered, to discuss it once it has been articulated, and to make reasonably discriminating choices. The distance between expert and nonexpert on these matters is not so great as to make the latter incapable of grasping the conceptions of aims or the reasons behind them elaborated by specialists. Specialization in the articulation of conceptions of aims is not based on technical knowledge. So, assuming some rough natural equality of competence in matters of morals and interests, roughly equal educational conditions for all, and a wide array of alternatives discussed by different associations, the fact of the division of labor per se need not undermine the equality of citizens in the process of deliberation.

Therefore, the division of labor by itself need not threaten equality. It need not threaten equality in the area of deliberation about aims because here the division of labor is merely one between those who develop and elaborate the ideas and those who use the ideas once they are developed. It is not a division between those who understand and those who do not understand. Specialization in technical deliberation and monitoring the process of legislative decision-making does not threaten equality either. Citizens can reasonably rely on the judgments of those, supported by properly constituted interest groups and parties, who specialize in assessing the legislative process.

Equality in the System of Associations:
The Deliberative Agenda

In a properly ordered democracy, the primary function of interest groups and political parties is deliberative. These groups engage in technical as well as political deliberation about aims. Putting aside the issues of technical deliberation, political deliberation involves formulating the aims of citizens. The proper standard of equality in a process of deliberation is qualitative equality, so resources ought to be distributed equally among views and not persons. Only such a distribution can be said to treat persons equally.

This argument is amplified by the observation in Chapter 7 that organization in the process of developing knowledge is important. The best way to develop understanding about interests is not to have each person try to figure things out for himself or herself. Resources among persons interested in developing the understanding of interests as well as points of view ought to be pooled in order to support specialization and expertise. But if we distribute resources to persons equally, then those who share interests with greater numbers of persons will have more resources devoted to understanding their interests and points of view. This constitutes an important form of unequal treatment among individuals. Therefore, we must apply the principle of qualitative equality to the distribution of resources to secondary associations. Resources for developing understanding should be distributed equally to each kind of *view*, not to each *person*. Since organizations are formed for the purpose of articulating conceptions of the interests and moral aims individuals have in the society, each must have roughly equal resources for developing its point of view. In this way each citizen has the same resources devoted to the cultivation of his or her understanding. The understanding of interests can be shared in the same way by larger and smaller groups. They exhibit the property economists call "jointness of supply."[6] The information does not have to be divided among all the interested citizens in the way that land, money, or even power must be. One piece of information can serve a thousand persons as well as one.

A commonsensical example of qualitative equality is the distribution of time and resources allotted by a parent to understand what is best for his children. Imagine that a parent has three children; two are boys and one is a girl. Suppose he must choose which boys' school to send the boys to and which girls' school to send the girl to. He need not spend twice as much time reflecting on boys' schools as on girls' schools. He gives roughly equal time to both.[7] This is not because the parent thinks less of the boys but because the knowledge that helps him figure out what boys' school is best for one boy also helps him understand what is best for the other. To treat each child equally he must spend as much time on learning about the choices for the girl as on the choices for the two boys, which is the only way of giving equal consideration to the interests of the girl and the two boys. To give twice as much time to the choice of school for the boys would seem to amount to spending twice as much time on each as on the girl.

The principle of qualitative equality is the guiding principle for organizing the system of secondary associations since the function of these associations is deliberative and an egalitarian process of deliberation requires qualitative equality. In order to defend particular institutions of deliberation, however, we need to lay out two further relevant conditions. First, egalitarian institutions of deliberation must be sensitive to the variety of relevant interests and points of view as well as to their relative importances. Second, such a system must be able to accommodate the many disagreements in a society about which interests should be counted and what their relative importances are. In the next section, I will lay out some of the main dimensions of complexity in the system of interest groups and show how disagreement is likely to arise in this context. This explanation will set the stage for our discussion and evaluation of different institutional mechanisms of deliberation.

Dimensions of Complexity of the Deliberative Agenda

To get a handle on the complexity and variety of interests in a society as well as the disagreements that arise about them, let us look at the complexity of the systems of associations in modern democracies and the extent of disagreement about interests and points of view among them.

One main dimension on which associations might differ is the *importance* to the members or the society of the issues they are concerned with. Some associations are concerned with issues that are of manifestly less significance to anyone in the society than others. Associations that are concerned with the distinctive interests of groups that have been largely assimilated in the society, such as groups of European Americans, are not seen as very important by most citizens. The interests of these people are important but not qua European American. Most European Americans would not think of the fact of their being such as being particularly salient to their interests. More subtly, though most do think it relevant, some African Americans may not think of their ethnic heritage as relevant to their interests. They may see the difference between white and black as not very salient to their points of view. They do not identify themselves as African American. Thus the groups that claim to "represent" them are not very important to them. Presumably, all of these claims of importance will be matters of controversy.

Another kind of variation in importance is the difference in scope of the concerns of an association. Some are concerned with only a few issues in politics. For instance, antiabortion groups are often concerned with only that issue. Environmental groups are concerned with wider issues, but they are not usually concerned with the whole gamut of political issues. Business and labor groups are also quite diverse. They can, as does the AFL-CIO, concern themselves with the whole range of political issues in society.[8] The question is, Ought points of view on matters of greatly different importance be treated equally? Obviously, they should not, but it is not clear how we can properly accommodate this fact since the matter of importance will be a subject of controversy.

A second dimension is the extent to which interest groups are *significantly different* from others. Two groups may be concerned with very similar issues and may have views that are very close. Surely, in this case it would be unfair to treat these groups as on a par with some other association that represents a very different view on the issue at hand. It would, for those who think that the points of view of the groups are similar, be a case of having twice as many resources devoted to a particular point of view. As with the matter of importance, there may be a lot of controversy about whether the views or interests of two groups are relevantly different in a particular case. In many cases, some groups will see their interests as being quite different from each other, whereas many outside those groups may not see much difference between their concerns.

A third difficulty is that groups in the society encounter different *obstacles* to organization. First, there are collective action problems that are more and less difficult to solve for different groups, depending on their size. Consumer groups have always been more difficult to organize than business groups. In many cases, the former have had no voice at all. Second, poverty may make it quite difficult for some groups to organize. It has been hard, though not impossible, for poor people's groups, such as groups of welfare recipients or migrant farmers, to organize because of lack of resources. In some cases, parts of society with distinctive interests and points of view do not have the ability to form associations. Indeed, the interests for which there is no organizational support may go unrecognized even by those who share them.[9] Surely, many of these interests and points of view ought to be taken into account in an egalitarian process of deliberation. But what these interests are and the nature of the groups that have them are likely to be subjects of considerable contention within the society.

A fourth kind of variation is in the *credibility* of groups. Some interest groups simply do not advance credible claims on the society. The proverbial Flat Earth Society is one that advances no credible claim to be heard by everyone in society. But more controversially, many argue that those who insist that the theory of creation ought to be treated on a par with evolutionary biology in the school curriculum, or that it should be given precedence, do not advance credible claims. Ought these groups really to be treated on a par with others? Ought the principle of qualitative equality require that these groups have as many resources as other more credible associations? Clearly this would be illegitimate. Yet, serious disagreement about which groups are credible is to be expected.

A fifth important kind of variation is among groups that hold to tyrannical conceptions of the aims of society. Such groups refuse to treat some other groups in the society as equals. Their positions are based on a denial of equal consideration of interests to certain citizens. An example is the Nazi party in the United States. They refuse to grant equal status to many of their fellow citizens. Surely such groups are not entitled to be treated on a par with those whose views are compatible at least with some rough interpretation of equal status among citizens. Views that imply that some people's interests ought not be treated equally need not benefit from a scheme of equality. Only nontyrannical views ought to be treated as equals in an egalitarian deliberative agenda. Even here, however, there is likely to be some disagreement.

Some may think that a sixth dimension ought also to be taken into account. Associations might be distinguished by whether they advance *special interests* or *the common good*. Religious, ethnic, and socioeconomic associations promote the concerns of sectors of the society on the assumption that they have distinctive interests and points of view. The parts of the society they "represent" are independent of the existence of the associations, and they claim to represent the interests of those who are not members of the group but who are in the relevant sector of the society. By contrast, environmental, consumer, and other general reform associations do not claim to represent the interests or points of view of any particular sector of the society; they are united on the basis of shared opinions about the common good. They cannot claim to represent the points of view of anyone outside the group, and they do not represent anyone's interests; they have opinions about what the common good is. That some groups take positions on the common good and others on the good of a particular sector of society would appear to make a difference to the appropriate allocation of resources to groups in the process of discussion. The difference between public and special interest groups, some would say, ought not to be ignored in our conception of what equality in the process of social discussion comprises.

Contrary to these views this distinction is problematic in a number of ways. Many so-called special interest groups advance points of view about the common good of the entire polity. For example, unions as well as trade associations make claims to speak for the public interest, and these claims ought not to be dismissed merely as bad faith. Though they tend to be biased towards their own interests, they do offer legitimate contributions to debates about how the society ought to be structured. Furthermore, socioeconomic, ethnic, and religious groups usually offer judgments about what fairness demands in accommodating their interests. Thus, they advance claims about the society as a whole. Moreover, public interest groups are not free of bias towards particular interests either. Environmental groups, for example, tend to reflect the interests of the upper-middle-class members who support them and downplay the interests of working-class persons. This is not a cynical observation on the concealed motives of these individuals, but rather a remark on the necessary cognitive bias involved in any assertion of important social goals.

Public interest groups and special interest groups may be distinguished on the basis of the claims that the former advance *judgments* about the common good whereas the latter advance the *interests* of a sector of the society. But this distinction is not cut-and-dried since "special interest" associations do not uncontroversially represent the interests or views of sectors of the population except the members. In some cases, alternative associations have different views about the interests and views of the same sector of the society. Indeed, the very idea that the associations represent groups is problematic. What associations of ascriptive groups do in their deliberative function is express judgments about the interests and points of view of their constituencies as well as the importance of such interests and fair ways of accommodating those interests in the society. The claim to represent the people whose interests they describe is not much better than the claim of public interest groups to represent the interests of the citizenry as a whole. Each of these kinds of groups offers controversial judgments about interests and fairness. Thus, those groups ought not to be thought of as simply advancing the interests of particular citizens. These points diminish the importance of the distinction between public interest and special interest groups for a specification of the deliberative agenda. The proposed sixth dimension of complexity can be safely ignored in our attempt to define a viable principle of qualitative equality.

The five dimensions of complexity must have an influence on how an egalitarian deliberative agenda is to be structured. They suggest how the principle of qualitative equality must be modified. If a set of issues that some association is concerned with is relatively unimportant, then it is hard to see why we should be worried if it receives less support than organizations that treat more important issues. Such an organization ought not to have as prominent a place on the agenda for discussion. Furthermore, if two organizations are concerned to advance nearly indistinguishable points of view on various issues, we should not be disturbed if one or both do not occupy as important a position in the deliberative process as a group that advocates a distinctive set of ideas. Giving all three groups equal attention would violate the principle of qualitative equality. And groups with ideas that lack credibility ought not to have the same status on the agenda as the more credible. Finally, only associations advocating nontyrannical points of view ought to be guaranteed an equal place on the deliberative agenda.

Thus, the principle of qualitative equality must be quite complex. It states that nontyrannical and credible groups must be given an equal hearing with other views on issues of the same importance as long as the views are sufficiently distinct; it also requires that no important sectors of the society be excluded from the process of discussion. Tyrannical groups need not be banned, but they may not make a claim to equal support.[10] The same conclusion should hold for groups whose claims are not credible. Furthermore, issues of less importance ought to be given less of a hearing. Let us call this modified idea the principle of plural qualitative equality.

The Deliberative Agenda Problem

The principle of plural qualitative equality is a reasonable principle for evaluating an egalitarian deliberative agenda, but we should expect considerable controversy regarding the importance, distinctness, credibility, latency, and sometimes even the tyranny of different views. The setting of an egalitarian deliberative agenda itself is likely to be the subject of considerable dispute on all the dimensions. Moreover, this controversy is similar to the kind of disagreement and conflict that motivates the demand for democratic equality in the first place. It concerns the relative importance and nature of the interests that individuals have. Therefore, the disagreement and conflict that calls for a democratic solution also seems to put the characterization of democratic equality into question in any particular case.

The problem to be solved for the democrat is how to establish an egalitarian deliberative agenda in accordance with plural qualitative equality in a manner that takes account of the considerable disagreement on what the proper structure of such an agenda should be. Democrats require that citizens themselves make the decisions in these circumstances of disagreement. The deliberative agenda must be chosen by the citizens. It ought not to be determined from above. Such a method would be inconsistent with the basic principles that underlie democratic equality: that each must have a say in collectively binding decisions when there is considerable disagreement among them. This is the deliberative agenda problem.

Note that the system of political parties has less complexity on this score than interest groups. Political parties generally take stances on most of the important issues of the day. Their function in the system of associations is to take positions on the overall aims of the society. Thus the variation in importance of issues is relatively small. As a consequence, the principle of qualitative equality applies more easily to the support of the deliberative activities of political parties. The principle requires that nontyrannical and credible parties should receive equal funding in their efforts to persuade citizens to support the overall conceptions of aims that they stand for. Here we have solid ground for a principle of equal campaign finance laws supplemented by the requirement that parties demonstrate that their platforms deal with at least most of the major issues confronting the society. Also, political parties in a system of party list proportional representation will tend to distinguish themselves from each other as we have seen above. Therefore, the problem of significant difference is not pressing. Conversely, evaluating the system of interest groups in terms of the principle of qualitative equality will prove to be a serious problem. It is to this problem that we shall now turn.

In the next section I consider two general ways to solve the problem of the deliberative agenda. First, we will explore the familiar idea that institutions of deliberation ought to be a marketplace of ideas. The flaws in this view will show why some system of public support is necessary to sustain an egalitarian deliberative process in a complex society, such as our own. Second, we will explore an egalitarian modification of the marketplace of ideas that has been proposed recently. Both of these views propose a market method for choosing the deliberative agenda. We will see how they fall afoul of some important requirements of democratic equality. Third, we will review democratic collective decision-making methods for solving the deliberative agenda problem. Though this method is the most desirable for organizing the process of deliberation, I will argue that it too encounters difficulties of practical as well as theoretical significance. The problem of the deliberative agenda only permits a partial institutional solution.

Institutional Arrangements: The Marketplace of Ideas

The basic idea behind the marketplace of ideas is to make institutions of deliberation like economic markets and consequently to bring the virtues of efficiency and productivity of the market to the process of discussion. Oliver Wendell Holmes gave a classic formulation of this hope: "When men have realized that time has upset many fighting faiths, they may come to believe even more than they believe the foundations of their own conduct that the ultimate good desired is better reached by free trade in ideas—that the best test of truth is the power of thought to get itself accepted in the competition of the market."[11] Just as bad products are driven out and replaced by better products in economic markets, so bad ideas are driven out and replaced by better ones in the marketplace of ideas. The idea however is ambiguous and involves a number of different thoughts that ought to be separated out. There is a metaphorical ideal of the marketplace of ideas and a more literal conception of the marketplace of ideas. On the one hand, the idea is often used as a metaphor for a set of institutions in which ideas are exchanged freely and in which each person has the right to make up his or her own mind about which are the best ideas. Thus, a seminar might be a marketplace of ideas if all are permitted to say what they think is right and to advance reasons for what they think and each is permitted to make up his or her own mind. Buying, selling, competition, cost, and benefit are all metaphors for agreeing, persuading, disagreement, and the demerits and merits of ideas, respectively. The productive efficiency of markets is a metaphor for the optimistic idea that the good ideas will ultimately drive out the bad in free discussion. This metaphor provides an attractive ideal of social discussion inasmuch as it is egalitarian and open and it suggests that the cause of truth will be served. But it fails to provide institutional guidance since it does not include a description of the social costs in time and resources of discussion or the distribution of those costs. Thus, it cannot help solve our problem.

On the other hand, the idea of a marketplace of ideas is used in a more literal sense when it is thought of as a method for allocating resources to particular points of view. The idea is that there ought to be a market in the production and consumption of ideas just as there is in the production and consumption of any other good. Accordingly, the process of discussion should be funded in much the same way as other economic activities. It should be paid for by those who benefit from it. The beneficiaries will pay only on condition that it is worth their while, and they are well placed to know whether it is worth their while. Consumers pay for the food they consume, the stereo equipment they use, and the clothes they wear; this arrangement ensures that only things that consumers desire will be produced at the price at which consumers find it worthwhile to pay. This same logic is applied to the supply of information. A consumer will buy a book on a subject he or she is interested in only if it is worth the price. The price reflects the cost of production to a great degree, so in effect the consumer supports the production of the information. If the consumer does not desire the information sufficiently to pay the price for it, then it is more worthwhile to produce something else: either some different information or some noninformation product for which people are willing to pay. Though producers must decide what to produce, their decisions will be based on what consumers wish to consume at the prices that must be paid for the objects. The consumer is ultimately sovereign in the marketplace.

The theorists of the marketplace of ideas in a literal sense argue that the institutions of deliberation and discussion we are presently contemplating ought to be organized along the same lines as any other market institution. Thus, organizations for elaborating and articulating the interests and points of view of citizens ought to be paid for by those who consume the information. Only if it is worthwhile to them to pay for the information will it be useful information to produce. The very same efficiency that results from markets in general will also result here.

The cause of truth is served since citizens have an interest in hearing what is true and in telling the true from the false. Citizens will not support those organizations that are unreliable in producing good information and will transfer their resources to organizations that are more reliable in this respect. The process is highly competitive and rewards innovation. The producers of information have incentives to improve their products by developing new and more defensible ideas. And since citizens are diverse there will be a great diversity in the kinds of ideas that are expressed. Consequently, the citizens will have a lot to choose from and in the long run the good ideas will drive out the bad.

The market can also determine how many resources to devote to the development and articulation of each kind of knowledge about the different interests and points of view in the society. If citizens find certain kinds of information unimportant then they will be willing to expend fewer resources on them. More resources will go to elaborate more important ideas. And citizens will not be willing to support sources that produce roughly the same information because they would just be getting the same information twice. In a marketplace of ideas, entrepreneurs are rewarded for their awareness and responsiveness to citizens' views on these matters. Citizen consumers decide whether information is credible and pay only those groups that are credible; they decide how important it is and pay only as much as they think the information is worth; they decide whether it is sufficiently distinct from the information they already have to be worth their purchase. All of these discriminations are adequately handled in a marketplace of ideas of the sort we have described. The problem of the deliberative agenda seems to be solved here.[12]

But there are two serious objections to this view. The first objection is that the uneven distribution of resources in the society undermines equality in rational social deliberation to the extent that it enables some to support the kinds of organizations necessary to developing and communicating their interests to others while it disables others from developing and communicating their views. The ability and willingness to pay for anything is partially a function of wealth. As a consequence the wealthy contribute more resources to organizations that are devoted to the development of the understanding of their interests and points of view. Naturally, the same holds for large economic organizations, such as corporations.[13] So a system of organizations structured by the marketplace of ideas is biased towards the interests and points of view of wealthy consumers. The marketplace of ideas proves to be deeply inegalitarian.

These observations imply that the marketplace of ideas may fail to ensure the diversity of opinion that advances the basic epistemic aims of social discussion and deliberation. It limits what Mill called "the clash of ideas" and the testing of ideas because of its limitations on sources of ideas outside the wealthier parts of society. Inasmuch as the testing of ideas by competition with other ideas is an essential condition for enhancing the understandings of everyone in society, the uneven distribution of resources is an obstacle to the basic aim of rational social deliberation. Since the epistemic aim of rational social deliberation and equality in the process of discussion can be achieved only when active support is given to a diversity of groups to organize and articulate their views, the marketplace of ideas cannot be endorsed as the best institutional arrangement for democratic deliberation.

The second objection has to do with the fact that political information is a collective good. Recall that the main purpose of improving one's understanding of political and social matters is to have an impact on the outcome of collective decisionmaking. But for the great majority of citizens, there is little incentive to develop this understanding because they will make little difference to the ultimate outcome. Citizens desire that a lot of information about their interests be available to voters and that voters use that information wisely; but each citizen is far less concerned with personally having that information. He or she does not desire to pay the price for it because either enough others are paying or not enough others are paying the price; in either case it makes little difference whether a particular individual does or not. Thus, although each would like everyone else to be well informed, each has little reason to inform

him or herself. Thus, self-interested citizens are rationally ignorant.[14] This reasoning suggests that most citizens radically undersupport the system of secondary associations even if they approve
of the aims of such a system. In general, the principle of consumer
sovereignty operates rather poorly in this kind of context.

Given this problem of low information among a large proportion
of the electorate, it is not clear how citizens can be in a position to
evaluate ideas in the way that is required by the theory of the marketplace of ideas. Although it is true that self-interested citizens desire that flawed ideas be rooted out and that good ideas replace
them, they do not have the incentive to make the evaluations on
their own. Therefore, there is little reason to expect that citizens will
drive out the bad ideas and favor the good ones. And there is little
reason to think that citizens will have the incentive to develop nuanced conceptions of their interests and points of view with regard
to the collective properties of society. Thus, at least on the self-interest assumption, the theory of the marketplace of ideas seems to
fail to bring about the desirable outcomes promised by the theorists.

Furthermore, Downs's four sources of inequality described in
Chapter 3 will arise.[15] Those who are in professional, large business,
and governmental occupational positions in the society tend to receive much more political information than others as a by-product
of their work than those who are, say, construction workers, wait
persons, or unemployed. Their jobs bring them into contact with
government policy quite often. They also tend to be better educated
and more able to process the information they receive. As a consequence they tend to be more politically sophisticated and active.[16]
Thus, the government and the entrepreneurs who organize interest
groups and parties are likely to be more responsive to their interests
and points of view than those of the less well-to-do. Also, certain
groups whose interests are affected in highly concentrated and narrowly circumscribed ways by the government have incentives to
sponsor the generation of knowledge about their narrow interests
and points of view and communicate it to the government. They
tend to be overrepresented in the system of interest groups. For example, firms that employ many workers have interests in becoming
narrowly informed about occupational regulation; those that experience competition from foreign firms wish to know about laws reg-

ulating imports; and potential beneficiaries of public subsidies have interests in knowing about government policy in these areas. But only some have these incentives. Finally, since most citizens are not willing to pay for their political information but often receive it from other sources, the groups that have a special interest in government policy have an incentive to subsidize the production and communication of whatever information the citizenry at large receives. That information will tend to be biased in favor of the interests of the groups that do the subsidizing.[17] For example, advertisers have a substantial impact on the political information aired on television and published in the newspapers. Here is a revealing case:

> Coca-Cola tried unsuccessfully to persuade NBC to change a documentary depicting unfair treatment of migrant workers by Coca-Cola and others. When its efforts at persuasion failed, Coca-Cola withdrew all of its billings from NBC, in the amount of several million dollars. It did so even though the President of Coca-Cola acknowledged in later congressional testimony that the documentary had accurately depicted housing and worker conditions, and that as a result the company would change the situation. In the next eight years, NBC did not air any documentary on any controversial issue involving an important advertiser.[18]

Private subsidization of political information tends to bias the production of information towards the interests and points of view of the wealthy at least as much as the other mechanisms described above. As a consequence, it appears that the process of social discussion in a large democracy will tend to be deeply inegalitarian if the marketplace of ideas is the main institutional method for organizing it.

I have proceeded as if citizens act on the basis of self-interest alone. Although we have seen that this assumption is false in Chapter 4, it provides illumination into the case in which motives of fairness also play a role. For even if we suspend the strong self-interest assumption, we can see that important inequities result from the fact that the cultivation of understanding is a collective good. First, even if citizens are willing to cooperate in supporting organizations that develop and communicate knowledge of their own interests and points of view, they still face what is called an assurance problem. They do not wish to contribute resources to an organization if not enough others contribute to it. Such a contribution would be a waste of their resources. But if they cannot tell whether others will contribute to such an organization, they will be wiser to allocate their resources to other things. Thus, I may be willing to do what I think is my fair share in supporting some cause that I think is important, but if I do not think enough others will do the same, then I prefer to invest my efforts and resources in other more private areas.

This uncertainty poses a special problem for most people in the society. Since they do not know what organizations will receive sufficient support from others, they cannot tell whether the organizations they favor will receive such support. In short, they experience a massive coordination problem. Coordination problems themselves are difficult and costly to solve. Their solution requires that one become informed about what others are doing and that one informs the others of what one intends to do. Ordinary citizens may well be willing to support collective organizations as long as enough others do, but they do not know what the others will support. Thus, they will reasonably tend to be cautious in their support for an organization. As a consequence, even individuals who are not fully self-interested tend to undersupport such organizations and are disinclined to be innovative. Thus, the principle of consumer sovereignty fails to operate properly for the vast number of people in society.

Again, these obstacles will be smaller for the well-to-do. First, because of their greater wealth and the diminishing marginal value of each extra bit of wealth they will be more willing to contribute resources to organizations; they will be a bit less cautious.[19] Second, given their better education and the much greater amount of political information they receive as a by-product of their occupations, they have more knowledge about the interests they share with others and its relation with politics. Third, some of these people are associated with firms and corporations that receive highly concentrated benefits from the government. These firms have clear-cut incentives to cultivate knowledge and understanding of political matters regardless of what others do, so they do not face an assurance problem.

Most important, they have incentives to subsidize the information that the rest of society receives and to enlist other parts of the society in tasks that advance primarily their interests and points of view. The coordination problems so difficult for the rest of society to solve are in part solved with the help of those who are well-to-do and who have special interests in doing so. We see many examples in modern U.S. politics. When a large firm desires some change in government policy, they lay out enormous funds to find every other person in the society who might also think they can benefit from this change in policy. Then they pay for the organization of those persons in the forms of letter writing campaigns, telephone banks, and campaigns for raising money for the cause. It is the large firm that is willing and able to support the costs of coordination, and it is their interests and points of view that are primarily expressed. For example, the auto industry in the United States managed to defeat provisions of a clean air bill in 1990 by hiring a lobbying firm that "scoured six states for potential grassroots voices, coaching them on the 'facts' of the issue, paying for the phone calls and plane fares to Washington and hiring the hall for a joint press conference." This firm

> has a "boiler room" with three hundred phone lines and a sophisticated computer system, resembling the phone banks employed in election campaigns. Articulate young people sit in the little booths every day, dialing around America on a variety of public issues, searching for "white hat" citizens who can be persuaded to endorse the political objectives of Mobil Oil, Dow Chemical, Citicorp, Ohio Bell, Miller Brewing, U.S. Tobacco, the Chemical Manufacturers Association, the Pharmaceutical Manufacturers Association and dozens of other clients.[20]

Thus, much of the organization that ordinary, well-meaning citizens are involved in is coordinated by and in the interests of large private economic interests.

Therefore, in a society in which the institutions of deliberation are structured by a marketplace of ideas, the wealthy and powerful private economic institutions will dominate the process of discussion, which will reflect their interests and points of view primarily.[21]

Such a society simply cannot live up to the egalitarian ideals of democracy. It undermines the diversity of voices necessary for a fully informed process of discussion, and it undermines equality of citizenship in the process. Ironically, the very ideals embodied in the metaphorical marketplace of ideas are betrayed in the actual marketplace of ideas.

Public Support for Political Parties and Secondary Institutions

The previous considerations suggest that some public support is necessary to advance the epistemic aims of rational social deliberation in a democracy as well as the demand for equality in the process. This social support could be in the form of public expenditures for political parties and secondary associations that represent broad sectors of the society. We have already argued for public support for election campaigns in Chapter 7 because of the deliberative function of parties and interest groups. Two further considerations undergird and expand the argument for special public support for political parties and interest groups.

First, the public support guarantees that a number of different voices from different parts of the society have the opportunity to develop and articulate their points of view and interests as well as the ability to communicate them to other parts of the society. It guarantees a diversity of voices by supporting efforts at organization of groups that might not otherwise be able to organize. It can help solve the problems of resource inequality and coordination. Second, public support guarantees greater equality in the process of deliberation and discussion by underwriting and giving public recognition to the diversity of interests and points of view in the society in such a way that it encourages members to make a contribution to the process of social deliberation. It supports broad participation by means of redressing the effects of resource inequality in society and by underwriting the cost of coordination among ordinary citizens.[22]

There are different ways in which public support can be provided, and we shall consider two: a publicly sponsored voucher system for paying for the costs of secondary associations and a direct subsidy for secondary associations decided upon by the democratic legislature. The first attempts to preserve the idea of the marketplace of ideas, whereas the second uses a collective decision procedure to make this choice.

An Egalitarian Marketplace of Ideas?

Some have argued recently that the state ought to distribute vouchers to all citizens that may be used only for the purpose of supporting secondary associations. According to this scheme, citizens allocate their vouchers to the associations of their choice, which in turn cash them in for resources with which to develop the association.[23] Citizens receive many vouchers, so they can allocate them in a nuanced way to associations of their choice, giving more to those they see as more important.

The voucher scheme solves some of the problem of resource inequality by giving equal resources to all citizens with which to support organizations. This system enables organizations concerned with articulating the interests and points of view of the less well-to-do to flourish. It increases the presence of different voices and interests in the process of discussion and contributes to equality of citizenship as well as the clash of ideas so important to the democratic process. It mitigates the problem of collective action by disallowing the use of these resources for purposes other than political organization. Citizens have no choice but to use vouchers to support the associations they prefer. Therefore, some of the inequalities that arise as a result of the problem of collective action are mitigated. The problem of coordination remains to some extent since vouchers spent on organizations that receive too little support from others will be wasted, but it is mitigated by the fact that there is no opportunity cost to the political use of the voucher. Since citizens have nothing to lose in trying to support organizations of their choice, they will not exhibit the same kind of caution as they would with their own money. At the same time the virtues of the marketplace remain. The support each organization receives will be more nuanced in the sense that it will reflect the importance citizens associate with the interests and points of view advanced by the organization. It will also reflect citizens' judgments as to the distinctness of the different organizations. And citizens will not support organizations that they do not regard as credible. This system has some of the virtues of the marketplace but has fewer of its vices.

The distribution of vouchers does not eliminate inequality by any means. The use of private funds to support organization would still be available to citizens, and these would be subject to the same logic as in the unmodified marketplace of ideas. This alternative source of funding would bring about inequalities on its own, but it would also skew the distribution of vouchers. This problem would arise because organizations would have to campaign for the receipt of vouchers from citizens. And this campaigning would inevitably be dominated to a great extent by those with greater funds to dispose of. Thus those with large private funds as well as those with funds from previous distributions of vouchers would be favored over the less well-to-do and those who have not entered into the system. All the difficulties affecting the unmodified marketplace of ideas would come in at the stage of persuading citizens to contribute vouchers to organizations.

In order to rectify this problem the process of campaigning itself would have to be publicly funded, and private funds would have to be excluded both from the campaigns and from the funding of the organizations. But in order to ensure that this funding was done in an egalitarian way, some nonmarket process would be necessary in order to decide on the allocation of resources for the campaigns for raising money. Thus, the voucher scheme must fall short of the ideal of equality it attempts to achieve, or it must rely on a prior nonmarket method of ensuring equality in the process of social discussion.

There is another problem with the marketplace of ideas schemes. If we suppose that individuals always allocate more resources to those organizations they think are the most important, then the system of associations satisfies the principle of numerical equality appropriate for voting systems and systems for distributing the means for exerting pressure on collective decisionmaking, but it does not satisfy the principle of qualitative equality appropriate for institutions of deliberation. The voucher system ensures that those interests and points of view favored by a larger group of people receive more resources with which to cultivate and develop the understanding of those interests. But this result means that some people's interests will be treated more than equally by such a system.

So any literal marketplace of ideas, whether privately or publicly sponsored, must fall afoul of basic norms of democratic equality. It favors the better-off who are more likely to consume and produce information, and it fails to satisfy the standard of qualitative equality, which is at the heart of egalitarian deliberation. We must therefore turn our attention to a democratic method for determining the deliberative agenda.

A Democratic Solution

Recall that the kinds of disagreements about the credibility, importance, and distinctness of interests and points of view are similar to the very problems that led us to accept a principle of democratic equality in the first place. Democratic equality embodies equal consideration of interests when there are severe and inevitable epistemic limitations on our abilities to assess and compare the interests individuals have in collective properties of the society and when we require a coordinated method for deciding on these properties. But equality in the process of discussion is itself a problematic ideal due to the difficulty of publicly ensuring that plural qualitative equality is satisfied. The marketplace of ideas is unable to provide a coordinated method for establishing equality in the process of social discussion. Thus, to establish an egalitarian deliberative agenda seems to require a coordinated and egalitarian collective decision-making process.

The natural solution to this problem is to make ultimate decisions on the deliberative agenda democratically. In this account, the democratically elected legislature decides on the proper distribution of resources to the various secondary associations. They subsidize organizations on the basis of a principle of plural qualitative equality, taking into account differences in importance, credibility, and qualitative distinctness and assessing which interests and points of view are merely latent in the society. Their decisions have a remedial function in that they merely have to subsidize those groups that need help. Private funding is not excluded, it is merely supplemented. Thus the problems of inequality and coordination are partly solved by this method.

The coordination problem is solved because the method of sponsoring secondary associations does not depend on the coordination of citizens, as it did in the market institutions. The problem of equality is solved in two ways. First, legislators take themselves to be deciding on the deliberative agenda in accordance with their conceptions of the qualitative equality. They do not merely put forward an agenda on the grounds that they agree with the positions advanced by the associations; they put forth their best interpretation of what all the various interests, issues, and points of view in the society are. Hence they attempt to implement equality. But this method of deciding on the deliberative agenda is also egalitarian in the way that all democratic decisionmaking is. To the extent that there is disagreement on how to compare and accommodate all the different interests and points of view in the society and to the extent that collective decisionmaking is necessary to solve the problems of coordination in constructing the deliberative agenda, an egalitarian method of solving the problem is to give each equal resources in the decisionmaking. This solution is an application of the basic principle of democratic equality I defended in the first part of this book. A deliberative agenda that is chosen through an egalitarian decisionmaking process is thereby made egalitarian. "Groups so authorized inherit the legitimacy of the authorization."[24]

The Problem of Circularity

However, this solution implies that the system of secondary associations is both a condition of genuine equality in democratic decisionmaking and the outcome of democratic decisionmaking in a democratic society. This solution seems to imply practical and theoretical problems.

The idea that an egalitarian system of secondary associations is a condition of democratic equality is fairly clear by now. Only if citizens have the wherewithal to develop their understanding of their interests and their points of view on the society can they genuinely be thought to have some ability to have a say in the direction of their society. Furthermore, only if citizens' interests and points of view are somehow equally explored in organizations can they be said to have an equal say in their society.

This raises the problem of circularity. The system of secondary associations has a significant impact on democratic decisionmaking. In the long run, it affects the composition of the legislature. For example, a society with very strong business associations and weak associations from other parts of the society will have a legislature dominated mostly by business interests.[25] But a legislature that is dependent for its composition on the current system of associations has a strong bias in favor of retaining it. Inasmuch as individual legislators owe their positions to the persuasive powers of the associations in place, they may be inclined to maintain the arrangement, which the democratic solution gives them some ability to do. Such a system of associations could well become "locked in" or "sclerotic," thus undermining the democratic aspirations of the society. This can happen when the system of associations straightforwardly overrepresents certain interests and points of view. The problem is not unusual in political societies that give substantial support to secondary associations.[26] It is a serious practical problem for the ideal of democratic equality. It suggests a strong tendency away from democratic equality inherent in the very institutions of democracy.

We should not overstate this problem. The idea is that legislators are concerned with implementing qualitative equality in the process of deliberation. Legislators do not merely decide to support associations on the grounds that doing so makes their reelection more likely. Nevertheless, given the inevitability of cognitive bias that we have been assuming throughout our discussion, even when legislators decide in good faith on the deliberative agenda, they make decisions that reflect their bias. And those who benefit from that bias are those who contribute to the process whereby those legislators are elected.

In addition to this problem, a democratic legislature is bound to have difficulty making the complex decisions necessary to set up or reasonably alter a system of associations satisfying the principle of qualitative equality. The number of such associations seems to be unlimited, and the nuances between them are very fine. Perhaps we ask too much of such a system if we ask it to make such fine-grained decisions. To be sure, the decisions of the legislature need only be remedial, so it will not be the basis on which all associations are supported. As a consequence, the legislature will not be responsible for all the decisions on how to allocate funding for secondary associations.

There is a serious theoretical problem here as well. It is hard to see how the system of associations can acquire its legitimacy from being chosen by a majority in the democratic legislature at the same time as being the very condition under which the democratic legislature is legitimized. Disagreement about the deliberative agenda will imply disagreements about whether the society is fully democratic or not. Those who do not think that the system of associations is egalitarian, or that the deliberative agenda it supports is democratic, would regard the legislature that is elected partly as a function of such a system as nondemocratic at least to some extent. They can argue that the legislature has been elected under circumstances in which not everyone has had the chance to become informed, and they will conclude that the interests of everyone are not given equal weight. This criticism suggests that even in a democratic society in which everyone agrees on the basic principles of democracy, there is inevitably disagreement about whether that society is fully democratic. There is permanent ambiguity and uncertainty about whether the society is fully treating the interest of all of its citizens with equal consideration.

Requiring the legislature to decide the deliberative agenda unanimously would not improve the situation. First, a unanimity rule would work as much as majority rule against groups of increasing prominence that do not have representation in the legislature. Second, unanimity rule invariably works to the benefit of certain groups. A unanimity rule requires that there be a default rule for those occasions when consensus cannot be reached. One default rule might be that the system will remain the same unless there is consensus on change. With this default rule a single party or a small group of parties could hold the system hostage if they wished to retain the status quo. Another possible default rule might be that support for the system of associations would simply end if no agreement could be reached. But such a rule would favor those who can do without public support for the system of associations: the wealthy groups who tend to do well under the unmodified marketplace of ideas. They might be able to hold the system hostage so as to receive greater allocations of resources from the state. These problems are the familiar difficulties of unanimity rule: It is inegalitarian when some specially benefit from the status quo.

How serious is this problem for democracy? Since equality in the deliberative agenda is a necessary component of political equality, citizens will disagree on whether the society is fully democratic. And since democratic equality is the embodiment of equal consideration of interests, it is likely that many citizens will have reason to think that their interests are not being taken equally into account. There is a threat that some citizens will think that they are being treated as inferiors, which can lead to instability in the society if everyone is committed to democracy. The equal public status of citizens will always be obscured to some degree.

Nevertheless, the problem may not always be overwhelming. First, recall that the system of political parties is more easily regulated by the principle of qualitative equality and the effects of the system of interest groups on the composition of the legislature come as a result of their participation in deliberation since electoral campaigns are publicly funded. As a consequence, these effects are uncertain and difficult to predict, thereby making the possibilities of circularity and sclerosis somewhat uncertain. Second, as long as the electoral and legislative systems are set up along egalitarian lines and individuals are confident that their fellow citizens are doing their best in trying to accommodate the interests of all in the deliberative agenda, then even those who believe their interests are not being given equal attention must acknowledge that it will be hard to do better in terms of equality without making others even worse off. This problem is one that lies at the heart of any conception of democracy that takes equality in the deliberative process seriously; it is not distinctive of the particular conception of democracy that I have presented, and thus it can be eliminated only by doing away with some of the institutions of democracy. Those who contemplate such actions cannot often have the realization of equality as their aim. They would only be sacrificing the interests of others to achieve a lesser gain for themselves. Third, those who do not think that their interests are being given equal consideration in the process of social discussion can most likely be assured that their situation is not permanent. Given the shifting distribution of opinions in the society, the chances are that in the future they will either find themselves in a more powerful position to affect the agenda or more citizens in the society will see that their views are legitimate and important (if their own views do not undergo change). Thus, over time the significance of these inequalities will be mitigated for many groups.

Nevertheless, it is clear that there is no permanent or fully satisfying solution to the problem of the deliberative agenda. This problem explains perhaps more than anything else the permanent proneness of democracies to self-examination and reassessment. Democratic societies are and must always be restless and changing.

Notes

1. It should go without saying that equal access to education both in and out of schools is an elementary condition of democracy inasmuch as it requires equality in cognitive conditions for participation. No society that makes the possession of an adequate education for many of its citizens extremely difficult or even impossible to acquire can be said to be concerned with the interests of all its citizens. The shocking disparity of access to adequate education in the United States is incompatible with the most widely held beliefs about equality among citizens as well as democracy.

My discussion focuses on democracy among educated adults, but I want to make three observations with regard to education. First, such education must include an introduction to the principles of democratic government, including the basic norms of citizenship we are attempting to understand and a well-rounded coverage of the histories and cultures of the various peoples and groups in our society. Second, the analysis here makes a contribution to a more egalitarian conception of education insofar as it attempts to describe the framework within which democratic discussion about education can take place. Moreover, this framework ought to increase the understanding of the diversity of interests and points of view in the society as well as facilitate acceptance of it. Third, the norms outlined in this chapter are applicable to educational institutions to the degree that they are concerned with enhancing the skills in discussion and deliberation of citizens.

2. The locus classicus of this argument is Robert Michels, *Political Parties* (New York: Dover Publications, 1959 [1915]).

3. See Paul Sabatier, "Interest Group Membership and Organization: Multiple Theories," in *The Politics of Interest Groups Transformed*, ed. Mark Petracca (Boulder: Westview Press, 1992), pp. 99–129, for a discussion of solidary motives in interest groups. See also Alan Ware, *Citizens,*

Parties, and Democracy (London: Polity Press, 1990), for a review of evidence regarding constraints on party leaders. See also Joshua Cohen and Joel Rogers, "Secondary Associations and Democratic Governance," *Politics and Society* December (1992): pp. 393–472, for evidence of large groups not submitting to the tendency of oligarchy.

4. See John Plamenatz, *Democracy and Illusion* (London: Longmans, 1973), and Robert Dahl, *Democracy and Its Critics* (New Haven: Yale University Press, 1989), p. 276, for their arguments.

5. For the importance of opinion leaders in the political thinking of ordinary citizens see Anthony Downs, *An Economic Theory of Democracy* (New York: Harper and Row, 1957), p. 214, as well as John Zaller, *The Origins of Mass Opinion* (Cambridge: Cambridge University Press, 1992). See Stuart Hill, *Democratic Values and Technological Choices* (Stanford: Stanford University Press, 1992), for an extensive discussion of the importance of trusting elite opinion in the context of one very important kind of technical deliberation: discussion about the impact of new technologies.

6. See Paul Samuelson, "The Pure Theory of Public Expenditure," in *Rational Man in Irrational Society?*, ed. Brian Barry and Russell Hardin (Beverly Hills, Calif.: Sage Publications, 1982), pp. 171–179, for the original characterization of this notion.

7. This assumes that there are no relevant differences between the boys.

8. See David Greenstone, *Labor in American Politics* (New York: Vintage, 1970), for an account of the comprehensive nature of union participation in politics in the United States after World War II.

9. See Mancur Olson, *The Logic of Collective Action* (Cambridge, Mass.: Harvard University Press, 1960), for the seminal discussion of the extensive implications of these difficulties. See also Francis Fox Piven and Richard Cloward, *Poor People's Movements* (Boston: Pantheon Press, 1980), for evidence of success and failure in these efforts.

10. The fact that it is reasonable to permit tyrannical groups to say what they think but not to have a share in the resources that are devoted to the promotion of democratic discussion undermines the idea that principles of free speech are defensible on grounds of promoting democratic deliberation alone. It also undermines the idea of those who think that a requirement of fair access to the means of communication is inherent in the right to free speech. The American Nazi Party has a right to think and say what it believes, but it does not have a right to an equal share of resources that give it access to social discussion. For examples of the democratic discussion argument for free speech, see Alexander Meiklejohn, *Political Freedom* (New York: Oxford University Press, 1965), part 1, and Cass Sunstein, *Democracy and the Problem of Free Speech* (New York: Basic Books, 1993). These theorists generally defend a fair access provision as part of free speech. For

another argument that includes the fair access condition in the ideal of freedom of expression, see Joshua Cohen, "Freedom of Expression," *Philosophy and Public Affairs* Summer (1993), p. 216.

11. Cited in Sunstein, *Democracy and the Problem of Free Speech*, p. 24.

12. See David Kelley and Roger Donway, "Liberalism and Free Speech," in *Democracy and the Mass Media*, ed. Judith Lichtenberg (New York: Cambridge University Press, 1991), for a defense of the literal marketplace of ideas; see also Giovanni Sartori, *The Theory of Democracy Revisited: Part I, The Contemporary Debate* (Chatham, N.J.: Chatham House Publishers, 1987), p. 98.

13. See Sunstein, *Democracy and the Problem of Free Speech*, for an elaboration of this kind of argument.

14. See Downs, *An Economic Theory of Democracy*, p. 246.

15. See Downs, *An Economic Theory of Democracy*, p. 221, as well as Samuel Popkin, *The Reasoning Voter: Communication and Persuasion in Presidential Campaigns* (Chicago: University of Chicago Press, 1991), pp. 22–28.

16. See H. Russell Neuman, *The Paradox of Mass Democracy* (Cambridge, Mass.: MIT Press, 1990), for evidence that these are the most important factors behind political sophistication.

17. See Downs, *An Economic Theory of Democracy*, p. 235, and Charles Lindblom, *Politics and Markets* (New York: Basic Books, 1977). See Robert Entman, *Democracy Without Citizens* (New York: Oxford University Press, 1990), for a very good critique of the marketplace of ideas along these lines as it applies to discussions of the mass media.

18. Sunstein, *Democracy and the Problem of Free Speech*, pp. 64–65.

19. See Russell Hardin, *Collective Action* (Baltimore: Johns Hopkins University Press, 1980), for evidence of the greater willingness of the well-to-do to contribute to collective goods.

20. See William Greider, *Who Will Tell the People? The Betrayal of American Democracy* (New York: Simon and Schuster, 1992), pp. 39–40, for this and many other examples of this kind of corporate-led coordination.

21. See Lindblom, *Politics and Markets*, for arguments to the same conclusion.

22. See Danilo Zolo, *Democracy and Complexity: A Realist Approach* (University Park: Pennsylvania State University Press, 1992), for skepticism about public support for parties and secondary associations.

23. See Philippe C. Schmitter, "The Irony of Modern Democracy and Efforts to Improve Its Practice," *Politics and Society* 20, no. 4 (December 1992): pp. 507–512, especially pp. 511–512. See also James Fishkin, *Democ-*

racy and Deliberation (New Haven: Yale University Press, 1991), as well as *The Dialogue of Justice* (New Haven: Yale University Press, 1992), for an endorsement of this kind of institutional setup.

24. Joshua Cohen and Joel Rogers, "Secondary Associations and Democratic Governance," p. 451.

25. See Lindblom, *Politics and Markets,* for an extensive argument to this effect in the United States. See also Thomas Ferguson and Joel Rogers, *Right Turn: The Decline of the Democrats and the Future of American Politics* (New York: Hill and Wang, 1986).

26. See Schmitter, "The Irony of Modern Democracy and Efforts to Improve Its Practice," pp. 507–512.

SELECTED BIBLIOGRAPHY

Arendt, Hannah. 1963. *On Revolution.* Harmondsworth, Eng.: Penguin Publishers.

Aristotle. 1981. *The Politics.* Trans. T. A. Sinclair (rev. Trevor J. Saunders). Harmondsworth, Eng.: Penguin Books.

Arneson, Richard. 1993. Democratic Rights at National and Workplace Levels. In *The Idea of Democracy,* ed. David Copp, Jean Hampton, and John Roemer. Cambridge: Cambridge University Press.

Bacharach, Peter. 1967. *The Theory of Democratic Elitism.* Boston: Little, Brown.

Barber, Benjamin. 1983. *Strong Democracy: Participatory Politics for a New Age.* Berkeley: University of California Press.

Barry, Brian. 1979. *Sociologists, Economists, and Democracy.* Chicago: University of Chicago Press.

Barry, Brian. 1991. *Democracy and Power: Essays in Political Theory I.* Oxford: Oxford University Press.

Barry, Brian, and Hardin, Russell, eds. 1982. *Rational Man in Irrational Society?* Beverly Hills, Calif.: Sage Publications.

Beitz, Charles. 1989. *Political Equality: An Essay in Democratic Theory.* Princeton: Princeton University Press.

Berlin, Isaiah. 1969. Two Concepts of Liberty. In *Four Essays on Liberty.* Oxford: Oxford University Press.

Brennan, Geoffrey, and Buchanan, James. 1985. *The Reason of Rules: Constitutional Political Economy.* Cambridge: Cambridge University Press.

Brennan, Geoffrey, and Lomasky, Loren, eds. 1989. *Politics and Process: New Essays in Democratic Thought.* Cambridge: Cambridge University Press.

Buchanan, James, and Tullock, Gordon. 1962. *The Calculus of Consent: The Logical Foundations of Constitutional Democracy.* Ann Arbor: University of Michigan Press

Burnheim, John. 1985. *Is Democracy Possible? An Alternative to Electoral Politics.* Berkeley: University of California Press.

Christiano, Thomas. 1990. Freedom, Consensus, and Equality in Collective Decision Making. *Ethics* (October): pp. 151–181.

Christiano, Thomas. 1990. Political Equality. In *NOMOS XXXIII: Majorities and Minorities,* ed. John Chapman and Alan Wertheimer. New York: New York University Press.

Christiano, Thomas. 1993. Social Choice and Democracy. In *The Idea of Democracy,* ed. David Copp, Jean Hampton, and John Roemer. Cambridge: Cambridge University Press.

Christiano, Thomas. 1994. The Incoherence of Hobbesian Justifications of the State. *American Philosophical Quarterly* (January): pp. 23–38.

Christiano, Thomas. 1995. Democratic Equality and the Problem of Persistent Minorities. *Philosophical Papers* (January): pp. 169–190.

Christiano, Thomas. April, 1996. Is the Participation Argument Incoherent? *Philosophical Studies,* pp. 1–12.

Cohen, G. A. 1969. Capitalism, Freedom, and the Proletariat. In *The Idea of Freedom,* ed. Alan Ryan. Oxford: Oxford University Press.

Cohen, G. A. 1989. On the Currency of Egalitarian Justice. *Ethics* (July): pp. 906–944.

Cohen, Joshua. 1986. Autonomy and Democracy: Reflections on Rousseau. *Philosophy and Public Affairs* 15: pp. 275–297.

Cohen, Joshua. 1986. An Epistemic Conception of Democracy. *Ethics* (October): pp. 26–38.

Cohen, Joshua. 1989. Deliberation and Democratic Legitimacy. In *The Good Polity,* ed. Alan Hamlin and Philip Pettit. New York: Basil Blackwell.

Cohen, Joshua, and Rogers, Joel. 1983. *On Democracy: Towards a Transformation of American Society.* New York: Penguin Books.

Cohen, Joshua, and Rogers, Joel. 1992. Secondary Associations and Democratic Governance. *Politics and Society* (December): pp. 393–472.

Coleman, Jules, and Ferejohn, John. 1986. Democracy and Social Choice. *Ethics* (October): pp. 6–27.

Dahl, Robert. 1959. *A Preface to Democratic Theory.* Chicago: University of Chicago Press.

Dahl, Robert. 1979. Procedural Democracy. In *Philosophy, Politics, and Society,* 5th ser., ed. James Fishkin and Peter Laslett. New Haven: Yale University Press.

Dahl, Robert. 1989. *Democracy and Its Critics.* New Haven: Yale University Press.

Dent, N.J.H. 1989. *Rousseau: Psychological, Social, and Political Theory.* New York: Basil Blackwell.

Downs, Anthony. 1957. *An Economic Theory of Democracy.* New York: Harper and Row.

Dworkin, Ronald. 1981. What Is Equality? Part I: Equality of Welfare. *Philosophy and Public Affairs* (spring): pp. 185–246.

Dworkin, Ronald. 1981. What Is Equality? Part II: Equality of Resources. *Philosophy and Public Affairs* (summer): pp. 283–345.

Dworkin, Ronald. 1987. What Is Equality? Part IV: Political Equality. *San Francisco Law Review* 22.

Elster, Jon. 1983. *Sour Grapes: Studies in the Subversion of Rationality.* Cambridge: Cambridge University Press.

Elster, Jon. 1986. Self-Realization in Work and Politics: The Marxist Conception of the Good Life. In *Marxism and Liberalism,* ed. John Arens, Fred Miller Jr., Ellen Frankel Paul, and Jeffrey Paul. New York: Basil Blackwell.

Elster, Jon, and Hylland, Aanund, eds. 1986. *Foundations of Social Choice Theory.* Cambridge: Cambridge University Press.

Estlund, David. 1993. Making Truth Safe for Democracy. In *The Idea of Democracy,* ed. David Copp, Jean Hampton, and John Roemer. Cambridge: Cambridge University Press.

Feld, Scott, and Grofman, Bernard. 1988. Rousseau's General Will: A Condorcetian Perspective. *American Political Science Review* 82: pp. 567–576.

Ferejohn, John, and Kuklinski, James, eds. 1990. *Information and Democratic Processes.* Chicago: University of Illinois Press.

Fishkin, James. 1992. *Democracy and Deliberation: New Directions for Democratic Reform.* New Haven: Yale University Press.

Gamson, William. 1992. *Talking Politics.* Cambridge: Cambridge University Press.

Goldman, Alvin. 1987. Foundations of Social Epistemics. *Synthese* 73: pp. 109–144.

Gould, Carol. 1988. *Rethinking Democracy: Freedom and Social Cooperation in Politics, Economics, and Society.* New York: Cambridge University Press.

Graham, Keith. 1986. *The Battle of Democracy.* London: St. Martin's Press.

Habermas, Jurgen. 1975. *Legitimation Crisis.* Trans. Thomas McCarthy. Boston: Beacon Press.

Hardin, Russell. 1980. *Collective Action.* Baltimore: Johns Hopkins University Press.

Hardin, Russell. 1988. *Morality Within the Limits of Reason.* Chicago: University of Chicago Press.

Hardin, Russell. 1993. Public Choice Versus Democracy. In *The Idea of Democracy,* ed. David Copp, Jean Hampton, and John Roemer. New York: Cambridge University Press.

Hegel, G.W.F. 1977. *The Phenomenology of Spirit,* ed. A. V. Miller. Oxford: Oxford University Press.

Hobbes, Thomas. 1968 [1641]. *Leviathan,* ed. C. B. MacPherson. Harmondsworth, Eng.: Penguin Books.

Hudson, Thomas. 1994. Self-Determination, Decentralization, and Political Diversity. Ph.D. thesis, Department of Philosophy, University of Arizona.

Hume, David. 1965. Of the Original Contract. In *Hume's Ethical Writings,* ed. Alasdair MacIntyre. Notre Dame, Ind.: University of Notre Dame Press.

Jenkins, J. 1970. Political Consent. *Philosophical Quarterly* 1: pp. 60–66.

Jones, Peter. 1983. Political Equality and Majority Rule. In *The Nature of Political Theory,* ed. David Miller and Larry Siedentop, pp. 155–182. Oxford: Oxford University Press.

Lindblom, Charles. 1977. *Politics and Markets: The World's Political-Economic Systems.* New York: Basic Books.

MacPherson, C. B. 1973. *Democratic Theory: Essays in Retrieval.* Oxford: Oxford University Press.

Manin, Bernard. 1987. On Legitimacy and Deliberation. *Political Theory* 15: pp. 338–368.

Mansbridge, Jane. 1980. *Beyond Adversary Democracy.* Chicago: University of Chicago Press.

McMahon, Christopher. 1994. *Authority and Democracy: A Theory of Authority in Government and Management.* Princeton: Princeton University Press.

Mill, John Stuart. 1991. *Considerations on Representative Government.* Buffalo, N.Y.: Prometheus Books.

Nelson, William. 1980. *On Justifying Democracy.* London: Routledge and Kegan Paul.

Neuman, H. Russell. 1986. *The Paradox of Mass Politics.* Cambridge, Mass.: MIT Press.

Olson, Mancur Jr. 1965. *The Logic of Collective Action: Public Goods and the Theory of Groups.* Cambridge, Mass.: Harvard University Press.

Page, Benjamin L., and Shapiro, Robert Y. 1992. *The Rational Public: Fifty Years of Trends in Americans' Policy Preferences.* Chicago: University of Chicago Press.

Pateman, Carole. 1970. *Participation and Democratic Theory.* Cambridge: Cambridge University Press.

Piven, Francis Fox, and Cloward, Richard. 1988. *Why Americans Don't Vote.* New York: Pantheon.

Plamenatz, John. 1973. *Democracy and Illusion.* London: Longmans.

Plato. 1974. *The Republic.* 2nd ed. (revised). Trans. Desmond Lee. Harmondsworth, Eng.: Penguin Books.

Popkin, Samuel L. 1990. *The Reasoning Voter: Communication and Persuasion in Presidential Campaigns.* Chicago: University of Chicago Press.

Rainsborough, Thomas. 1986. The Putney Debates: The Debate on the Franchise (1647). In *Divine Right and Democracy,* ed. David Wootton. Harmondsworth, Eng.: Penguin Books.

Rawls, John. 1971. *A Theory of Justice.* Cambridge, Mass.: Harvard University Press.

Riker, William. 1982. *Liberalism Against Populism: A Confrontation Between the Theory of Social Choice and Democracy.* San Francisco: William Freeman Co.

Rousseau, Jean-Jacques. 1967. *The Social Contract and Discourses.* Trans. G.H.D. Cole. London: J. M. Dent.

Sartori, Giovanni. 1987. *The Theory of Democracy Revisited.* 2 vols. Chatham, N.J.: Chatham House Publishers.

Schattschneider, E. E. 1960. *The Semi-Sovereign People: A Realist's View of Democracy in America.* New York: Holt, Rinehart and Winston.

Schumpeter, Joseph. 1956. *Capitalism, Socialism, and Democracy.* New York: Harper and Row.

Sher, George. 1989. Three Grades of Social Involvement. *Philosophy and Public Affairs* 18: pp. 133–157.

Simon, Herbert. 1983. *Reason in Human Affairs.* Stanford: Stanford University Press.

Singer, Peter. 1974. *Democracy and Disobedience.* Oxford: Oxford University Press.

Sunstein, Cass. 1985. Interest Groups in American Public Law. *Stanford Law Review,* 38: pp. 29–87.

Sunstein, Cass. 1993. *Democracy and the Problem of Free Speech.* New York: Free Press.

Taylor, Charles. 1985. *Philosophical Papers.* 2 vols. Cambridge: Cambridge University Press.

Thompson, Dennis. 1970. *The Democratic Citizen.* Cambridge: Cambridge University Press.

Walzer, Michael. 1981. Philosophy and Democracy. *Political Theory* (August): pp. 379–399.

Williams, Bernard. 1967. The Idea of Equality. In *Justice and Equality,* ed. Hugo Adam Bedau, pp. 116–137. Englewood Cliffs, N.J.: Prentice Hall.

Wootton, David, ed. 1986. *Divine Right and Democracy: An Anthology of Political Writings in Stuart England*. Harmondsworth, Eng.: Penguin Books.

Young, Iris Marion. 1991. *Justice and the Politics of Difference*. Princeton: Princeton University Press.

Zaller, John. 1992. *The Nature and Origins of Mass Opinion*. Cambridge: Cambridge University Press.

Zolo, Danilo. 1992. *Democracy and Complexity: A Realist Approach*. University Park: Pennsylvania State University Press.

ABOUT THE BOOK
AND AUTHOR

There is no problem more crucial to contemporary political thought than the status of democracy, its role, and its problems in the contemporary world. In this survey of democratic theory, Thomas Christiano introduces the reader to the principles underlying democracy and to the problems involved in applying these principles to real-life situations.

Beginning with the simple, democratically inspired presumption that the interests of all citizens are to be treated equally, Christiano argues that the implications of such a minimal commitment clarify the nature of democracy and what must be demanded of democratic institutions. He argues that it is the collision of this demand for equality with the fact of pluralism of interests that determines how democratic institutions ought to be designed. This strong sense of reality will be welcomed by those interested in practical questions of transition in newly democratizing states.

Christiano combines a broad coverage of important positions taken by others with the exposition of his own ideas, allowing his text to appeal to a wide range of readers, from introductory students to experienced scholars. Clear, accessible, and often elegant, *The Rule of the Many* is a splendid introduction to democratic theory, one that will take its place as both an important scholarly contribution and an effective text.

Thomas Christiano is associate professor of philosophy at the University of Arizona and the author of several influential papers on ethics and political philosophy.

INDEX

Accountability. *See* Responsibility
Administration/administrators. *See* Bureau-
    cracy
Agenda, 26, 34, 87–92, 97, 199, 200, 220, 221,
    222, 227, 229, 230, 231, 252, 261, 266,
    275–279, 281, 290–295
    deliberative, 92, 266, 271–279, 281,
        290–295
Aims
    articulation of, 4, 112, 114, 187, 231, 244,
        247, 259, 266
    choice of, 9, 167–168, 169–194, 199–200,
        207, 215, 218, 233
    discrimination of, 18, 42, 188–189, 259
    and means, 18, 19–20, 55, 63, 79, 167–168,
        169–171, 175–178, 187, 207, 208, 217,
        218, 222, 223, 233, 236, 248, 266–267
    objectivity of, 181–183
    reasonableness of, 24, 48, 121, 187, 188,
        245, 259, 260
Aristocracy, 15, 30
Aristotle, 45(n22), 75
Arneson, Richard, 43(n2), 100(n16)
Arrow's theorem, 95

Bargaining, 49, 87, 89, 91, 117, 179–180, 218,
    236, 248–253
Barry, Brian, 43(n2), 202(n3)
Beitz, Charles, 101(n25), 232–234, 240(n8)
Brennan, Geoffrey, 162(n21), 163(n38),
    164(nn 40, 42)
Buchanan, James, 159(n1), 162(nn 19, 21),
    163(nn 29, 38)
Bureaucracy, 123, 237, 238–239
Burke, Edmund, 214, 240(n8)
Burnheim, John, 202(n4)
By-product theory, 109–110, 110–115, 141,
    158

Campaign finance, 222, 244, 257–258, 268
Citizenship
    economic conception of, 9, 106–116,
        131–159

formalist conception of, 133, 134–140, 146
normative conception of, 165–201,
    172–175
pluralist conception of, 133, 140–143, 146,
    172. *See also* Pluralism
Coalition building, 68, 88, 89–90, 115,
141, 142, 235–236, 254
Cohen, G. A., 44(n5), 99(n8)
Cohen, Joshua, 20–21, 36, 45(n22), 99(n11),
    101(n29), 129(nn 16, 17), 162(n20),
    202(n7), 262(n9), 263(n15), 295(n3),
    296(n10), 298(n24)
Cole, G.D.H., 202(n4), 263(n13)
Collective property of society, 59–93,
    105–106, 131, 169
Common good, 29–35, 39, 45(n24), 135, 136,
    140, 141, 151, 170–194, 218, 244,
    275–276
Competence, 3, 32, 34, 74, 192–194, 270
Compromise, 49, 50, 51, 89, 167, 168, 218,
    248, 251, 254. *See also* Fair compromise
Condorcet method, 45(n22), 95
Consent, 27–28
Consensus, 19, 35, 36–39, 45(n24), 47, 57,
    61–62, 68, 69, 117
Constitutions 41, 82
Constructive view, 19, 24, 35–43
Contractarianism, 9, 134
Corporatism, 252–254
Countermajoritarian institutions, 82

Dahl, Robert, 98(n4), 100(n18), 141, 162(n17),
    262(n8), 263(n11), 296(n4)
Delegate, 171, 213–214, 215–219, 224, 227
Deliberation, 10, 83–87, 91–128, 178–190. *See
    also* Discussion
    democratic conditions of, 10, 123–128,
        215–218
    egalitarian conditions of, 6, 10, 91–92, 132,
        218, 258, 274–275, 276–277
    rational conditions of, 48, 116–125
    social conditions of, 116–128, 135, 244

307